INSTITUTIONS AND THE POLITICS OF SURVIVAL IN JORDAN

SUNY SERIES IN MIDDLE EASTERN STUDIES

Shahrough Akhavi, editor

INSTITUTIONS AND THE POLITICS OF SURVIVAL IN JORDAN

Domestic Responses to External Challenges, 1988–2001

RUSSELL E. LUCAS

STATE UNIVERSITY OF NEW YORK PRESS

Published by
STATE UNIVERSITY OF NEW YORK PRESS, ALBANY

© 2005 State University of New York

All rights reserved

Printed in the United States of America

No part of this book may be used or reproduced in any manner whatsoever without written permission. No part of this book may be stored in a retrieval system or transmitted in any form or by any means including electronic, electrostatic, magnetic tape, mechanical, photocopying, recording, or otherwise without the prior permission in writing of the publisher.

For information, address the State University of New York Press,
194 Washington Avenue, Suite 305, Albany, NY 12210-2365

Production, Laurie Searl
Marketing, Anne M. Valentine

Library of Congress Cataloging-in-Publication Data

Lucas, Russell E., 1970–
    Institutions and the politics of survival in Jordan : domestic responses to external challenges, 1988–2001 / Russell E. Lucas.
       p. cm. — (SUNY series in Middle Eastern studies)
    Includes bibliographical references and index.
    ISBN 0-7914-6445-8 (hardcover : alk. paper)
    1. Jordan—Politics and government—1952–1999. 2. Jordan—Politics and government—1999– 3. Political culture—Jordan. 4. Structural adjustment (Economic policy)—Jordan. I. Title. II. Series.

JQ1833.A58L83 2005
956.9504—dc22
                                                  2004014215

10 9 8 7 6 5 4 3 2 1

for Camelia and Aman

If there were a single hair

Between me and my people

I would not let it break

If they pull the hair

I lighten my hand

If they let it go

Then I pull it tight

– Muawiyah ibn Abi Sufiyan

CONTENTS

List of Tables	XI
Acknowledgments	XIII
Note on Translation and Transliteration	XV
1 Institutions and the Politics of Survival	1
2 Regime-Led State Building in Jordan: 1921–1988	13
3 Economic Crisis and Political Liberalization	25
4 Institutionalizing Political Liberalization	51
5 Managing Peace and Its Discontents	71
6 Normalization and Structural Adjustment	87
7 Press Restrictions and the 1997 Elections	99
8 A New King and a New Intifada	127
9 Institutions and the Politics of Survival: An Appraisal	137
Notes	157
Bibliography	173
Index	181

TABLES

3.1	Distribution of Election Districts and Representation	29
3.2	Results of the 1989 Election	31
3.3	Members of the Royal Committee for Drafting the National Charter	34
4.1	Political Parties Legalized, 1992–1993	59
4.2	Opinions on the Success of Political Work by Parties	60
4.3	Prosecutions for Press Violations, 1993–1997	65
4.4	Violations by Selected Weekly Newspapers, 1993–1997	66
5.1	Comparison of Election Results, 1989 and 1993	80
6.1	Will Peace Lead to Economic Benefits for Jordan?	95
6.2	Do Israelis Remain Enemies?	95
6.3	Percentage Change of Select Economic Indicators, 1994–2000	97
7.1	Maximum Fines for Violations of Press Laws, 1993 versus 1997	104
7.2	Results of the 1997 Election	116

ACKNOWLEDGMENTS

This project traces its roots to my being assigned to play the role of King Hussein in a simulation of Middle Eastern politics as an undergraduate student. That classroom experience prompted me to write a research paper, which led to a master's thesis, which then led to a doctoral dissertation, and now to a book.

In a project like this, especially one that has developed over so many years, I owe thanks to numerous people. I hope to remember all of them. However, there may be some I forget; I hope that they will forgive me if I do so. While everyone has helped me make this the best work possible, any faults that remain in this project I claim for my own.

Financial support from the following sources has supported my research and writing: Georgetown University, the USIA Fulbright program, the American Center for Oriental Research, the U.S. Institute of Peace Jennings Randolph program, the Research Authority of the University of Haifa, and the Truman Institute for the Advancement of Peace at the Hebrew University of Jerusalem. I kindly thank all of these donors for their aid.

Parts of this work have previously appeared in other forms. Some portions are reprinted with the permission of Cambridge University Press and draw from my article "Monarchical Authoritarianism: Survival and Political Liberalization in a Middle Eastern Regime Type," *International Journal of Middle East Studies* 36, no. 1 (February 2004): 103–119. Some portions draw on "Deliberalization in Jordan," *Journal of Democracy* 14, no.1 (January 2003): 137–144. Other portions have appeared in my articles "Press Laws as a Survival Strategy in Jordan," *Middle Eastern Studies* 39, no.4 (October, 2003): 81–98, and "Jordan: The Death of Normalization with Israel," *Middle East Journal* 80, no.1 (Winter 2004): 93–111. I would like to thank the publishers for their permissions to use this material that they have previously published.

I would like to especially thank Joseph Nevo for mentoring my postdoctoral research and Daniel Brumberg for mentoring my dissertation.

Ellen Lust-Okar deserves special praise for joining my dissertation committee in hurried circumstances. I have known her since Ann Arbor, and I have benefited from her advice all along the way.

I would like to thank many people for their help during my fieldwork in Jordan: Alain McNamara and the staff of the Bi-national Fulbright Commission, the entire staff of the American Center for Oriental Research, Hani Hourani and his staff at Al-Urdun Al-Jadid Research Center, Mustapha Harmarneh and the staff of the Center for Strategic Studies at the University of Jordan, the staff of the archives of the *Jordan Times*, the late Adnan Faraj, Adnan Abu Odeh, and Bassam Asfour. I would also like to thank HRH Prince Ra'ad bin Zeid. Nahla Abu Khalaf of the Center for Strategic Studies at the University of Jordan deserves special praise for her assistance. I know that some in Jordan may disagree with my analysis and conclusions about Jordan. However, even King Abdullah II wishes to compare Jordan to the developed and democratic West, and not Jordan's dictatorial neighbors.

At Georgetown, I would like to thank: Maria Alves, Jen Boone, David Boyer, Victor Cha, Liz Kepferle, Charles King, Jerry Mara, Sam Mujal-Leon, Kerry Pace, George Shambaugh, John Voll, Mark Warren, and Patricia Wrightson. I would like to thank my friends and colleagues who were with me in the graduate program—you are all too many to name.

In Jerusalem and Haifa I would like to thank: Mahdi Abd al-Hadi, Amatzia Baram, Michael Clark, Zach Levy, Moshe Ma'oz, Paul Scham, and the staff of the Truman Institute Library. I would also like to thank my wife's family for the warm welcome to a foreign son-in-law.

I would like to thank for their friendship and advice through the years: Jill Crystal, Peter Furia, Jefferson Gray, Phil and Mary Ann Haar, Catherine and Bob Haar, Amanda Klekowski von Koppenfels, Fr. Daniel O'Connell, Kathy Smith, Peter Siavelis, and Catherine Sweet.

I would like to thank Holly Reason and Meredith McRoberts for their assistance. I would also like to thank the anonymous reviewers and my editors at SUNY Press.

I wish to also recognize the great support I have received from my entire family—emotional and otherwise. My grandparents, Robert and Norma Lucas, have been especially helpful in the otherwise department. Without the aid of my grandfather, the late Jere Lustig, and my grandmother, Deborah Lustig Ozer, I would not have finished my doctorate. For that, I owe them a lot.

Finally, I am even more indebted to my wife, Camelia Suleiman. Aside from all of her help on the Arabic data, she has given me great insight into Arab culture and society. But she has given me so much more than that. I am sure I could fill another few hundred pages trying to put all of it into words. Camelia has also given me her daughter, Aman, who is now my daughter too. Aman has opened up a whole new side of life to me. She has also helped with editing the notes. For all of their efforts in helping me in this project I dedicate this book to them. Robert Sari, our son, will get his turn later.

NOTE ON TRANSLATION AND TRANSLITERATION

With the translation and transliteration of Arabic names and terms I have focused first on consistency and readability. If names and terms are commonly used in English, I have followed their spelling. Next, I have relied on the practice of the *Jordan Times*. In other cases, I have generally tried to follow the transliteration system of the *International Journal of Middle East Studies*. For translation, the final texts of all the laws studied in this book have been officially translated by the Hashemite Kingdom of Jordan. For most of the debates over these laws and the debates over the National Charter, the translation is my own. I would like to thank Camelia Suleiman for her assistance in translation, but in the end, I am solely responsible for their content—and any errors they may contain.

ONE

INSTITUTIONS AND THE POLITICS OF SURVIVAL

The monarchs of the Hashemite Kingdom of Jordan have endured in the face of economic crisis and regional political instability by following the spirit of Caliph Muawiyah ibn Abi Sufiyan's strategy. But how has the Jordanian regime managed to survive external challenges and control domestic threats at the same time? Can the Jordanian monarchy's success help explain the surprising durability of authoritarian regimes in the Arab world? And how can the lack of democracy in Jordan, and in the rest of the Middle East, be accounted for?

This book takes an institutional approach to answering these questions. Previously, some scholars have answered these questions by highlighting the lack of cultural or economic prerequisites for democracy in the Arab world. Other scholars, in contrast, have pointed to the evolution of civil society in the Middle East. But unlike other regions of the world, processes of political liberalization in the Arab world have not resulted in transitions to democracy. Yet, instead of tracing the persistence of authoritarian regimes to Islamic fundamentalism or to the uniqueness of Arab societies and economies, perhaps scholars must come to grips with the simple fact that democratization does not always lead to democracy.

By using an institutional focus, this book investigates the features of authoritarian regimes that facilitate the stability of autocracy. This approach blends the culturalist, structuralist, and rationalist accounts that are familiar in the social sciences. It highlights the way particular trajectories of institutional, ideological, and social interactions create distinctive paths of regime stability. In the face of external crises, the Jordanian regime has frequently used manipulations of domestic political institutions as a coping mechanism to quiet discontent caused by unpopular policies—especially during the 1990s. This book investigates the forms that these strategies have taken and the factors behind their success or failure in Jordan.

Today, the main threats to the Jordanian regime come in two forms. Jordan, like many developing countries, faces a severe debt crisis because of a poor resource base and exploding demographics. Secondly, like many countries in the Middle East, regional war and peace threaten more than the kingdom's borders. In the past, security crises threatened to remove Jordan from the map. But today security threats and economic crises pose a different challenge to the Hashemite regime. Both threaten to disturb the balance between the monarchy and the constituent members of the regime coalition, thus empowering the opposition to stoke popular resentment against the government and, potentially, the monarchy. In the face of such existential threats, the regime has been forced to undertake domestic institutional manipulations in order to limit popular discontent, to contain the opposition, and to maintain the unity of the regime coalition—maneuvers that can be labeled "regime survival strategies."

The regime's catalog of survival strategies in the 1990s has included both moves toward and away from political liberalization. Since 1989, the regime has focused its survival strategies on three main centers of political and civil society: political parties, the parliament, and the press. The Jordanian regime has managed the rules of these institutions when it saw the need to contain opposition to unpopular existential policies. The monarchy in Jordan, however, is not alone in using the management of political rules to its advantage. Political incumbents, regardless of regime type, use institutional rules to their political advantage. However, studies of the Middle East have frequently neglected these features of domestic politics.

The success of the Jordanian regime in implementing these survival strategies has been varied. This book investigates three factors that have influenced the success or failure of survival strategies: the resourceful use of constitutional rules by the regime, the reinforcement of the opposition's disunity of collective action against the survival strategy and the regime's policies, and the attention to not imposing costs on sectors of the regime coalition that could fray its unity. In highlighting these three factors, this book hopes to further scholarly debates about the stability of autocracy and the limits of democratization.

EXPLAINING AUTHORITARIANISM AND DEMOCRACY IN THE ARAB WORLD

Many attempts at explaining the lack of democracy in the Middle East have highlighted the lack of economic and cultural prerequisites for democracy in the region. The political culture argument finds that the fragile flower of democracy cannot grow in the desert of Islamic and Arab culture. The political economy argument finds that dependent economic development has caused structural deficiencies in Arab societies. Arguments such as these drive most popular analyses of Middle Eastern politics—especially the first.[1]

However, reducing the complexities of politics in the Middle East—or elsewhere—to a single variable has so far failed to yield useful and compelling explanations of the weakness of democracy in the region—or anywhere.[2]

In recent years, with the growth of democracy in southern Europe, Latin America, and Eastern Europe, many social scientists have come to see democracy as a contingent process brought about by decisions within the regime and the opposition. While today this approach suffers from a number of detractors, its contribution as the base for current literature on democratization in the Middle East—and its difficulties—nevertheless stands as intellectually relevant.

In this approach to democracy, the primary object of study has become the choices of actors—especially elites—in negotiating the change of power from authoritarian regimes to democratically elected politicians.[3] Democracy is viewed as the outcome of a political process in which groups reach a political compromise to install an institutional framework in order to settle their differences. Authors in this approach see these agreements as contingent upon situations and choices; thus, no transition to democracy results from deterministic systemic requisites.

Authors of this more contingent and short-run approach to democracy draw a distinction between processes of liberalization and democratization. Perhaps Guillermo O'Donnell and Philippe Schmitter best express the distinction between political liberalization and democratization. Liberalization is "the process of making effective certain rights that protect both individuals and social groups from arbitrary or illegal acts committed by the state or third parties."[4] Democratization, for O'Donnell and Schmitter, centers on the greater inclusion of citizens into the political process. Analysts of Middle Eastern politics have adapted this distinction between political liberalization and democratization. They have found that, in the Arab world, while the former process sometimes exists, the latter generally does not.[5]

Transitions from authoritarian rule usually occur when the regime loses legitimacy, often through failed economic reform efforts or military misadventures. The regime may attempt a project of political liberalization in an attempt to regain its legitimacy.[6] For some proponents of the contingent choice approach, the possibility that a liberalization project would stabilize without a transition to democracy is theoretically possible but not elaborated upon. For Adam Przeworski, liberalization without a regime transition can occur only if liberalizers within the regime open the political system while attaching a high probability to the success of repression (if necessary). Moreover, the regime will choose repression if civil society organizes an autonomous mobilization. Civil society, knowing that the liberalizers will choose repression (which would probably be successful), chooses to enter the opening and to forgo mobilization outside the regime's desired limits.[7]

Yet, according to Przeworski, liberalization is inherently unstable because the regime's institutions cannot accommodate the opposition's demands.

In this manner, a full transition to democracy generally results from splits within a regime between soft- and hard-liners that widen under the instability of political liberalization. Liberalization leads to a resurgence of civil society beyond the regime's control. Thus, the contingent approach to democracy sees the choices of political actors in a transition as the key to understanding the development of democracy.

That political liberalization is "inherently unstable" provides the fulcrum in the contingent choice model of regime transitions.[8] Yet this book will argue that political liberalization did not lead to democratization in Jordan. The regime was able to use political liberalization as a survival strategy when it was needed. Political liberalization was reversed when it later produced undesirable results for the Jordanian regime. The contingent choice model of democratization generally does not account for a stable political liberalization that does not lead to democratization. It cannot because it assumes a particular type of relationship between the state, the regime, and society—one that was present in southern Europe and in Latin America—but may not be elsewhere.

Under the bureaucratic authoritarian regimes of Latin America, the regime attempted to eradicate civil society. Yet, in the end the regime was only able to freeze the shape of society.[9] Civil society bloomed again once the authoritarian regime began the thaw of political liberalization. However, the global variation in the structures of state-society relations is far wider than this model of regime transition literature considers. Political liberalization may not be such a risky proposition to an authoritarian regime when a different pattern of relations between the state and society exists. The trajectory of regime-led state building that took place in Jordan (and in many other Middle Eastern countries) contrasts with the capturing of an already existing state by bureaucratic authoritarian regimes in Latin America. Chapter 2 will discuss the historical paths of regime and state building in the kingdom.

This book joins with critics of the contingent choice model of democratization in focusing on two problematic aspects of this model. First, authors within the contingent choice tradition tend to discount the role that external factors play in bringing about regime change. Second, with this model's focus on agency and contingency, political legacies and institutional contexts are often ignored. This book will use these lines of critique to help uncover how the Jordanian regime has survived numerous external crises during the 1990s. In sum, this book explores the roots of the stability of authoritarian regimes and the difficulties of democracy in the Middle East.

EXTERNAL FACTORS AND DEMOCRATIZATION

Explanations of the global growth of democracy have highlighted disciplinary boundaries within political science. Scholars of international relations have tended to overstate the unity of factors in causing this wave of democratization—up to the point of seeing the "end of history."[10] Scholars of comparative politics can also be critiqued for ignoring variables external to the state in causing democracy.[11] The contagion of democratization has thus been both overplayed and underplayed by scholars. However, there is no shortage of scholars that will point to the Middle East's immunity to the recent spread of democracy. In explaining this resistance, a key task for analysts lies in incorporating external factors while leaving room for domestic actors and institutions.[12]

Both war and peace in the Middle East have buffeted Jordan's domestic politics since the state's creation. Some argue that Jordan's shifting external alignments in the 1990s—first with Iraq during the Gulf War, and then with the U.S. and Israel in the Middle East peace process—were caused by King Hussein trying to steer a rocky course between domestic discontent and external security. Alternatively, others explain Jordanian foreign policy as the quest for "budget security" and external rents to prop up Jordan's meager resource base.[13]

This need for external financial support of the kingdom has been a feature of Jordanian politics from its inception. Subsidies have come from Britain, later the U.S., changing to Arab states, and then switching back to the U.S. Yet the necessity for foreign subsidies has also had a dramatic impact on Jordan's domestic politics. Jordan can be classified as a "rentier state" since such a large share of the state's budget is drawn from fiscal sources outside the kingdom, not from taxing domestic production.

The rentier state model argues that since states have enormous financial resources from nonproductive activities (oil revenues, large amounts of foreign aid, etc.), the state does not have to rely on taxation for its activities. As a state centered on the allocation of fiscal benefits, not on the extraction of taxes on production, the state has no need for representative institutions, "no taxation, no representation."[14]

Analysts have used the rentier state model to argue that the ending of external rents due to the fall in world oil prices—and the related declines in aid from oil states (to states such as Jordan)—has caused economic crises to lead to political crises.[15] In the "post-rentier" argument, the return of the necessity for taxation will lead to the return of representation. Democratization and political liberalization will be used by incumbent regimes to expand the base of support for necessary economic reforms, as well as to share the blame for such unpopular measures as cuts in subsidies and higher taxes. Yet, even if the post-rentier argument correctly sees economic and political crises as linked, the argument cannot predict the direction of the regime's reaction to the political crises: by using political liberalization or by using deliberalization (or even coercion). Jordan is thus similar to cases in Africa where Michael Bratton and Nicholas van de Walle found that "to the extent that economic and international forces were important to regime transitions, they were mediated by domestic political and institutional considerations."[16]

The effects of war-making in the Middle East, likewise, have produced varying effects on the paths of state and society building in the region—a variation that can be linked to regime type.[17] Has regime-led political liberalization allowed the leaders of Jordan and Egypt to pursue policies of conflict resolution with Israel—allowing the regime to mitigate both domestic and international conflicts? Or has political liberalization opened the door to sometimes quarrelsome public discussions of Jordan's best foreign policy interests?[18] The Jordanian regime, in the face of regional war and peace, first opened itself up for political liberalization in the late 1980s and early 1990s. It then reversed the process later in the decade. This raises questions of how the Jordanian regime was able to: first, liberalize politically without a resulting transition to democracy; and second, deal with unpopular foreign and economic policies in the context of stabilizing authoritarian rule.

LEGACIES OF REGIME TYPES AND DEMOCRATIC TRANSITIONS

These questions return us to the second major criticism of the contingent choice model of democratization: that the model tends to ignore the political and institutional context where "contingent choices" take place. Is there a relationship between the institutional features of the monarchical regime in Jordan which facilitates its survival?

Przeworski, for example, argues that agency is central to regime transitions since "conditions only structure conflicts, they do not make choices. But the structure of choices is the same."[19] However, a number of authors have responded to Przeworski by demonstrating that the structure of choices is *not* the same in different paths of transitions. In other words, political institutions have been the "missing variable in theories of regime change."[20]

Since regimes are generally seen as "the formal and informal institutions that structure political interaction," the institutional features of the regime in Jordan may explain why it has been able to liberalize politically without losing control over the process.[21] Richard Snyder and James Mahoney find that incorporating institutional variables into theories of regime change helps explain both how incumbents fail to survive and how challengers can succeed in transforming regimes. Perhaps investigating institutions can also help explain the opposite situation that has occurred in Jordan—incumbents surviving and challengers failing to transform the regime. In other words, an institutional approach toward the Jordanian monarchy would seem especially suited for investigating the factors influencing the success or failure of a regime's survival strategies.

A number of recent works on regime change have begun to remedy the lack of attention to the legacies of previous regime types that plagued the contingent choice model of democratization. Juan Linz and Alfred Stepan argue that "it should be clear that the characteristics of the previous nondemocratic regime have profound implications for the transition *paths* available and the *tasks* different countries face when they begin their struggles to develop consolidated democracies."[22] Within this institutional approach, Linz and Stepan use a two-track research method. They first taxonomize the characteristics of the various regime types. They then delineate the possible paths from those regimes toward democratic transition and consolidation.

The monarchies of the Middle East, however, are generally left out of these general classification schemes. Moreover, there are a number of institutional differences between Middle Eastern monarchies and Latin American bureaucratic authoritarianism, Eastern European post-totalitarianism, and African neopatrimonialism. A near comprehensive survey of democratization by Barbara Geddes includes all authoritarian regimes lasting three years or more, except for monarchies.[23] As most current monarchical authoritarian regimes are in the Arab world, she neglects both a region and an important subtype of authoritarian rule. This book hopes to help remedy this neglect.

The regime in Jordan can be taxonomized with the other examples of monarchical authoritarianism in cases such as Morocco, Kuwait, Saudi Arabia, and Iran under the shah. In this type of regime, the monarch is a personalistic ruler, however, he does not rule alone. The king stands at the center of a regime coalition that may be diverse and can include a broad social base. A degree of political pluralism is allowed—if not encouraged—both within the regime coalition and the legal opposition. The mass population generally remains politically quiescent and is mobilized along communal or clientelistic lines. The monarchy is generally constitutionally organized and legitimized, but the constitution formally grants the monarchy unchecked power. However, informal constraints on the monarch's power come from social norms and protected spaces—such as the home and the mosque. Finally, a mentality (not quite an ideology) of the regime may be based on anticolonial leadership, religious prestige, or "traditional" privilege.[24]

SURVIVAL STRATEGIES

How does a monarchical authoritarian regime react to external crises that threaten to destabilize its rule? Like many other authoritarian regimes, the monarchy's reaction takes the form of a "satisficing" strategy to deal with these crises. The regime meets the crises with piecemeal reforms that privilege the regime's survival over making sweeping reforms that may upset the status quo.[25] These survival strategies vary with the nature of the crisis and the ability of the regime to successfully carry them out.

This book concerns itself with the Jordanian regime's manipulation of institutional rules in three venues: political parties, the Jordanian Parliament (specifically the elected House of Deputies), and the press. These three venues have been chosen because they are the three major objects of domestic political discussion among the Jordanian public and elite. Debates over the proper institutional rules for political parties, elections for Parliament, and newspapers dominated the political attention of Jordanians in the 1990s. The regime has focused on these three institutional venues because they offer the best potential to contain the opposition and to limit popular discontent while maintaining the unity of the regime coalition and still appearing to outsiders to be offering a "march towards democracy." Political scientists have also focused on the role that civil society (in this study exemplified by the press) and political society (parliaments) and the linkage between the two spheres (political parties) have all played in political liberalization and democratization elsewhere in the world. Thus, this book focuses on these three institutional areas to help argue that democratization does not always lead to democracy. Rather, manipulations of the press, political parties, and elections for Parliament have helped insure the continued rule of the Jordanian monarchy. This book, however, will not only point out that survival strategies can maintain a regime's power. It also discusses some of the factors behind the success of regime survival strategies. Why do some institutional manipulations work in capturing the opposition while others fuel public discontent?

This book investigates three factors that have influenced the success or failure of survival strategies. The first factor is the resourceful use of constitutional rules by the regime. Actors, in choosing the venue for implementing or contesting institutional changes, seek the arena that will most likely yield positive results for that particular actor. Different institutional venues contain specific rules for behavior. In some institutional environments, actors may have incentives to "switch to neighboring institutional codes should their behavior prove incompatible with the rules of one institution."[26] Thus, it is up to the actors involved to use these sets of rules creatively for their strategic advantage. If, in implementing the institutional manipulation, the regime can more resourcefully use constitutional rules than the opposition, the more likely it is that the survival strategy will succeed. This factor behind the success or failure of survival strategies captures this idea of institutionally enabled action.

A second factor behind the success of survival strategies is the regime's manipulation of institutions to reinforce the disunity of the opposition's collective action against the regime's policies and the survival strategy itself. The contingent choice literature of democratization has highlighted the explanatory power of the agency of political actors. While this argument can be taken too far if the institutional context is ignored, agency nevertheless remains a useful explanatory tool when discussing contests over institutional rules. Often—especially in reference to Latin American cases of democratization—the unity of the opposition is assumed. In Jordan however, this assumption does not always hold. Ideological differences divide the Islamist opposition from Arab nationalists and leftists. Plus, within each trend, personal and programmatic disputes cause further fragmentation. One should not assume the unity of the opposition nor its choice to act.[27] Thus, regime survival strategies in limiting the role of the opposition accentuate these divisions within the opposition—in other words, to divide and rule. The regime attempts to sow the seeds of disunity through selective incentives or disincentives to specific opposition groups or by institutionalizing rules that can capitalize on the variety of ideological trends within the opposition. The more likely the institutional manipulation's ability to promote disunity among the opposition, the more likely it is to succeed.

The third factor behind the success of regime survival strategies can be seen as a mirror image of the second. If the institutional manipulation does not impose costs on sectors of the regime coalition—which fray its unity—the more likely the survival strategy is to succeed. The contingent choice model of democratization highlights the role that divisions within an authoritarian regime coalition have in leading toward a regime transition. If institutional manipulations can be found to resolve—or at least contain—natural divisions within the regime coalition, then a major cause of regime failure can be avoided. The institutional structure of monarchical authoritarianism aids in this project—as the king stands in the center of politics and builds policy coalitions around him. However, policy differences in Jordan have threatened to tear the coalition apart. Thus, survival strategies aim to minimize this potential by providing a clear policy agenda for the regime coalition, as well as minimize ideological disputes within the regime coalition that could be capitalized on by the opposition.

These three factors combine to explain the success or failure of a regime survival strategy. As these factors vary, so does the potential for the success of an institutional manipulation by the regime. However, the success or failure of a survival strategy does not stand alone in time. Background and context do matter. Thus, regime survival strategies in Jordan are investigated historically in this book. Past events—especially past successes or failures of survival strategies—can influence the outcome of a later episode by offering new interpretations of institutional rules, by creating differing degrees of opposition disunity, or by resulting in various levels of regime coalition unity. Thus, this book will pay careful attention to the historical sequence of events surrounding the regime's survival strategies in Jordan between 1988 and 2001.

Chapter 2 offers a historical background to this study. This chapter briefly explains the process of regime-led state building in Jordan. It will pay special attention to critical junctures in Jordan's history such as the founding of the state in the 1920s, the challenge of Arab nationalism in the 1950s, and the civil war with the Palestinian *fedayeen* in 1970. The legacies of these junctures set the stage for the events studied in this book by empowering the monarchy, creating a set of social allies for the regime, and by setting the institutional, economic, and cultural contexts in which events after 1998 played out.

Chapter 3 will begin the book's discussion of regime survival strategies. It focuses on the domestic ramifications of King Hussein's 1988 decision to sever administrative ties with the Palestinian West Bank and the resulting economic crisis in Jordan. The regime responded to riots in April 1989 with a series of survival strategies that offered greater political liberalization. The two main survival strategies were the 1989 parliamentary elections and the National Charter pact of 1990. The domestic impact of the 1991 Gulf War will also be noted in this context.

The analysis of the period of political liberalization continues in chapter 4. After the end of the Gulf War, the Jordanian regime joined the U.S.-led Middle East peace process. The Madrid conference and the following Washington talks offered the hope for a peace treaty between Jordan and Israel. On the domestic front, however, the regime was involved in a number of institutional debates with the opposition. The legislation of laws relegalizing parties (1992) and allowing greater press freedom (1993) institutionalized the process of political liberalization. However, both laws privileged the regime's desire for limits to public freedoms.

The summer of 1993 offered a crucial turning point in the process of political liberalization as discussed in chapter 5. As a peace treaty with Israel began taking form, the regime moved to curtail political liberties. Through the decree of amendments to the election law the regime dramatically reduced the opposition's role in the Parliament. This new Parliament quickly ratified the Jordanian-Israeli peace treaty in 1994.

Chapter 6 explains how, over the next few years, opposition grew to the regime's existential policies of normalizing relations with Israel and implementing economic structural adjustment reforms. Moreover, the Middle East peace process began to slow and promised economic rewards failed to appear. These events resulted in greater domestic discontent that would be addressed through later survival strategies.

Chapter 7 describes how the regime cracked down on political liberties in order to contain domestic discontent. The most notable of these survival strategies was the legislation of laws to curtail press freedom. After failing to make a decreed amendment to the press law stand in 1997, the regime succeeded in 1998. In the meantime, the opposition boycotted the November 1997 parliamentary elections. As a result, an even more progovernment parliament took office. Thus, on the eve of King Hussein's death, relations between the regime and opposition had reached a nadir.

The succession of King Abdullah II in 1999 promised a return to greater political liberalization. The results of this promise are discussed in chapter 8. The press law of 1999 offered fewer limits on press freedoms than the 1997 and 1998 versions of the law. However, the collapse of the Middle East peace process and the second Palestinian intifada presented the new king with significant external challenges that called for domestic survival strategies—and a return to the process of deliberalization. The regime delayed parliamentary elections and further manipulated the electoral and press laws to keep regional tensions from overflowing into the kingdom.

The concluding chapter will recap the discussion of the factors behind the success and failure of regime survival strategies. It will also put regime survival strategies in Jordan in a comparative perspective with cases of authoritarianism in Morocco, Kuwait, Egypt, and Iran under the shah.

TWO

REGIME-LED STATE BUILDING IN JORDAN: 1921-1988

This book makes the argument that the institutional features of monarchical authoritarianism can help explain the Hashemite regime's survival of external crises during the 1990s. This chapter provides a historical background to recent events by outlining the process of regime-led state building in Jordan. External crises and domestic opponents have constantly challenged the Jordanian monarchy during its eight decades of rule. Critical historical junctures have shaped the current structure of Jordan's regime and its coalition of supporters. Moreover, these legacies of the past both help and hinder the regime's ability to implement survival strategies today.

The historical process of state building by authoritarian regimes, while not unique to the Middle East, nevertheless has received less attention than warranted in the general literature on regime transitions. In southern European, Latin American, and, to a lesser extent, Eastern European examples of regime transitions, an authoritarian or totalitarian regime had taken over an already existing state apparatus. However, in many Middle Eastern (as well as African) countries, the regime predates the existence of the modern state. Thus, authoritarian regimes have built a state around themselves. In contrast, Latin American authoritarian regimes often inherited the political legacies of previously democratic states—making redemocratization an easier task once the bureaucratic authoritarian regime weakened.

Thus, this chapter argues that the process of regime-led state building explains the survival of authoritarianism in Jordan and other Middle Eastern states through three important legacies. First, tracing the process of regime-led state building more clearly delineates the actors who comprise the regime coalition and the roots of their links to the monarchy. Second, exploring historical developments also shows the effect of established constitutional rules on the distribution of institutional prerogatives—for example, the balance of power between executive and legislative institutions in Jordan. Third, delineating the path of regime-led state building helps uncover the resources—material, symbolic, institutional, and otherwise—that are available for both the regime coalition and the opposition. These factors will be explored through a short summary of some of the critical junctures in the process of regime-led state building in Jordan.

ESTABLISHMENT OF THE STATE

Jordan, like many states of the Middle East and Africa, owes its existence to the process of European colonialism. Before World War I, the areas that would become the Kingdom of Jordan were peripheral provinces of the Ottoman Empire. In the aftermath of the war, the British and the French carved the Middle East into zones of imperial influence. The British created the mandate territory of Transjordan and awarded it to the Hashemites in 1921. Amir Abdullah, with the help of the British, built the apparatus of a state in Transjordan. Abdullah and the British fended off threats to the existence of the state from various powerful tribes, eventually consolidating government rule over all of the mandate's territory. With independence from Britain in 1946, the mandate became a kingdom, and Amir Abdullah became King Abdullah I. From 1920 until 1947, Abdullah and the British established the core of the Jordanian state, monarchical authoritarian rule under the Hashemites, and nominal independence for the new entity.

The Ottoman Empire generally neglected the areas that were to become Jordan. The semi-arid geography of Jordan favored nomadic pastoralism over settled agriculture and centralized administration. Peasants eked out livings on the few areas for agriculture in the north of the country, but they always faced the constant threat of Bedouin incursions. In the final century of Ottoman rule, however, direct state authority from Istanbul via Damascus began to expand over the area. With advances and retreats, the Ottomans first brought the north of Transjordan under direct control and later attempted to subdue the south. On the eve of World War I, the Ottoman state firmly held Ajloun and Salt in the north, was attempting to regain control in Karak, and had failed to assert its authority in Maʿan in the south.[1] When the Ottoman state collapsed after the war, the British moved into the region.

The Hashemites of Arabia, under the leadership of Abdullah's father, Sharif Hussein, sought rewards for their leadership of the Arab revolt against the Ottomans and for their cooperation with Britain in the war effort. Meanwhile, the British were eager to have a buffer between their direct rule in Palestine and both the expanding Saudi power in Arabia to the south and the French mandate in Syria to the north. The two wishes were fulfilled with the creation of a new entity in Transjordan.

In 1920, Abdullah had come to Amman with the hope of regaining his brother Faisal's throne in Damascus. The French had put Syria under their direct rule, pushing the Hashemites out to Iraq and back to Arabia. The British carved a mandate for Transjordan out of the mandate for Palestine and handed its control to Abdullah in Amman in 1921. Mary Wilson describes the relationship between Britain and Amir Abdullah:

> Within Transjordan the close association of Abdullah and Britain was a product of mutual utility. That Transjordan existed at all as a separate state was in response to Britain's strategic and political needs; as it was Abdullah's ties to Britain, his position as the keystone in the arch between British mandate authority and local society that lifted and maintained him above the indigenous leadership of the territory. As far as British interests were concerned, Abdullah was useful as the 'native facade' behind which it was able to ensure its interests without unduly stimulating opposition.[2]

The nascent Jordanian state, however, faced threats from restless Bedouin tribes. Abdullah's regime eventually crushed local rivals, but only after having to rely on direct British military intervention. In the early 1920s, revolts in the Jordan Valley and an uprising by the powerful Adwan tribe tested the new state's ability to assert its autonomy. Incursions by Saudi Wahabbi forces in the south forced Abdullah to define the state's borders in the desert. British military officers, led by John Bagot Glubb "Pasha," began to forge the unity of the various Jordanian tribes by including them in the Arab Legion.[3]

The new state also owed its fiscal survival to the British. The British subsidy to Amir Abdullah allowed him to buy support among indigenous leaders. In addition to the military subsidy, the British also began to aid the new state's expansion of the administration of taxation over the mandate's territory. Local grievances gained a voice through a national conference of opponents of the British (and to a lesser extent, Abdullah), which produced the 1928 National Pact. With the formalization of the mandate under Jordan's 1928 Organic Law, the British and Abdullah reluctantly accepted the need for an elected legislative council. In 1929, the first Legislative Assembly was elected—but the council was rigged to pose no threat to the executive authority's power.[4]

The period of the establishment of the state of Jordan thus left a number of important legacies. Most important was the existence of the state itself. During this period, the British and Abdullah also eliminated or subdued local rivals—many who preferred their autonomy under the tribal "anarchy" of earlier times.[5] For the state to exist, it relied first on rent from outsiders and then later on the support of friendly tribes on the inside. The building of the state revolved around the person of Abdullah and his embryonic court.

However, a competing legacy from Jordan's early constitutional development was a reoccurring popular demand for elected legislative accountability and constraints on, if not control over, the monarch's executive powers. Yet, unlike Morocco or Egypt, this popular desire did not take the form of a 'national party' along the lines of the Moroccan Istiqlal or Egyptian Wafd parties. Private local interests prevented the signatories of the National Pact from presenting a coherent unified program in opposition to the British and to Abdullah.[6] The power of social forces in Jordan also could not compete with the relative fiscal superiority of the externally funded mandate state—a more severe handicap than what faced nationalists in Egypt of Morocco.

THE WAR IN PALESTINE

Despite Abdullah's growing strength inside Transjordan, his ambition remained for control of a larger Arab entity—either greater Syria, or an even larger Hashemite-led Arab state. Until 1948, the British had kept Abdullah's ambition in check with its control over his military. However, with the British withdrawal from Palestine looming, and the failure of the United Nations partition plan for Palestine, the British allowed for Abdullah to expand his kingdom.[7] Transjordan's role in the 1948 war can be debated, but most accounts now show that Abdullah had reached some form of agreement with the leaders of the nascent Israeli state in dividing the territory of mandatory Palestine. At the conclusion of the war, Transjordan's Arab Legion controlled the West Bank—a lion's share of Arab Palestine under the UN partition plan.

Transjordan annexed the West Bank following the war. Transjordan thus became the Hashemite Kingdom of Jordan. Jordan's population tripled with the addition of the West Bank and of Palestinian refugees. Palestinians were quickly given full Jordanian citizenship. However, the more urbanized and settled Palestinians were generally less willing to submit to Abdullah's personalized patrimonial authoritarianism. In 1951, a Palestinian gunman assassinated Abdullah.

Jordan's intertwinement with Palestine had begun with the mandate. After 1948, however, Jordan's role in Palestine was magnified. The three-sided relationship between Jordan, Israel, and the Palestinians continues as a legacy until today.[8] For Jordan, the Arab-Israeli conflict became not only a matter of foreign policy, but an issue of domestic politics as well. The addition of the West Bank and its Palestinians inhabitants also changed Jordan's society and economy. A Palestinian private sector took its place alongside the institutions of the state with their East Bank focus. Over time these lines blurred, but the legacy of such a dualism remains. Moreover, the addition of the Palestinians into Jordanian politics expanded membership in both the regime coalition and the opposition.

THE TALAL INTERLUDE

After the assassination of King Abdullah, his son, Talal, ascended to the throne. However, Talal's rise proved contentious because of his history of mental illness and because of palace intrigue. Talal's reign would be brief for the same two reasons. The prime minister, Tawfiq Abd al-Huda, exploited the weak position of the king and expanded the powers of his office. However, Abd al-Huda alienated not only the ideological opposition in parliament, but the conservative supporters of the palace as well. King Talal was deposed for his mental illness in August 1953 after a many-sided struggle for power. With the removal of Talal, the palace faction, led by Talal's wife Zayn, gained power in the name of Talal's son Hussein at the expense of Abd al-Huda.[9] The balance of power between the king and the prime minister, however, remained contested even after the dismissal of Abd al-Huda.

During his reign, Talal promulgated a new constitution in January of 1952. The constitution made Jordan a constitutional monarchy with power divided between the king, the prime minister, and the elected parliament. The 1952 constitution would be Talal's main legacy in Jordanian politics. Despite the fact that the regime has often ignored or suspended many of its provisions, the constitution provides norms regarding the division of powers and the processes of lawmaking that are frequently invoked in Jordan. The resulting institutional venues created by the constitution are discussed below. However, the replacement of Talal by Hussein marked the beginning of the consolidation of power in the throne. Yet, as politics in the Middle East polarized in the 1950s, the young King Hussein would have to survive challenges from prime ministers other than Abd al-Huda for the crown to rest easily on his head.

THE ARAB NATIONALIST CHALLENGE TO THE REGIME

The early years of King Hussein's reign coincided with a period of ferment in the Arab world. A number of postcolonial regimes were replaced by Arab nationalist coups as socioeconomic growth and the repercussions of the loss of Palestine in 1948 spread across the region. The Hashemites in Jordan survived due to timely Western help and the young Hussein's skill and luck. Domestic and foreign crises aligned in the second half of the 1950s to nearly sweep away the Jordanian monarchy.

In 1955, Britain brought Turkey and Iraq into the Baghdad Pact military alliance as a response to the growing power of Arab nationalism and its related Soviet interest in the region. Both the signatories of the pact and their Arab nationalist opponents in Egypt and Syria courted Jordan to join their side. In Jordan, the public generally tended toward the Arab nationalist opinion. The regime, however, was split between its historical dependence on Britain and the new king's own vague notion of an independent Hashemite Arab nationalism.

As 1955 turned to 1956, rioters heeded Egyptian President Gamal Abd al-Nasser's call for Jordan to join the Arab nationalist line in rejecting the Baghdad Pact. Through considerable coercion King Hussein and his army put down the riots. But deft diplomatic maneuverings allowed Jordan to stay out of the pact without alienating its British patron.[10]

In a gesture to show his independence from Britain, in March 1956 Hussein dismissed Glubb "Pasha," the Arab Legion's British chief. King Hussein's popularity in Jordanian and Arab public opinion skyrocketed. However, it took the voice of Glubb himself to restrain British resentment.[11] With the departure of its British leadership, control of the Arab Legion fell to young Arab officers, many of whom held Arab nationalist sentiments.

The rise of Arab nationalist army officers coincided with the rise of civilian politicians of various opposition stripes as well. In October 1956, parliamentary elections produced a House of Deputies with an absolute majority of the various opposition groups. The National Socialist Party was the largest party in the Parliament, which in alliance with the Communist and Baʿath parties constituted the opposition National Bloc. In a nod to constitutional monarchy and British parliamentary procedure, King Hussein appointed the head of the National Socialist Party, Suleiman al-Nabulsi, as his prime minister. As the Nabulsi government took office, the 1956 Suez War began when Israel, France, and Britain attacked Egypt.

The struggles among outside powers, public opinion, army officers, the prime minister, and the king cumulated in a showdown in April 1957. In the wake of the Suez War and the general rising tensions in the region, King Hussein and Prime Minister Nabulsi pulled in opposite directions. Alignments toward patronage from Britain or Egypt twisted foreign policy commitments as the king and prime minister attempted to use outside powers against their domestic rivals. The army joined the fray but aborted a coup on April 2, 1957. Aware of the multiple threats to his rule, King Hussein sacked Nabulsi. Then on April 13, the king, with the help of loyal Bedouin rank-and-file soldiers, fended off a second coup by Arab nationalist officers. With a return to his conservative supporters, Hussein declared martial law and banned political parties. Hussein returned Jordan to a pro-Western foreign policy by aligning with the U.S. under the Eisenhower Doctrine.[12]

The Hashemite regime barely survived the crises of the 1950s. The regime proceeded to forcefully crush Arab nationalist opposition, and, as a by-product, domestic political pluralism. Jordanian politics remained in stasis until 1967. However, the legacy of the monarchy's fear of pluralism lasted until the 1990s. During the intervening three decades, martial law froze the institutions of political society. Although the regime paid lip service to the rule of the constitution, some of its provisions were ignored. Yet the regime generally amended troublesome constitutional provisions rather than suspending the entire constitution.

As a result of this critical juncture, Hussein returned to Abdullah's regime coalition. However, he also added new allies like the Muslim Brotherhood. Over time, many of the king's Arab nationalist enemies were even rehabilitated, becoming loyalist politicians. In the late 1960s however, the Arab-Israeli conflict returned to endanger the survival of the Hashemite monarchy.

WAR AND CIVIL WAR

In the spring of 1967, Jordan joined Egypt and Syria in preparations for war against Israel. Although King Hussein foresaw defeat, he joined the Arab alliance for fear that his inaction would cause a domestic revolt. By joining the Arab alliance, Jordan lost the most from Israel's surprise attack in the June 1967 war. The Israeli military quickly seized control of the West Bank, as well as the Egyptian Sinai and the Syrian Golan Heights. However, Uriel Dann argues that losing the West Bank in 1967 may have been worth the price, as the threat of Arab nationalism to King Hussein's survival then subsided.[13]

Ideological threats to the survival of the Hashemites in Jordan did not end with the embarrassment of Arab nationalism in 1967. Palestinian nationalism grew out of the Arab states' defeat as a force in organizing resistance to Israel. As the Palestine Liberation Organization (PLO) grew and related Palestinian guerrilla groups multiplied in the late 1960s, they began to cause the Jordanian regime discomfort. The *fedayeen* militias, with their raids across the border, invoked Israeli reprisals against Jordanian targets. Moreover, as the Palestinian groups gained confidence they began to take an active role in Jordanian domestic politics. The Jordanian regime began to feel that the *fedayeen* were a threat to its sovereignty.[14]

After nearly two years of rising tensions between the Palestinian *fedayeen* and the Jordanian regime, the two forces clashed in September 1970. "Black September" was triggered by the People's Front for the Liberation of Palestine's (PFLP) hijacking of two Western airliners and bringing of the planes to Jordan. The regime responded with force and eliminated the militias positioned across the country—killing up to 3,400 Palestinians in the process.[15] By July 1971, the Jordanian regime had eliminated the PLO's military presence in Jordan.

However, not all Palestinian elements in Jordan sought to join the *fedayeen*. Many Palestinians had joined the monarchy's regime coalition in the decades of the state's growth—especially between 1948 and 1967. Palestinian businessmen were especially prominent in the Jordanian private sector and sought stability for economic growth under the monarchy and continued to do so even after Black September.

The losing of the West Bank to Israel in 1967 removed Jordan's direct control over events in Palestine, but not its key role in Arab-Israeli affairs. However, the legacy of the 1970 civil war may prove more important for the survival of the Hashemite regime in Jordan. The Arab nationalists and Palestinian nationalists both represented organized and ideological opposition movements that sought to remove the Hashemites from power.[16] With the elimination by force of the Palestinian *fedayeen*, the Jordanian regime succeeded in removing the most significant nationalist threats.

OIL BOOM AND THE POLITICS OF THE RENTIER STATE

In the 1970s, Jordan's economy received a welcomed boost with the rise in oil prices by the Arab petroleum producing states. Although Jordan itself produces no oil, Jordan exported many educated workers—most of whom are of Palestinian lineage—to the Gulf countries. These workers sent back remittances to their families in Jordan. With the enormous wealth accruing to the state through customs and indirect taxes, Jordan's economy could thus be seen as a secondary rentier economy. A state behavior similar to that of oil producing countries emerged as the state accrued revenue from sources other than taxation of production. Moreover, foreign aid directed to Jordan by other Arab governments mushroomed in the 1970s and 1980s, leading to the categorization of Jordan as a full-fledged rentier state. Regardless, the Jordanian state's primary activity became centered on the distribution of economic benefits. According to the rentier state literature, the rentier state offers nearly unlimited economic opportunities. In return, the rentier state expects its citizens to remain politically quiescent. In Jordan, the main beneficiaries of the state's largess generally had East Bank origins. The size of the Jordanian state ballooned in the 1970s and early 1980s. The Palestinians in Jordan generally either went to the Gulf for employment or continued their role in the private sector of Jordan's economy. The politics of the Jordanian rentier state left the legacy of the perception, if not the fact, of a divide between the state-employed East Bankers, and the Palestinian private sector. Moreover, the state used the economic boom to buy out domestic opponents that it had not yet crushed.

Just as the economy based on oil boomed in the 1970s, it burst in the 1980s.[17] The state did not begin weaning Jordanians off of state support, since the population had grown accustomed to state intervention in the economy. Instead, Jordan turned to foreign lending to support the state's spending habits. However, the growing economic malaise was worsened by a crucial foreign policy decision in 1988.

WHO'S WHO AND WHO'S WHERE IN CURRENT JORDANIAN POLITICS

Thus, in 1988, the Hashemite monarchy controlled a broad and varied regime coalition that ran a solidified state apparatus. King Hussein's decision in July 1988 to sever ties with the Palestinian West Bank would have far reaching consequences for Jordanian politics. It would necessitate the use of institutional survival strategies to contain the Jordanian opposition and to maintain the balance of power within the ranks of the regime coalition. The remainder of this chapter will outline the major political actors in Jordan and the domestic institutional venues that they inhabit. The survival strategies used by actors in these contexts will be discussed in the subsequent chapters.

The monarchy is the linchpin of the Jordanian political system. In the process of regime-led state building, the Hashemite monarchs have created a political system where the king not only reigns but rules as well. Unlike the monarchies of the Arab Gulf, however, members of the Hashemite family do not publicly serve in the government. In fact, the Jordanian monarchy has built the appearance that the king stands above day-to-day politics. Yet all Jordanians know that the king sets major policy decisions and trajectories. Thus, the personality of the monarch remains an important factor in Jordanian politics. Since independence, only four men have worn the Hashemite crown in Jordan: Abdullah ibn Hussein, Talal ibn Abdullah, Hussein ibn Talal, and now Abdullah ibn Hussein. King Abdullah I and King Hussein have imprinted their personalities on Jordan through the process of regime-led state building, and King Talal bequeathed Jordan a constitution. They have created the political system that Abdullah II inherited in 1999. They also built a broad and varied regime coalition.

The East Bank tribes comprise the first pillar of the Jordanian regime coalition. Many of these tribes were pastoral Bedouin even until after the creation of the Jordanian state. Tribesmen have filled positions in most sectors of the Jordanian state. Ethnic and religious minorities, a second pillar of the regime coalition, were also early to join the Hashemites in building the Jordanian state. Christians (in a Muslim country) and Circassians and Chechens (in an Arab nation) can also be found in many important state positions.

The state bureaucracy and the military each have grown over the years since the formation of the Jordanian state. The process of regime-led state building has given each of these state institutions its own culture so that individuals associated with them have subscribed to an identity beyond their local, tribal, or ethnic origin. Each today can be called a pillar of the Jordanian regime coalition.

A fifth pillar of the Jordanian regime coalition generally has its origins outside of the East Bank. These are the Palestinians in the businesses of the Jordanian private sector. The Palestinian community in Jordan can be divided in many ways—by their point of origin in Palestine, by their time of arrival in Jordan, and by their economic status. However, a general sense of corporate identity remains. Yet the most important cleavages among Palestinians are between 1948 refugees who improved their economic situation by working in the Gulf, West Bank elites that joined the Jordanian state during the nineteen years of Jordanian control over the West Bank, and refugees who arrived in 1967 or in 1990–1991. The first two groups have clearly joined the Hashemites' regime coalition; the latter has not.

Social groups, like the Palestinian refugees, have given their support to a variety of political groups that have a complicated relationship with the

Jordanian regime. From the 1950s until the 1970s the strongest opponents of the Hashemites were Arab nationalists and leftists. Leftist and Arab nationalist parties and organizations were severely repressed after 1956. Political parties remained banned in Jordan until 1992. With the decline of these ideologies in recent years, however, some individuals associated with these trends have thrown their support behind the regime. The examples of Soviet and Baʿathist dictatorship have led some leftists and Arab nationalists to conclude that the Hashemite monarchy in Jordan is a benign alternative.

As leftists and Arab nationalists began moving into the regime coalition, Islamists began moving out of it. The Muslim Brotherhood organization in Egypt and Syria was a long-time opponent of these Arab nationalist regimes. In Jordan, however, the Muslim Brotherhood provided the Hashemites with a reliable ally during the turbulent 1950s and 1960s. With the growth of political Islam as a potent ideology in the 1970s and 1980s, the Muslim Brotherhood and other Islamist groups in Jordan began to lose confidence in the Jordanian regime's commitment to making Jordanian society more Islamic. Yet, the Muslim Brotherhood remained legal during the thirty-six-year ban on political parties because it was considered a "social organization," not a political grouping. Today the group still clearly opposes government policies, but not the regime itself. By 1988, this helped the Islamists become the most potent opposition force in Jordan.

These political actors reside and work in a variety of political institutional environments in Jordan. Six major venues are crucial to the implementation and success or failure of regime survival strategies under study in this book. The process of regime-led state building has shaped each of these venues. The 1952 constitution and its later amendments provide the basis for most of these institutions. However, forces in political and civil society have also shaped the rules of these institutions as they stood in 1988.

Under the Jordanian constitution, the executive branch has considerable powers to unilaterally control the political system in Jordan.[18] The king constitutes a venue to himself as he stands above the state machinery. The king appoints and dismisses the prime minister and the cabinet (Article 35), appoints the Senate (Article 36), calls elections for the House of Deputies, and can also dissolve the House (Article 34).

The prime minister and cabinet require not only the king's confidence, but the House's as well (Article 51). Individual ministers, as well as the entire cabinet, can be removed by a majority vote of the House (Article 53). Yet, the cabinet begins the legislative process by determining what draft laws will be submitted to the Parliament (Article 91).

The elected House of Deputies and the appointed Senate comprise the parliamentary venue. In the normal course of legislation, the House may accept, amend, or reject a draft law submitted by the cabinet (Article 91). After the House has decided upon a draft law, even if it is rejected, the Senate then decides upon the draft law. The draft law then proceeds to the king, who ratifies it. If the king vetoes a draft law, the veto may be overridden by a two thirds majority of each chamber of Parliament (Article 93).

In contrast to this normal course of legislation, in certain circumstances the ministerial cabinet can also decree laws. The cabinet can approve "provisional laws" which have the full effect of law (Article 94). However, the cabinet only has this power when the Parliament is not sitting or has been dissolved. Moreover, provisional laws should only cover matters which "admit of no delay or which necessitate expenditures incapable of postponement." (Article 94) The king ratifies the provisional law if he so chooses. Provisional laws must be submitted to the Parliament at the beginning of its next session; at that time the Parliament may nullify or amend provisional laws.

The judicial venue in Jordan is firmly under the king's control. The king appoints judges by Royal Decree (Article 98). Constitutionally, the courts are to be "free from any interference in their affairs" (Article 100), however, in practice the courts have only been staffed with staunch supporters of the regime. Yet judges are often drawn from the regime coalition's more liberal wing. Jordanian judges have taken their role seriously and may on occasion reject the government's dictates. If the king's will is clear, however, the courts generally will not try to challenge it.

Outside of the formal state structures, the press traditionally formed a venue that generally complemented rather than challenged the existing power relations. This, of course, changed with the expansion of press freedoms with the passing of the more liberal 1993 Press and Publications Law. Most of the daily newspapers, however, remained under state ownership through the 1990s. The mass media—television and radio—was also state owned and tightly controlled. The "street" occasionally saw mass mobilization. However, most public outbursts were on the order of the April 1989 riots—disorganized displays of dissatisfaction.

The riots in April 1989 were caused by the removal of subsidies on a number of everyday products. The necessity of implementing such economic reforms stemmed from the economic crisis Jordan was undergoing at the time. That economic crisis had its roots in a foreign policy decision made by King Hussein in July 1988—the decision to disengage Jordanian administrative ties to the West Bank. This sequence of events would lead to the need for institutional survival strategies to contain the domestic political fallout from these economic and foreign policy decisions.

THREE

ECONOMIC CRISIS AND POLITICAL LIBERALIZATION

King Hussein severed Jordan's administrative ties to the Israeli-occupied West Bank in July 1988. The move allowed for the declaration of a Palestinian state in the West Bank and Gaza by the PLO later that year. The foreign policy decision had far-reaching effects on the domestic politics of the remainder of the kingdom for the next decade. The disengagement from the West Bank quickly turned from a foreign policy maneuver into an economic crisis as the Jordanian economy nearly collapsed. The government introduced a number of unpopular economic reforms in order to please international lenders who were bailing out the economy. Average Jordanians protested the cuts in daily subsidies. In April 1989, riots erupted in a number of traditional strongholds of the regime coalition in response to the biting economic reforms.

With the riots the economic crisis turned political. The regime responded with a series of domestic political reforms that allowed greater political liberalization. The first was allowing long-stalled parliamentary elections in November 1989. The second was the signing of a National Charter where a spectrum of Jordanian elites agreed on a program of liberalizing political institutional reforms. These two survival strategies aimed to contain the discontent caused by the disengagement from the West Bank and the decision to pursue economic structural adjustment. This "democratic bargain" was the price to pursue existential foreign and economic policies. However, in both institutional maneuvers, the regime attempted to award advantages to its supporters and to limit the gains of the opposition in the process of political liberalization.

DISENGAGEMENT AND FINANCIAL CRISIS

King Hussein announced that Jordan would disengage its administrative links to the West Bank on July 31, 1988. King Hussein stated that this decision was made for the "benefit of the Palestinian cause and the Arab Palestinian people."[1] A number of international factors resulted in the severing of ties with the part of the kingdom annexed after 1948 but lost to Israel in 1967. The decision seemingly resolved the longstanding dispute between the Hashemite Kingdom and the PLO over the Palestinians of the West Bank in favor of the PLO. The Palestinian uprising, or intifada, which began in 1987, protested the Israeli occupation. But Palestinians also generally rejected a return to Jordanian rule. In contrast, most external plans for peace envisioned a role for Jordan in the West Bank. However, Israeli right-wingers began to argue that "Jordan is Palestine" when calling for a transfer of Arabs out of Israel and the occupied territories. By disengaging from the West Bank, Jordan sought to affirm a distinction between Jordan and the Palestinians. In the regime's eyes, this would then reduce the threat from both Israel and the Palestinians. As the PLO and Jordan had begun a rapprochement in the late 1980s, disengagement cleared the way for the PLO to declare a Palestinian state in November 1988. Finally, by allowing for the possibility of a separate entity in Palestine, Jordan could be allowed to concentrate on its own (Jordanian-East Bank) national identity.[2]

While the disengagement was seen by the Jordanian regime as a political success (despite the mixed public reaction to the decision), severing ties with the West Bank came with a high economic price. Palestinians residing on both sides of the Jordan River began to question if Jordan would remove their citizenship. Insecurity about their international status and domestic communal relations led to worsening consumer and investor confidence among the largely Palestinian commercial class of Amman. Palestinian capital began a flight out of Jordan's banks. Against the background of the bust of the oil economy, Jordan's currency, the dinar, lost nearly half its value. Jordan's external debt soared to nearly double its GNP in 1988–1989. In response to the fiscal crisis, Prime Minister Zeid Rifaʾi resorted to a lending program sponsored by the International Monetary Fund (IMF) to contain the economic crisis. In return for $275 million in standby credits, Jordan agreed to a five-year stabilization program with the IMF. "Jordan agreed to strength foreign reserves, reduce inflation through tight credit policies and improve the current account balance. It also pledged to reform the tax system and reduce its budget deficit."[3] To do this the IMF called on the Jordanian government to reduce subsidies on fuel and food.

The removal of subsidies led the economic crisis to become political when rioting erupted on April 18, 1989. Yet the rioting did not begin in the Palestinian refugee camps around Amman. Rather, the riots began in the traditional heartland of Hashemite support, the city of Maʿan in the south of the country. Through the process of regime-led state building the Hashemites had gained the acceptance of the tribes in the 1920s and 1930s. As politicians and military leaders, southern East Bankers had been pillars of the regime. However, rank and file East Bankers in the south of the kingdom generally relied on fixed incomes from government service and had less general economic opportunities than residents of the capital. The protesters called for economic and political reforms. The combination of fiscal and international crises had led to calls for a change in the frozen Jordanian political arena—yet these calls came most loudly from within the regime coalition. The protesters voiced their support for the monarchy as an institution but called for returning the subsidies, new parliamentary elections, and the sacking of Prime Minister Zayd al-Rifaʾi.

The regime chose to call for new elections instead of responding with massive force, as it had in the past. The decision to offer a return to parliamentary life was a capricious decision by King Hussein. His advisors had split on recommending a response to the riots. Malik Mufti argues that the decision to hold elections was a convenient response to the subsidy crisis, since an electoral initiative had been envisioned in 1986 by the passing of a new electoral law.[4] Thus, King Hussein responded on three tracks to the 1989 riots. First, he quickly sacked Prime Minister Rifaʾi and replaced him with the king's cousin, General Sharif Zeid bin Shaker. Second, the king expressed his desire for a political pact, the National Charter to draw up rules for a more liberalized political system. And third, he allowed the long delayed parliamentary elections to go forward. Many see the elections held in November 1989 as one of the most free and fair in Jordan's history—if not the fairest. This chapter investigates the latter two survival strategies in detail.

THE NOVEMBER 1989 ELECTIONS

With the riots of April 1989 the necessity of a political transformation became clear to the regime. Included among the many demands of the rioters was the desire for a new freely elected parliament.[5] King Hussein thus pulled the issue of electoral reform off of the back burner. Bin Shaker's new government hastily decreed amendments to the 1986 Election Law that recognized the disengagement from the West Bank. Electoral constituencies were realigned to an East Bank only electorate; special mechanisms for representing Palestinians were eliminated. The 1989 amendments to the 1986 Election Law were decreed as a provisional law in July 1989 (Number 23 for the year 1989).

The management of electoral rules in the 1990s to minimize the power of the opposition and to maximize the power of regime supporters in Jordan's Parliament was not a new phenomenon for the Hashemite regime. Jordan saw its first Election Law in 1928 with the creation of the Legislative Council.[6] The council was composed of members indirectly elected or appointed by Amir Abdullah. This mandate law established two precedents. First, the 1928 law gave a degree of overrepresentation to minorities—namely Christians, Circassians, and Bedouins. Second, electoral constituencies were based on geographical divisions that did not correspond to population distribution.[7]

These two factors have been present in some form in all subsequent electoral laws in Jordan since 1928.

With independence from Britain in 1946, King Abdullah promulgated a new election law in 1947. Two years later this law was amended to incorporate the annexed West Bank territories. Elections had been held just before the loss of the West Bank to Israel in 1967. When the term of this Parliament ended in 1971, parliamentary life was suspended for over a decade.[8] King Hussein recalled Parliament in 1984. Any vacant seats from the East Bank were filled through by-elections, while vacant West Bank seats were filled by appointment. In 1986, the Parliament passed an entirely new electoral law. The 1986 Election Law also continued the tradition of overrepresenting rural areas, as well as including quotas for the Christian, Circassian, and Chechen minorities, as well as certain Bedouin tribes.[9]

Many of the rioters in April 1989 demanded the implementation of the 1986 Election Law and the holding of elections under it. However, Prime Minister Bin Shaker amended the 1986 law removing all references to Jordanian administration of the West Bank. The 1989 amendments created an electoral system with 80 seats from 20 electoral constituencies. However, district magnitude varied from constituency to constituency. The seats and constituencies set up with the 1989 amendments remained mostly constant (with minor changes) during the 1993 and 1997 elections. The distribution of constituencies and seats can be found in Table 3.1. The electoral system of 1986/1989 warrants comment in four areas: voting procedures, apportionment of constituencies, minority quotas, and the voting list system.

A number of procedural features of the 1986 Election Law remained unchanged with the 1989 amendments. Voters had to be nineteen years of age (Article 3). Members of the military and security forces were barred from voting (Article 5). Also, in order to vote, potential voters must not have only registered to vote in advance (Article 8), but also have obtained a personal election card (a voting card), in order to vote (Article 35).

However, more important to the outcome for the 1989 elections was the distribution of seats and districts under the 1989 amendments. Constituencies were distributed based on administrative and geographical boundaries that often trace back to the 1920s, rather than on population. Thus, under the 1989 Election Law amendments, Jordan's electoral districts were severely malapportioned and remained so with the later 1993 amendments (see table 3.1). Consequently, most urbanized areas tended to be underrepresented. Rural overrepresentation generally has helped traditional regime allies in gaining seats in the Parliament. In contrast, urban underrepresentation tended to minimize the inclusion of Palestinians and ideological groups in Parliament.

Under the distribution of seats in the 1989 amendments, Christians, Circassians, Chechens, and Bedouins were again all overrepresented in comparison to their proportion of Jordan's population. Christians received 11.25 percent of the seats despite their comprising only 6 percent of the general

Table 3.1 Distribution of Election Districts and Representation

Constituency (Shaded Signifies Urban Area)	Muslim Seats	Christian Seats	Circassian Seats[a]	Total Seats	Malapportionment[b]
Amman 1 (Far Eastern Suburbs)	3	0	0	3	−2
Amman 2 (Eastern Amman)[c]	3	0	0	3	−7
Amman 3 (Center/West Amman)[d]	3	1	1	5	0
Amman 4 (Southern Suburbs)[e]	2	0	0	2	−1
Amman 5 (Far Western Suburbs)[f]	4	0	1	5	0
Madaba	2	1	0	3	+1
Balqa	6	2	0	8	+2
Karak	7	2	0	9	+4
Tafilah	3	0	0	3	+2
Ma^{c}an[g]	5	0	0	5	+3
Zarqa	4	1	1	6	−2
Mafraq	3	0	0	3	+1
Irbid	8	1	0	9	−1
Ajloun	2	1	0	3	+1
Jarash	2	0	0	2	−1
Ramtha & Bani Kinanah	3	0	0	3	0
Kourah & North Jordan Valley	2	0	0	2	−2
Northern Bedouins (Bani Khalid, Azamat)	2	0	0	2	+1
Central Bedouins (Bani Sakhr)	2	0	0	2	0
Southern Bedouins (Huwaitat)	2	0	0	2	+1
Total	68	9	3	80	0

Source: Data from Al-Urdun al-Jadid Research Center, *Intikhabat 1989: Haqa$^\gamma$iq wa-Arqam* [Election 1989: Facts and Figures] (Amman: Al-Urdun al-Jadid Research Center, 1993), 6.

[a] Includes the Chechen minority as well.
[b] Computed on the basis of actual seats assigned to the constituency less the number of seats hypothetically assigned if district magnitudes were proportional to their population.
[c] A high concentration of Palestinians live in this area.
[d] The most wealthy and politically active constituency.
[e] Includes some Eastern suburbs of Amman, a more industrialized, but tribally inhabited area.
[f] Includes Wadi Seir and Na^{c}our, a more tribally inhabited area.
[g] For the 1997 election, a district for Aquaba was carved out of the Ma^{c}an district. Aqaba received 2 Muslim seats, leaving Ma^{c}an with 3 seats.

population; Circassians and Chechens were allotted 3.75 percent of the seats despite their less than 1 percent of the population, and Bedouins of the scheduled tribes were assigned 7.5 percent of the seats compared to their 3.25 percent of the total population.[10] Rewarding these traditional allies of the regime has been a long established practice in Jordanian election laws.

However, given this malapportioned distribution of seats in geographically determined constituencies, the key factor in determining the make up of the Parliament elected in 1989 was the fact that voters were able to cast multiple votes under an open-list plurality system.[11] Voters were able to choose from among all the candidates in their district and vote for any combination of candidates up to the number of seats in the district for each quota category (Muslim, Christian, or Circassian/Chechen). Candidates won seats by receiving the highest total votes in each category of the district until the number of seats in each category was filled.[12] All voters could vote for minority quota candidates as well as for Muslim candidates, regardless of the voter's religion or ethnicity. Thus, for example, a Christian voter in Amman's third district could vote for up to three Muslim candidates, one Christian, and one Circassian/Chechen candidate, for a total of five votes. Likewise, a Muslim voter in Irbid could select up to eight Muslim candidates and one Christian.

In the 1989 election campaign, candidates ran as individuals since political parties remained illegal. However, the government decided not to enforce the ban on candidates with affiliations to "illegal political organizations," (Article 18, Paragraph E) which allowed a number of opposition candidates to participate in the election.[13] While voters could vote for candidates as they wished under the open-list system, this did not prevent candidates, especially ones affiliated with a political organization, from teaming up to make a list. Such alliances tended to do well in a field of 562 candidates running for 80 seats and with little to differentiate individual candidates. The Muslim Brotherhood often teamed with other independent opposition figures (often leftists or Arab nationalist Christians) in an electoral list. However, suggested election lists also derived from tribal alliances as well as ideological political affiliations. With so many individual candidates, voters tended to notice organized electoral lists. Thus, the electoral system in 1989 was one of the major factors that led to the success of the Muslim Brotherhood in the elections.

The Islamists emerged as the big winners of the 1989 elections. Candidates affiliated with the Muslim Brotherhood performed even better than expected. Twenty-three of twenty-six Muslim Brotherhood candidates won seats. In addition, approximately thirteen leftists and Arab nationalists won in 1989. Individual centrists, conservatives, and tribal figures—in general all strong supporters of the regime—filled the rest of the eighty seats. The regime greeted the opposition's success in the elections through such lists with dismay. The opposition nearly won a majority of seats in the 1989 election in spite of the severe malapportionment of constituencies to favor likely progovernment candidates.

Table 3.2 RESULTS OF THE 1989 ELECTION

Trend	Votes for Winners	% of Popular Vote	Seats Won	% of Seats Won
Muslim Brotherhood	292,279	14.54	22	27.50
Independent Islamists	105,027	5.22	11	13.75
Tribal or Centrist Independents	258,569	12.86	33	41.25
Leftists	59,425	2.96	6	7.50
Arab Nationalists	51,118	2.54	8	10.00

Sources: Data from Kamel S. Abu Jaber and Schirin H. Fathi, "The 1989 Jordanian Parliamentary Elections," Orient 31, no. 1 (1991): 67–86; al-Urdun al-Jadid Research Center, Intikhabat 1989: Haqa'iq wa-Arqam [Election 1989: Facts and Figures] (Amman: Al-Urdun al-Jadid Research Center, 1993), 17–19; and Tim Riedel, Who's Who in Jordanian (sic) Parliament 1989–1993 (Amman: Friedrich Ebert Stitung, 1993).

Despite the 1989 elections being the first national parliamentary elections in over twenty years, public turnout was moderate; 555,397 voters cast their ballots. 54.5 percent of registered voters participated in the elections.[14] This amounted to only 17 percent of the total population. Turnout was markedly lower in urban and more Palestinian inhabited areas.

The results of the November 1989 election not only determined the composition of the Parliament for the next four years, but also displayed the balance of political power in Jordan's first full election in over twenty years. The strong showing by the opposition in the elections was something the regime did not wish repeated, leading to the decree of amendments to Election Law in 1993.

THE NATIONAL CHARTER OF 1990

After the April 1989 riots, King Hussein also unveiled the idea of a National Charter—a pact to affirm the legitimacy of the monarchy, which he felt had been damaged by the riots. The regime would allow a degree of political pluralism for the opposition to participate in political society in return for the opposition acknowledging the monarchy's supremacy. In May 1989, well before the elections, the king publicly broached his desire for a National Charter. He formally called for such a pact in his speech from the throne at the opening of the Parliament in November. The use of pacts in Latin America prompted many scholars using the contingent choice model of democratization to focus on the role that pacts play in transitions from authoritarian rule.[15] In Jordan, however, the pact followed the Tunisian example since "far from representing a response to the collapse of the previous regime, the pact here is advocated by a government still firmly in power. Indeed, the rulers set out the initial terms of the debate and initiated the discussion."[16]

In other words, the Jordanian regime used the National Charter as a survival strategy to quiet opposition to the regime's existential policies.

TALKS ABOUT TALKS

Behind-the-scenes discussions between the king's advisors and potential committee members took place before the appointment of the Royal Committee that would write the charter. Adnan Abu Odeh, a political advisor to the king at the time, held informal talks with many opposition figures in the months leading up to the appointment of the Royal Committee. Abu Odeh was a former member of the Communist Party. His talks attempted to reopen a dialogue, formally closed since the 1950s, between the regime and its historical opposition from the leftist and Arab nationalist trends. Abu Odeh offered the opposition a basic proposition: if the opposition recognized the legitimacy of the Hashemite monarchy, the regime would allow a reemergence of political party pluralism in Jordan underneath the power of the king.[17]

Generally, the various sectors of the opposition responded positively to the regime's overtures. The Islamists agreed to the groundwork for the charter because of their historical ties to the regime. Moreover, the Muslim Brotherhood felt confident with the organization's strong showing in the November 1989 parliamentary elections.[18] On the other hand, leftists and Arab nationalists agreed to participate—but with some reservations. By 1990, most leftists and Arab nationalists had accommodated themselves to at least living with the Jordanian monarchy. Many analysts noted the decline in the goals of the historical opposition from replacing the regime to merely being recognized by it.[19] Regime coalition members and allies, unsurprisingly, were quite willing to participate in drafting the National Charter.

By opening the informal dialogue about the charter, the regime held the initiative in two main areas that would help determine the course of the talks. First, the regime chose to whom among the opposition it wished to talk. The regime generally covered the political spectrum in its informal talks. However, some groups remained excluded from political society (e.g., Hizb al-Tahrir, which views all Arab regimes as un-Islamic). Second, the regime also determined the ground rules for the talks. The regime set the tone for the charter by offering the basic deal of recognizing the legitimacy for the regime for political pluralism.[20] Those who could not accept the basic condition of granting legitimacy to the monarchy were not included when the dialogue became formalized with the appointment of the "Royal Committee for Drafting the National Charter" in April 1990.

COMPOSITION OF THE ROYAL COMMITTEE

The "Royal Committee for Drafting the National Charter" included sixty members. The membership of the committee covered the range of political opinion in Jordan. However, the majority of the committee members selected could be counted as regime supporters. Table 3.3 lists the members of the Royal Committee.

Categorization of the political tendencies of the members is inexact. Ali Abu Nowar, for example, was an Arab nationalist general who led the 1956 coup attempt against King Hussein. After the failure of the coup, Abu Nowar fled to Egypt, but was later pardoned by King Hussein. By 1990, he had served as the Jordanian ambassador to France and had just been appointed as a senator. Thus, Abu Nowar had come full circle and returned from "opposition to the regime" to part of the establishment.

With such caveats in mind, a general classification of the political orientation of the members of the committee is also included in table 3.3. Based on a modified categorization of *Al-Destour* newspaper, the committee contained: 16 conservatives, 15 liberals, 8 independents, 8 Islamists, 8 Arab nationalists, and 5 leftists. As one moves across the categories in table 3.3, from leftist to conservative, one is more likely to find members of the regime coalition—the conservative and liberal categories mostly being exclusively composed of supporters of the regime. Thus, the regime and its allies held an easy majority in the Royal Committee that would draft the National Charter.

The Royal Committee also drew heavily from the newly elected House of Deputies. Sixteen members of the committee were House deputies, another seven had been appointed to the Senate. Many of the deputies were representatives of the Muslim Brotherhood. However, just as the committee's membership claimed to cover the political spectrum, it also contained some gaps.

Among the Islamists, the committee's membership drew mainly from the Muslim Brotherhood's more liberal wing. Hard-line Islamists who took a more critical view of the regime, such as independent Islamist Layth Shbeilat or Muslim Brotherhood hawk Abd al-Munʿam Abu Zant, were not included in the Royal Committee. Likewise, of the two Baʿathists selected for the committee, one had moderated his views toward the regime and served as a senator (Shuqir), the other came from a large Southern tribe (al-Tarawnah). Through the selection of the membership of the Royal Committee the regime helped to eliminate hazardous outcomes from the negotiations over the National Charter. Membership in the committee also rewarded and strengthened the regime's supporters.

AGENDAS FOR THE NATIONAL CHARTER

Many individuals selected for the committee had expressed their agendas for the talks through newspaper articles and public speeches before the meetings began. However, the clearest statements came from within the early meetings of the Royal Committee itself. After resolving some procedural issues, most members made statements of their agenda for the charter in front of the

Table 3.3 MEMBERS OF THE ROYAL COMMITTEE FOR DRAFTING THE NATIONAL CHARTER

Leftist	Arab Nationalist	Islamist	Independent	Liberal	Conservative
Ibrahim Bakr	Ali Abu Nowar	Abdullah al-Akaylah	Ahmed Awad	Adnan Abu Odeh	Mohammed Abu Olim
Theib Marji	Hammad al-Farhan	Mohammed al-Alawnah	Hamadah Faranah	Hosni Aish	Fowaz Abu Tayah
Issa Mdanat	Samir Habashnah	Abd al-Latif al-Arabiyat	Fowzi Gharibah	Ibrahim Badran	Hani Abu Hijlah
Abd al-Rahim Omar	Suleiman al-Hadidi	Yousef al-Athem	Sultan Hattab	Tahir Hikmat	Isam Badir
Taysir al-Zibri	Labib Kamhawi	Ahmed al-Azaiydah	Asmah Khader	Mahmoud al-Kayd	Adnan al-Bakhit
	Amin Shuqir	Ishaw Farhan	Sahban Khleifat	Abdullah al-Maliki	Abd al-Halim Khaddam
	Muna Shuqir	Jumʿah Hammad	Jamal al-Tahat	Aidah al-Matlaq	Awad Khleifat
	Mohammed Faris al-Tarawnah	Majid Khleifah	Fawzi al-Tuʾaimah	Tahir al-Masri	Jamal al-Khreishah
				Ali al-Shimat	Abd al-Salam al-Majali
				Abdullah al-Nsour	Mohamed Kheir Mamsir
				Iyad Qattan	Ahmed Obeidat
				Wahid al-Shaʿir	Subhi al-Qasam
				Layla Sharaf	Khalil al-Salam
				Mahmoud al-Sharif	Jamal al-Sarirah
				Sʿaid al-Tal	Saʿad Halil Srour
					Akram Zʾiter
5	8	8	8	15	16

Sources: Data from *Al-Destour*, April 24, 1990, 11; *Jordan Times*, April 10, 1990.

committee. A handful of these presentations will highlight the agendas of the different political trends in Jordan.

AGENDA OF A REGIME LIBERAL: IYAD QATTAN

Iyad Qattan served as the director of the Royal Cultural Center and was an advisor to the king during the period of the writing of the National Charter. A regime supporter with a liberal view of politics, Qattan expounded what seemed to be the king's basic agenda in drafting the National Charter.

Qattan argued to the Royal Committee that the National Charter should be a short document with a narrow purpose—to make a political deal to allow the "democratization" process to continue. Qattan's central goal was to transform the opposition from an "opposition to the regime" to an "opposition to the government." The role of the Royal Committee, in Qattan's words, was to function as the "honest broker" in making a deal between the regime and society.[21]

For Qattan, the charter should only focus on one issue—reforming the political process. Within this realm, he saw three points for dialogue within the committee. First, the Royal Committee should discuss the defining principles of the state by taking the constitution as a reference. Second, the committee should define the necessary rules of the political process by delineating the roles of political parties, the regime, and individuals. Lastly, the committee should discuss general freedoms with the constitution as its starting point.[22]

According to Qattan, other issues that the committee could discuss—economic, social, and identity issues—should be left until after the three proposed points of dialogue had been resolved. Only with a political agreement in place could Jordanians successfully resolve the other issues. Moreover, Qattan did not see the Royal Committee as the proper venue for "nonpolitical" dialogue on issues such as identity or foreign policy. Qattan felt that these topics would be better left to the elected House of Deputies.[23]

Qattan, as a regime liberal, wished the National Charter to be an explicit political blueprint for further democratization. He saw democratization as a "learning process" in which the National Charter would only be the first step.[24] By restricting the agenda of the Royal Committee to narrow political bargaining, Qattan perhaps saw the process as being quick and painless—attributes of the National Charter that the regime most desired.

A REGIME HARD-LINER'S AGENDA: AWAD KHLEIFAT

Awad Khelifat, the President of M'uta University in Kerak and a former cabinet minister, took a harder line than regime liberals such as Qattan. Whereas regime liberals saw the National Charter as a pact for further democratization, regime hard-liners, like Khleifat, saw the charter as litmus test for Jordanian nationalism.

In Khleifat's presentation to the Royal Committee he stated that some issues were not up for discussion. As a Hashemite monarchy with the powers of the king specified in the constitution, Jordan's political system was not open for interpretation. According to Khleifat, the constitution was clear enough on these issues.[25] Thus, regime hard-liners did not see the legitimacy of the regime as part of the bargaining process; instead the legitimacy of Jordan's current political order was assumed as a fact. For Khleifat, the Royal Committee existed to discuss the secondary issues of the limits of freedom and pluralism, and the delineation of Jordan's identity.

While the structure of the regime, as laid out in the constitution, was beyond discussion, the proper limits to freedoms were negotiable. Khleifat questioned the meaning of the constitution's grant of the right to form political organizations. He asked if this right extended to all parties, "Jordanian and foreign." He also asked if there should be a finite number of parties that could be formed. Khleifat also argued that the committee should discuss if there were limits to the "general freedoms" of Jordanians. Moreover, he sought elaboration of the constitutional principle of equality of Jordanians in their rights and duties.[26] In general it seemed that Khleifat's purpose was to limit the definitions used in these issues rather than to expand freedoms.

Khleifat also differed from Qattan on the National Charter's need to discuss the role of the identity of Jordan and Jordanians. While liberals sought an explicitly political deal, hard-liners wanted to clarify the preeminence of a "Jordanian identity." Such an identity would put Jordan first in relation to Arab unity. For Khleifat, the constitution's statements that Jordan is "a branch of the Arab Nation," and "Islam is the religion of the state," were clear. However, he wanted the Royal Committee to elaborate on these principles. Moreover, he asked the committee to clarify the relationship between Jordan and Palestine. In terms of religion, Khleifat noted "Islam's distinctive presence in a country that is ruled by a descendent of the Prophet."[27]

Thus, one can see that regime hard-liners, such as Khleifat, viewed the National Charter not as a pact on the legitimacy of the regime—they assumed that as a precondition for sitting at the bargaining table. Instead, they saw the Royal Committee as a place were the regime obtained both the acquiescence of the opposition to limits on political pluralism and the abandonment of claims to identity that superseded that of a "Jordanian identity." This would guarantee that Jordan in the 1990s would not return to the political instability of the 1950s.

AN ISLAMIST AGENDA: ISHAQ FARHAN

Ishaq Farhan was a senator who had previously served as Minister of Religious Affairs and as Minister of Education. Farhan represented the dovish wing of the Muslim Brotherhood organization. This current in the organization felt amenable to cooperation with the regime, if the government of the time was acceptable. Five other members of the Muslim Brotherhood—all moderates—were Royal Committee members. Farhan saw the project of the Royal Committee as less of a political deal to restore pluralism than as a chance to affirm Jordan's Islamic identity.

Farhan, in his remarks to the Royal Committee, recognized the pluralism inherent in the committee and in Jordan's political system as a whole. Senator Farhan and his Muslim Brotherhood counterparts in the House of Deputies, however, most likely saw this pluralism from a position of strength. The organization had won twenty-two seats in the November 1989 elections—the largest share of seats of any organized group. Farhan later noted that the organization had been intentionally holding back a full display of its power. The Muslim Brotherhood feared intimidating the regime if it ran candidates in all districts in the 1989 campaign.[28]

Farhan displayed the Muslim Brotherhood's acceptance of the structure of the regime. In terms of the political system, he agreed with regime liberals that the Royal Committee should focus only on political pluralism. The fact that Jordan was run by a monarchical regime received no comment in his early remarks. Farhan, however, drew a limit to political pluralism in Jordan. He demanded that there be no place in the political system for secular, atheistic parties.[29] Thus, the Islamists did not oppose the granting of legitimacy to the regime. Rather, they focused their energy on combating the more secular opposition currents.

The Islamists saw the task of the Royal Committee as promoting the place of Islam in Jordan's political system and in the country's political identity. Farhan remarked that the most important issue the Islamists wished to pursue in the Royal Committee was the promotion of Islamic law from *a* source of legislation to *the* source of legislation.[30] Moreover, Farhan argued to the committee that Jordan's Arab and Islamic identities were not mutually exclusive, but rather complementary. Farhan, who was of Palestinian origin, exemplified how Islamists in Jordan were able to use an Islamist ideology to bridge divisions between Jordanians of East Bank origins and Palestinians. For Farhan, Jordan lay at the center of overlapping circles of interests and identities that encompassed first the Arab world and then the larger Islamic world. Farhan saw agreement between the Islamists and some of the Arab nationalists—those who would be willing to align Arabism with Islam.[31] Atheistic secularism, however, remained unacceptable for Farhan.

Thus, the Islamists in the Royal Committee wished to use their status as the strongest political current in the Jordanian political arena. On one hand, the Islamists stood opposed to recent governments of the time, a position that allowed them to critique the regime and not be tainted by the crises that had led to the political opening in 1989. On the other hand, the Muslim Brotherhood did not oppose the structure of the regime per se, and seemed prepared to grant legitimacy to the regime through the National

Charter. The Islamists instead used the Royal Committee to pursue their agenda against the secular opposition.

An Arab Nationalist Agenda: Labib Kamhawi

Labib Kamhawi, an Arab nationalist of Palestinian origin, represented a constituency of Palestinian opposition activists in Jordan. Kamhawi had joined the Arab Nationalist Movement during his studies in Beirut. He later joined the Popular Front for the Liberation of Palestine (PFLP) as Palestinian Arab nationalists began to focus more on the Palestinian issue. By 1990, Kamhawi had become a businessman—like many of his Palestinian counterparts. His views are cited in this section because he represents a segment of the population that the regime had feared from the 1950s and 1960s—Arab nationalist Palestinians.

In Kamhawi's view, he and other opposition figures joined the Royal Committee in 1990 because they "were not in the business of overthrowing the regime."[32] To Kamhawi, the regime's desire for a grant of legitimacy from the opposition was clear. Kamhawi saw a loss in confidence in the government by the people that had stemmed from a gap between the regime and the public. He suggested a reformist response; the opposition would grant the regime a bounded legitimacy. In return the opposition would seek a new contract between the "regime and the people of Jordan" where "we (the opposition) would grant (the regime) legitimacy and take everything else and give it back to the people."[33]

For Kamhawi, however, the charter was not just a political document. He held that the charter should be a comprehensive document that reflected the shared bases of thought in Jordan. Politically, Kamhawi desired the participation of the people in the decision making in the kingdom. In addition to the political contract, however, Kamhawi saw other dimensions for the charter—especially economic, social, and educational. The identity of Jordan vis-à-vis Palestinian and Arab identities was at the center of Kamhawi's statement of his agenda to the Royal Committee.[34] He challenged the committee to agree upon Jordan's relationship to the Arab nation.

Strategically, Kamhawi recognized the minority role of the Arab nationalist opposition on the committee. He remarked that while the committee represented the political spectrum in Jordan, the selection of the committee's members was "done in a tricky manner."[35] Thus, Kamhawi asked for a baseline of common desires among the various political trends of the committee. Kamhawi's desire for agreement did not extend to a consensus imposed by the regime. Seeing that the opposition was far outnumbered by regime supporters, he helped push for a super-majority voting rule on all issues of substance in the decisions of the Royal Committee.[36]

Thus, Kamhawi's agenda for the National Charter had more than just a political dimension. Kamhawi was willing to grant the regime legitimacy, but only in a limited sense. In return, he wished for a greater recognition of the role of Kamhawi's community, Palestinian-Jordanians, in Jordan's social and political systems.

AGENDA OF A LEFTIST: ISSA MDANAT

Issa Mdanat had paid a price for his role as one of the founding members of the Communist Party in Jordan. From 1959 to 1965—and later on for shorter periods—he was imprisoned in Jordan for his political views. Communism in Jordan had been banned since 1953. Mdanat, however, was elected to the House of Deputies in 1989 as the Christian Deputy for Kerak. In the Royal Committee, Mdanat had a narrow agenda—to regain the right for the Left to legally organize in the political arena. Mdanat framed this right in terms of his goal for the National Charter to improve "the people's life."[37] Educating the people in democracy would do this. In this regard Mdanat's agenda had three points.

First, Mdanat argued that freedom was enshrined in the Jordanian constitution—especially in granting Jordanians the right to form political organizations. For Mdanat, restrictions on this right violated the constitution.[38] For Mdanat, the Royal Committee should reaffirm the right of political parties to organize—regardless of political tendency. In this way, the Left could be rehabilitated and return to normal political life.

Second, Mdanat expanded his call for freedoms to all public liberties and equal rights. In Mdanat's remarks to the Royal Committee, he argued that the constitutional guarantee of equal rights for Jordanians had been ignored. He called for equal rights to not only be talked about, but practiced as well. For Mdanat, if the constitution guaranteed political rights to Jordanians, the National Charter should as well.[39]

Third, Mdanat argued that parties and freedoms should allow the people of Jordan a role in the political decision making process. He argued that a parliament without political parties would be ineffective. Moreover, without an effective parliament, democratic institutions in Jordan would be meaningless.[40]

Thus, Mdanat saw the National Charter as reaffirming the constitution's grants of rights and freedoms. However, by focusing on the constitution, intentionally or not, Mdanat granted the regime legitimacy. External events had led to the weakening of Soviet support for Communism in the Third World. Thus, Mdanat and other leftists began to recognize the need to move from opposition to their countries' regimes and to begin to work within the political system to achieve social justice.[41]

PROCEDURES AND PROCESS IN
DRAFTING THE NATIONAL CHARTER

The Royal Committee began its work on April 10, 1990 with a speech from King Hussein. Former Prime Minister Ahmed Obeidat, who had been chosen by the king to preside over the committee, followed with a speech of his own. The committee began its work in earnest on April 21. The committee would meet regularly until producing a draft of the National Charter in December 1990. The Royal Committee faced four major procedural controversies in the process of drafting the National Charter.

Before the committee even began to meet, the issue of the constitutionality of a charter became hotly debated in the Jordanian press. Some among the opposition feared that the National Charter would replace the constitution, thus limiting even more the narrow freedoms contained in the constitution's text. The king tried to calm such fears in his speech to the committee by stating "the charter is not a substitute for the constitution."[42] The debate over the relationship between the charter and the constitution was a major feature of the first few meetings of the Royal Committee.[43] The debate continued in the press as well into May 1990.[44] The debate over the issue subsided as most members of the committee agreed that the National Charter was an explanation of the principles of the constitution—not its replacement.

The Royal Committee began its discussions with a debate over the rules of the committee's operations and its procedures for reaching an agreement in drafting the charter. The debates in the first two sessions, aside from the relationship between the charter and the constitution, mainly focused around two internal procedures for the committee. First, the threshold for agreement was agreed upon. While many regime supporters felt that a majority vote would be adequate for passing a draft, the opposition resisted. According to Kamhawi, the opposition—knowing its minority status—demanded a super-majority be required for including a text into the charter. The committee generally agreed to this logic. It decided upon a 75 percent threshold for agreement on accepting a draft text in the charter.[45]

A second major agreement on the internal structure of the committee was the discussion to break the sixty-member committee into subcommittees for discussions about specific issues. Despite the objections of some members, who proposed that the committee should discuss all issues in plenary, most agreed that the range of issues the charter could cover necessitated the formation of subcommittees.[46] Eventually, different subcommittees were formed to deal with the main topics of the charter. The reports of the subcommittees resulted in the various topical chapters of the National Charter.

A final controversy surrounding the process of drafting the National Charter was the issue of how to ratify the document. Some members of the regime coalition had proposed that the charter, once drafted, should be approved by a public referendum or plebiscite. This view seemed to stem from the Royal Court. However, the opposition argued that the constitution held no provisions for plebiscites.[47] Having the Parliament ratify the charter was also found unsatisfactory to all sides since the Parliament could only pass legislation—not a pact of principles like the charter was envisioned to be.

Eventually another subcommittee was formed to solve the ratification predicament. The subcommittee came up with the idea of a National Congress.

Although the Royal Committee had finished its work and produced a draft of the National Charter by December 1990, the ratification of the pact had to wait until after the Gulf War. In June 1991, a National Congress of over two thousand Jordanians convened to ratify the National Charter. The document was approved unanimously.

RESULTS OF THE NATIONAL CHARTER PROCESS

Once completed, the National Charter stood as a lengthy statement of the new era of political liberalization in Jordan. However, the pact itself contained little that one would consider surprising. The deal that was behind the regime's initial conception of the pact was at the document's core. The charter did cover a broad range of topics as exemplified by the headings of the charter's eight chapters.[48] Each of these chapters was the product of the work of the different subcommittees. However, the charter contained specific guidelines only in the chapters that explicitly discussed topics of political institutions.

General Principles of the National Charter

The National Charter's first principle sums up the central political deal that the regime intended the pact to endorse:

> The system of government in the Hashemite Kingdom of Jordan is parliamentary, monarchic and hereditary. Adherence by all to legitimacy (sic) and to respect of the letter and spirit of the Constitution shall enhance the union between the people and their leadership.[49]

The members of the Royal Committee thus endorsed the status quo in Jordan, recognizing the legitimacy of monarchy. The committee affirmed the constitutional right for the monarchy to hold veto power over all political processes in the country. The "letter and the spirit" of the constitution allowed for political pluralism—in the form of the Parliament. Constitutionally, however, the legislature cannot effectively veto the king's will.

In return for this grant of legitimacy to the monarchy, the charter allowed for the return of political parties after their decades of banishment:

> Strengthening the foundations of a state governed by the supremacy of the law, and firming up the democratic process based on political pluralism are an obligation of the state's institutions, of individual members of Jordanian society and all its other bodies.
>
> Political, party and intellectual pluralism is the means of strengthening democracy and ensuring participation by the Jordanian

> people in administering the affairs of the state. It serves to guarantee national unity and build a balanced civil society.[50]

Moreover, political pluralism was to take place in a liberal environment. The charter encouraged the notion that no one group holds the monopoly on the truth.

> Respect for the mind, belief in dialogue, recognition of the right of others to disagree, respect for the opinion of others, tolerance, and rejection of political and social violence are basic characteristics of Jordanian society. Pursuant to this, there is no compulsion in religion or recourse to fanaticism, sectarianism or regional bias.[51]

Thus, the National Charter generally envisioned a political system where a pluralistic system of parties stood under the power of the monarchy.

Relegalizing Political Parties

In the chapter "The State of Law and Political Pluralism," the details of the pact's core were spelled out. According to this chapter, "the Jordanian State is a 'State of Law' in the modern sense of a democratic state."[52] The chapter committed both the state and its citizens to the rule of law—as spelled out by the constitution.

However, the core of the chapter on political pluralism was the agreement of the Royal Committee members on "Principles and Limitations Governing the Establishment of (Political) Parties." Accordingly,

> Jordanians enjoy the right to establish and belong to political parties and groupings, provided that their objectives are legitimate, their methods are peaceful and their statutes do not violate the provisions of the Constitution. Laws regulating the operation of parties should not include any provisions which overtly or implicitly call for abrogating the constitutional right to establish political parties.[53]

Thus, the ban on political parties in Jordan would be replaced with a new law permitting, but regulating, the formation of parties. The National Charter spelled out four general limitations for the formation of political parties.

First, political parties would need to be committed to the principles of the constitution and political pluralism. This commitment insured that parties may oppose the government and the prime minister of the day. However, parties that opposed the regime would remain excluded from the political arena. Parties must also

> Employ democratic methods in their internal workings, choice of leadership and in the exercise of their activities within a framework of democratic dialogue and free competition among the political parties. The same shall apply to relations and dealings by any party with other political parties and groupings as well as with popular and constitutional institutions in a spirit of mutual respect for opposing views.[54]

Thus, the National Charter promoted liberal principles of tolerance and fair play. The different opposition trends—especially those of the Left and Arab nationalist leanings—could return to legal participation in the Jordanian political system, but only if they played by the regime's rules. Since the opposition members of the Royal Committee had already agreed with this principle by joining the committee, they easily made this compromise.

Second, and more controversially, the National Charter stated that parties should focus their political activities solely on Jordan.

> There shall be no structural or financial affiliation by the leadership or members of any party with any non-Jordanian. Also, no activities by any party or grouping shall be conducted upon instructions or directions from any foreign state or body.[55]

The opposition had objected to this restriction, but eventually relented.[56] In return, some exceptions were made.

> Taking into consideration what is stated in this paragraph and all principles and limitations governing the organization of parties, any provisions in the statute, internal regulations or programs of any licensed Jordanian party serving Palestine, Arab unity or Islamic solidarity shall be regarded as a national Jordanian undertaking.[57]

With this paragraph, the regime had intended to rule out some of the dangers that had threatened it when Arab nationalist and leftist opposition parties had nearly toppled the monarchy in the 1950s and in 1970. Under the limitations proposed by the charter, all parties needed to put Jordan first in their ideology and programs.

Third, the charter also included the principle that the finances of political parties be public. Moreover, the charter banned parties from relying on any financial support from outside of Jordan.[58] In this way the government would be able to keep tabs on the organizational strengths of the various parties.

Finally, the charter limited parties so that the regime's fears of a repetition of the 1950s would not occur. The National Charter demanded that political parties refrain from influencing the military or security forces, or from using public institution for party purposes.[59] In this way, the regime limited the possibilities for praetorian partisanship that had threatened the regime over the years.

Thus, with these four areas of limitations on political parties, the National Charter prepared the way for parties to be relegalized in Jordan. The rules for parties agreed upon in the National Charter reflected the regime's desires to avoid a repeat of the crises of the 1950s and of 1970. The opposition acquiesced to the regime's plans. These rules generally reflected either the limitations the parties already felt themselves or an acceptable price to pay for the ability to legally organize.

National Identity and the National Charter

The Royal Committee, however, did not stick with the narrow political agenda as Qattan had envisioned in the document. Rather, the National Charter spends a great deal of its text discussing Jordan's national identity through its relationship with Palestinians, the larger Arab world, and Islam. The charter, however, does not take any clear stands about Jordan's national identity. The committee agreed only upon general language with vague and innocuous meanings.

The role of Islam, however, did provoke some controversy in the discussions of the Royal Committee. The Islamists had desired to make a statement that Islamic law was the *only* source of legislation. Secular committee members, such as Kamhawi, fiercely objected. In the end, the committee agreed that, "Islamic law is the principal source of legislation."[60]

Despite the charter's great length, especially in areas of identity and foreign relations, the core of the charter lay in its chapter on the "State of Law and Political Pluralism." Only in this chapter was a detailed agenda for political action presented.

ECHOES OF THE GULF WAR

Even before the Royal Committee could finish its work in drafting the National Charter, external events again reverberated in Jordanian domestic politics. The August 1990 Iraqi invasion of Kuwait and the resulting military action by the U.S. and its allies threatened to further destabilize Jordan. King Hussein, nevertheless, managed to weather Operation Desert Storm. In the short run, King Hussein gathered popular support at home by tacitly supporting Iraq in the conflict and by bringing most political trends behind his foreign policy stance. His vague neutrality, however, angered Jordan's Western and Gulf financial supporters. Yet, in the long run, King Hussein regained the trust of the Americans by participating in the U.S.-led Middle East peace process with Israel.

Before the Iraqi invasion of Kuwait, Jordanian political groups had been consolidating in the wake of the November 1989 elections. The appointment of former Security Chief Mudar Badran as prime minister after the elections signaled the close watch the king was putting on the political liberalization process. Nevertheless, a mood of optimism grew from the beginning of the National Charter process and from the gradual consolidation of the disparate House deputies into political blocs. With ten deputies in his twenty-four-member cabinet, Badran easily won the confidence of the Parliament in January 1990. The Muslim Brotherhood, however, remained outside the government because the prime minister was unwilling to give the organization the education portfolio. As each of the newly congealed blocs in the Parliament—leftist, centrist, and Islamist—jockeyed for popularity, questions of Badran's ability to keep the House's confidence began to arise. However, the House's debate over the prime minister's economic policies was suddenly overridden by the events of August 2, 1990.

King Hussein's support for Iraqi President Saddam Hussein stemmed from a number of motivations; however, the seeds of political liberalization offered the roots for one of the major reasons behind Jordan's foreign policy during the Gulf War. Laurie Brand explains a number of the variables that influenced Jordanians' support for Iraq in the war.[61] The overwhelming fear of Israeli military power and large immigration of Soviet Jews caused the perception that Iraq was the only Arab state that would credibly deter Israel. Economically, many Jordanians welcomed Saddam Hussein's call to share Arab wealth, since many Jordanians viewed the Gulf Arabs as undeserving of their great wealth. Often the experience working as an expatriate in the Gulf and receiving poor treatment as payment for hard work caused these feelings of resentment. Even though the Gulf War showed the extent of fragmentation between Arab countries, many Jordanians believed that Iraq was leading the way toward Arab unity by beginning to erase the often artificial borders of the Arab world. However, in Jordanian eyes, the actions of the United States and its allies in turning an inter-Arab problem into an international conflict added to the already simmering anger of the American support for Israel. This anger grew with the perception of a double standard in the U.S.'s quick reaction to the invasion of Kuwait while allowing Israel's continued occupation of the West Bank and the Gaza Strip. However, Brand argues that "all these factors must be understood against the backdrop of what may be called the 1967 effect," which molds the generational memory of the large youth population in the Arab world, which reads Arab history since 1967 as a string of constant humiliations traceable to the West.[62]

The overwhelming public support for Iraq during the war affected the domestic political coalitions that had begun to form before the invasion. All three of the major opposition trends supported the king's position of supporting Iraq while seeking an Arab solution to the problem. The Islamists took a great risk by alienating their former backer, Saudi Arabia, by criticizing the

Saudi's decision to allow Western troops into the holy land. However, the Islamists saw working against Jordanian popular opinion as an even greater risk. The Left, still working to solidify their ranks, began to quickly mobilize support for their spin on the crisis. The centrists also helped cement the spectrum of support for Iraq. The totality of the crisis and the fears it generated dominated Jordanian politics during this period.

By the middle of December 1990, Prime Minister Badran had begun negotiations with some of the house deputies to form a new cabinet. After a couple of weeks of negotiations, Badran named a reshuffled cabinet. It included: five members of the Muslim Brotherhood—three of whom were members of the House, two independent Islamist deputies, and three members of the center-left National Bloc.[63] In drawing a large number of deputies into the cabinet, King Hussein and Prime Minister Badran sought support for their foreign policy while minimizing domestic political difficulties. The new cabinet also deepened the perception of democracy in the Jordanian public. By giving the Islamists a measure of power, including the Education Ministry, which the Muslim Brotherhood so desired in December 1989, Hussein attempted to neutralize the growing role of the Islamist opposition by putting them in a position where they needed to show results. With the new government, Jordan had, for the first time since the 1950s, a cabinet that mirrored the makeup of the House.

The events in the Gulf caused important domestic issues, such as unemployment and the economic situation, to receive less attention than before the crisis. Jordanians retained their pro-Iraqi stance even though Jordan's economy took a battering from the return of workers from the Gulf, the loss of their remittances, and the shut off of aid from the Gulf Arabs and the U.S. The threat to the existence of the country emanating from the Gulf removed economics, a long-term problem, from the top of the agenda of all the political trends' agendas.

This shift of the agenda of the opposition amounted to a turning point in the activities of the Parliament. The parliamentarians attempted to sway the king's foreign policy during the Gulf War by mobilizing public opinion. However, in addition to the tacit limits set by the regime, the opposition also put limits on itself to preserve its stake in the liberalization process.[64] Thus, the Gulf crisis deepened the political liberalization process in Jordan by reinforcing the needs of the regime and the opposition for each other. However, the regime, as the stronger player, managed to gain concessions on key issues, like economic policy, while conceding to open up foreign policy to a redundant debate.

SUCCESSFULLY SURVIVING EXISTENTIAL CRISES BY INSTITUTIONAL MEANS

By reacting to the April 1989 riots with a policy of political liberalization, the Jordanian regime ran the risk of allowing an "upsurge of civil society" which could have caused a democratic transition—as was the case in many Latin American examples from the 1980s. However, the process of regime-led state building had reduced that risk by gathering a large and diverse regime coalition around the Hashemite monarchy. The two survival strategies detailed in this chapter—the elections of 1989 and the National Charter—also demonstrate the initiative of King Hussein and his advisors in using political liberalization as a survival strategy. Both institutional manipulations aimed to bring discontented regime coalition supporters back into the fold. Both also minimized the risk of uncontrolled mobilization by the opposition through judicious institutional rules. Both survival strategies could be considered successful, but the National Charter proved to be more so for the regime because it better reinforced the disunity of the various opposition trends. Both strategies enabled the king to rally support for his foreign policy tightrope act during the Gulf War as the king returned to the center of the Jordanian political spectrum.

In 1989, the regime took a risk by organizing general parliamentary elections for the first time after twenty-two years. However, the risks of continued rioting or of using force in historic zones of regime support seemed greater to King Hussein and his advisors at the time. Thus, elections were held resulting in a near majority of opposition representatives in the House of Deputies. However, the regime successfully managed the use of constitutional rules by creating a distribution of seats and constituencies that rewarded tribal and conservative regime coalition supporters. The opposition—especially the Muslim Brotherhood—could have won a landslide had the seats in the House of Deputies more closely reflected population patterns. Moreover, the constitution provided another legislative safety valve for the king in the form of the appointed Senate.

With the National Charter, the regime's use of creating a new venue, the Royal Committee, and choosing its representatives appear to be the most significant two aspects of this episode. By creating a venue outside of the institutions ordained by the constitution, the regime avoided negotiating with some of its most prominent opponents by circumventing the newly elected Parliament where the opposition almost held a majority. In selecting members of the committee, the king and his advisors also weeded out individuals who would not agree to the pact's key deal. This is not to say that the majority of Jordan's political forces fiercely opposed the regime in 1990—most politicians of the time were willing to work within the monarchical system. The Royal Committee generally reflected Jordan's political spectrum. However, some of the most colorful of Jordan's politicians were excluded. Thus, the outcome of the process of drafting the National Charter, in terms of the core political bargain, was somewhat determined before the committee even met. Nevertheless, much of the work of bringing the opposition to the bargaining table had been done over the previous forty years through the process of regime-led state building. The regime made good strategic use of the rules of the venue as it created the rules of the game as well as the new venue. The opposition members of the committee realized this fact early in the discussions of the committee. By asking for super-majority voting rules, the opposition representatives sought to temper the regime's stacking of the deck. Thus, the opposition tried and also succeeded in making the most out of the Royal Committee venue.

In terms of reinforcing the disunity of the opposition, the 1989 elections were less than successful—despite the regime's best efforts. The opposition generally used the electoral system to its advantage. The open-list system of voting prompted candidates from the opposition to form coalition lists. A successful formula was the red-green list where a Christian leftist teamed with Islamists to maximize the support of each opposition trend.

In contrast, the National Charter helped promote the ideological divisions between the various opposition groups. The opposition displayed a split between the Islamists, on the one hand, and the leftists and Arab nationalists, on the other. The Islamists, being generally drawn from the ranks of the Muslim Brotherhood organization, usually acted in concert. The leftists and Arab nationalists on the committee also attempted to unify their ranks. Regular meetings outside of the Royal Committee were held by a number of committee members in order to coordinate their strategy.[65] Yet the differences between the Islamists and the other sectors of the opposition were generally over issues of identity—Jordanian versus Arab versus Muslim—and over the proper role of religion in public life. When it came to the political-institutional issues, however, all sectors of the opposition agreed to recognize the monarchical regime in return for the ability to organize political parties. Thus, in general, the opposition trends in the Royal Committee were not strongly united. But over the core of the charter, the opposition uniformly accepted the regime's terms.

Although some regime hard-liners questioned the king's wisdom in holding the 1989 elections, most sectors of the regime coalition willingly participated in the electoral process. Many regime coalition supporters were elected. Over 40 percent of the seats were filled with tribal, conservative, or centrist progovernment representatives. The government could rely on the support of a number of deputies from other trends as well—especially independent Islamists. The regime intended the elections to reward coalition supporters that had grown discontented during the crises of 1988–1989—in general it succeeded.

The regime coalition during the writing of the National Charter was generally cohesive and cooperative. Potential splits between regime liberals, such as Qattan, and regime hard-liners, like Khleifat, did not concern the issues of substance in the National Charter. Rather, differences within the regime coalition revolved around contrasting views on the emphasis of the charter's content. Personality differences between proregime individuals within the Royal Committee were also generally kept to a minimum. The unity of the regime coalition's representatives in the Royal Committee was strong, which helped produce the political deal the king had desired.

The process of political liberalization—inaugurated with these two survival strategies—helped King Hussein build a broad base of support during the Gulf crisis. However, the broad inclusion of the opposition into the government also limited King Hussein's ability to maneuver back into the good graces of the U.S. after the war. Soon after the defeat of Iraq, King Hussein replaced both the Islamists and Prime Minister Badran with a new center left-leaning cabinet headed by the Palestinian politician Tahir al-Masri. After six months of delay, the National Charter was ratified in June 1991. The regime then began to institutionalize the committee's consensus on the future of Jordanian political institutions.

FOUR

INSTITUTIONALIZING POLITICAL LIBERALIZATION

At the close of the Gulf War, Iraq lay defeated and Jordan found itself on poor terms with the Gulf Arab states and the Western powers. King Hussein's neutrality had garnered the support of his people. However, this could not cover Jordan's foreign exchange debts nor open up the sanctioned Iraqi economy. Moreover, the regime began to realize the extent of American power in the "New World Order." Thus, King Hussein eagerly welcomed President George H.W. Bush's initiative at resolving the Arab-Israeli conflict.

King Hussein had helped prepare the ground for a shift toward American diplomacy over the Palestinian problem by appointing Tahir al-Masri, a Palestinian by descent, as prime minister in June 1991. Masri led a cabinet in which leftist and secular centrist deputies were heavily represented. The king appointed the center-left government for three main reasons: to contain the growing power and popularity of the Islamists, to co-opt moderate Palestinians into supporting the U.S.-led moves toward a peace conference, and to deepen the process of political liberalization.

During the national mobilization of the public during the Gulf War, the main beneficiary, after the king, was the Muslim Brotherhood. The Islamists gained the ministries that they had desired when they joined Prime Minister Mudar Badran's cabinet in January 1991. However, Brotherhood deputies in the Parliament spent much of their time during the Gulf crisis demanding that the king take an even tougher line toward the Americans and the Israelis. Brotherhood ministers also accomplished little during their tenure in the cabinet. The minister of social development caused an uproar with his decision to segregate the sexes in his ministry. He eventually had to repeal the decision. After the Gulf War and King Hussein's preparations for participating in the Middle East peace process, the Islamists grew critical of the kingdom's new foreign policy tilt. The king decided that the inclusion of the Muslim Brotherhood in the government would be a potential liability. After being excluded from the cabinet, the Brotherhood's spiritual guide, Abd al-Rahman Khalifa, announced that the organization would never join a government designed for negotiating with Israel.[1]

The king also included the Left in the cabinet to help smooth relations with the PLO in the upcoming Madrid Conference. Masri's pro-PLO credentials had been built during his term in Parliament and as foreign minister. King Hussein made a historic move by allowing the inclusion of representatives from the Jordanian Arab National Democratic Alliance (JANDA), an umbrella of leftist and Arab nationalists. JANDA included the Jordanian wings of Palestinian parties such as the Popular Front for the Liberation of Palestine and the Democratic Front for the Liberation of Palestine, groups which had directly opposed the regime in September 1970. Masri, however, counterbalanced the Left by also including a number of regime liberals in the cabinet.[2]

The king charged Masri's government with deepening the process of political liberalization. The National Conference ratified the National Charter little more than a week before the appointment of the new cabinet. On July 7, 1991, Masri repealed most of the martial law regulations in force since 1967. His government also submitted drafts of laws that would relegalize political parties and liberalize the press. These two survival strategies are the focus of this chapter. However, Masri would not see these drafts into law, as controversies over negotiations with Israel would eventually topple his government.

MADRID IN AMMAN: THE BEGINNINGS OF THE MIDDLE EAST PEACE PROCESS

In 1991, Jordan abandoned its long-held demand that any Middle East peace conference be held under the auspices of the UN. Instead, it accepted the American's proposed format of concurrent negotiations between Israel and each of its individual Arab neighbors. Jordan also facilitated U.S. mediation efforts by agreeing to join Palestinian negotiators in a joint Jordanian-Palestinian delegation to the Madrid Conference. The fig leaf of the joint delegation allowed the Israelis to not formally negotiate with the PLO while still talking directly to Palestinians from the occupied territories. However, once the actual negotiations with Israel began, the two halves of the delegation split into separate negotiating teams—with the presence of a coordinating member from the other half of the joint delegation. King Hussein hoped that the realignment with American power would bring economic relief and an end to Israeli threats to turn Jordan into the alternative Palestinian homeland.

However, groups in the House, especially the Islamists and some leftists, opposed the government's policy of joining the peace process. Those opposed to the peace talks attempted to expand their power by resisting the foreign policy agenda of the government by placing the peace talks as an item on the Parliament's agenda. The opposition attempted to pursue this agenda by withholding confidence in Masri's cabinet and by accusing the government of sidestepping the will of Parliament.[3] However, most centrists remained silent on the issue of the peace talks.

Before the July 1991 vote of confidence on Masri's cabinet, the prime minister counted on the support of about thirty deputies from organizations represented in the cabinet. The Muslim Brotherhood and some other independents opposed the new cabinet. A newly formed "Constitutional Bloc" of regime hard-liners and conservative deputies decided to grant Masri confidence despite being excluded from the cabinet. With the assistance of lobbying from the king, Masri's government won the vote of confidence 47 votes to 31.[4]

As U.S. pressure on Jordan to participate in the peace talks grew, however, parliamentary support for Masri's government waned. In early October, four ministers resigned in protest to Jordan's participation in the peace talks. Masri did not replace them with parliamentarians. As leftists in Parliament began to strengthen their opposition to the peace talks, Masri's fragile coalition appeared in trouble. King Hussein delayed the parliamentary session from October until December to postpone a vote of confidence on the reshuffled cabinet and to quiet opposition to the Madrid Conference.

However, opposition deputies gave Masri notice that the postponed Parliament session only delayed the prime minister's day of reckoning. On October 7, a petition signed by forty-nine deputies, including the Muslim Brotherhood and the Constitutional Bloc and some independents, stated their loss of confidence in the government. Later some leftists from JANDA signed the petition. Although not binding on the government, the petition signaled that the Parliament intended to stand up to the government in calling for a change of policy, of leadership, or both. The opposition of the Muslim Brotherhood and the renegade leftists to Masri's peace policies is easily explained by ideology. However, many commentators saw the Constitutional Bloc's withdrawal of confidence as a blatant grab for ministerial power by regime conservatives.[5]

Throughout October the pressure mounted on the embattled government. On October 10, the government banned an Islamist rally and withheld circulation of *al-Ribat*, the Muslim Brotherhood's weekly newspaper. On October 12, King Hussein held a national congress to dictate the official Jordanian position on the peace talks, thus bypassing the Parliament. Another minister resigned from the cabinet on October 24. The government held the line through the Madrid Conference but Masri resigned and King Hussein again appointed Sharif Zayd Bin Shaker as prime minister on November 19. Through the next year and a half, Jordanian politics settled into debating the regime's liberalizing survival strategies of relegalizing political parties and overhauling the regulation of the press—the two survival strategies discussed in this chapter. Meanwhile, the Middle East peace process quietly proceeded in distant Washington.

THE POLITICAL PARTIES LAW

In 1957, King Hussein banned political parties in Jordan. The National Charter, however, paved the way for the return of political parties to Jordan's political arena. After the ratification of the National Charter in June 1991, Masri's government drafted a law to legalize political parties and regulate their licensing. It would take over a year for the bill to pass through constitutional channels to become a law. The 1992 Political Parties Law can be seen as an institutional survival strategy because it allowed organized pluralism back into political society. At the same time, the regime's draft law sought to regulate and narrow the range of groups that could claim to be political parties. The regime succeeded in implementing its general vision of the Political Parties Law through negotiations in the Parliament. However, the outcome of those negotiations relied heavily on the compromises made in reference to legalizing political parties in the National Charter. The political party system that evolved in Jordan after the relegalization of parties, however, never gained its full strength—partly because of the restrictions based in the Political Parties Law, partly because of decades of regime-led state building in a no-party system.

DEFINING POLITICAL PARTIES

Beginning in January 1992, the Law Committee of the House of Deputies met six times to write its recommendations to the draft law. At the time, the opposition strongly influenced the Law Committee, but liberal-leaning independent Hussein Majali sat as committee chair. In June 1992, the draft of the Political Parties Law made its way to the floor of the House for debate.

Before the House began to discuss the Law Committee's recommendations for the draft law, Jordanian nationalist Ahmed Abbadi sparked a debate to reject the proposed law entirely. Abbadi argued that Jordanians were not ready for political pluralism. For Abbadi, political parties were at a stage of political development that Jordan had not yet reached.[6] Abbadi was joined in this sentiment by Shaykh Abd al-Baqi Jammu, who argued that "pluralism is a foreign concept and we should not be importing Western and other foreign concepts to this culture."[7] However, only eight of the seventy-three deputies present supported Abbadi's motion to stop discussing the draft of the Political Parties Law.

Despite the Law Committee's list of changes and deletions to the draft law, the lengthiest debate about the Political Parties Law centered on the definition of political parties in Article 3. The draft law from the government provided a definition of a political party:

> A party is every political organization (*tandhim*) formed in accordance with the provisions of this law by individuals to group them-

selves on the principles and goals of endeavoring to participate in political life to realize a specific program related to political, economic and social affairs, and to work by legal and peaceful means in accordance with the rules of democratic practice based on political pluralism, freedom of thought, and the supremacy of law.[8]

The Law Committee, however, rejected this definition and proposed its own two-part definition:

A. A political party is every Jordanian political group (*jama'ah*) formed in accordance with the Constitution and the Law for endeavoring to participate in political life.

B. A party has a legal personality and it cannot be dissolved or dissolve its leadership unless in agreement with its basic governing rules or a decision from the court.[9]

In this debate, the government's definition of a political party was more narrow and restricted. The government's definition included three main features that limited the definition of a political party. First, a party must be an "organization." Pro-regime deputies, like Abd al-Majid al-Shreidah, argued that political parties must be "organized" in order to exist. Moreover, to some deputies, "organizations" were more developed than "groups." Second, according to conservative Abd al-Raouf al-Rawabdah, the Law Committee's change lacked a definition of a party's function because parties must be programmatic. For Rawabdah, parties functioned to achieve an ideological program, which was a component of the government's draft. Third, regime supporters argued that the definition of parties be restricted—by demanding that parties obey the "rules of democratic practice." This restriction was necessary because the era of "intellectual terrorism" by parties had ended.[10] For the regime coalition this meant that leftist and Arab nationalist parties would not be allowed to repeat the mass mobilizations of public support of the 1950s. In the 1990s, dialogue and tolerance were to be expected from parties—not street protests.

In contrast, the Law Committee sought to define political parties more broadly to incorporate features of the opposition that already existed. Thus, the Law Committee included "every Jordanian political group" in its alternative definition of a political party. This definition was designed to be more "broad" and "accurate." In support of this definition, some deputies argued that different groups, especially parties, have their own character. Therefore, parties may be more or less "organized," making the term "group" more appropriate in defining a political party. Moreover, Law Committee Chairman Hussein Majali based the committee's alternative text on previous Jordanian political party laws as well as party laws from around the Arab world—especially Egypt.[11]

The broader definition of a political party was designed to facilitate the speedy and easy legalization of the nascent (or, in the case of the Muslim Brotherhood, already existing) opposition groupings into political parties. Years of working underground had made their organizations flimsy, and since most opposition groups had been based on ideology rather than policy, their platforms were only weakly programmatic. Thus, the opposition felt that allegiance to the constitution was sufficient reason for their legal existence, and that "groups," not "organizations," should be the criteria for a political party.

Neither the supporters of the government's draft nor proponents of the Law Committee's alternative relented as the debate over Article 3 dragged on into its second session. However, the opposition's unity in support of the Law Committee began to fray as debate continued on June 24. Individuals from the opposition began to present their own definitions of political parties as additional alternatives or compromises. Regime liberal, Hosni al-Shyab, offered a compromise in which the term "organization" would be used in return for cutting the requirements for programs and platforms from the definition of a party. Communist Issa Mdanat echoed this sentiment by offering a definition of political parties as "organized political groups."[12] Momentum for a compromise between the government's draft and the Law Committee's alternative quickened when three prominent Muslim Brotherhood deputies proposed slight variations on the definition of a party as "all Jordanian political organizations or groups founded in accordance with the Constitution."[13] Debate between the weary deputies continued through the second session. By the end of the session on June 24, the House Speaker Abd al-Latif al-Arabiyat, a Muslim Brotherhood member, overruled demands to continue debate into a third session. He charged the House's administration to organize the various alternatives for voting in the next session.[14]

On June 29, the House held a third session to vote on Article 3 of the Political Parties Law. Arabiyat selected the proposal for a compromise by independent leftist Faris al-Nabulsi to be voted upon first. Nabulsi offered the definition that:

> A party is every political organization (*tandhim*) formed by a group (*jama'ah*) of Jordanians in accordance with the Constitution and the regulations of the Law for the purpose of participating in political life and realizing specific goals relating to political, economic, and social affairs and working by legal and peaceful means.[15]

The compromise definition passed with the support of 40 of the 61 deputies present. The final definition did lay closer to the original government draft, as it included both the term organization (*tandhim*) and the necessity for achieving goals. Yet the goals required were not specifically labeled a "program." The compromise definition broadened the definition from the government's original position but not as widely as the opposition had demanded.

PASSING THE POLITICAL PARTIES LAW

After the exhausting debate over the definition of a political party, the House moved on to discussing and passing the remainder of the draft law on June 29. The House passed few changes to the draft law from the government despite the many recommendations proposed by the Law Committee. Only a handful of exceptions to this trend were notable. First, Speaker al-Arabiyat broke a 30-30 tie to accept the Law Committee's recommendation for Article 6, Paragraph D. The draft law listed a number of social categories against which parties were prevented from discriminating. The Law Committee proposed the substitution that parties were required only to accord with the constitution in their terms of membership.[16]

The House also altered Article 21, a long list of principles that parties were to uphold. The draft law contained thirteen different points. The Law Committee recommended scrapping the entire article. Muslim Brotherhood deputy, Abd al-Rahim al-Akor, proposed to change the article into one paragraph to cover much of the same material. Only 7 deputies of 61 supported the Law Committee's motion, in contrast, Al-Akor's proposal passed by a wide majority.[17]

The House passed the entire law on July 5 by a vote of 43 of 53 deputies present. The speed with which the House passed the Political Parties Law surprised many in the press.[18] After spending two House sessions debating three articles, the remaining twenty-five articles were passed in only three more sessions.

COMPROMISE WITH THE SENATE

After the House passed the Political Parties Law, the Senate reviewed the law as well. The Senate passed the law on July 24, 1992. The Senate, however, made some changes that conflicted with the House's version. When a joint committee from the two chambers could not reach a compromise, the House and Senate met in a joint session on August 20, 1992.[19] In the joint session, the combined legislative chambers passed:

- The House's version of Article 5, Paragraph G which prohibited party members from being "a member in any other party, or any other non-Jordanian political partisan organization"
- The House's version of Article 18 which prohibited the searching of a party's headquarters
- The Senate's version of Article 21, which laid out principles by which parties needed to abide. The resultant list resembled the draft law, but did not contain the ban on religious or sectarian "extremism"
- A compromise on Article 24, which gave the penalties for violations of the law. The two chambers adapted the draft law, but kept the

punishment of violations within the Political Parties Law, without recourse to the Penal Code.[20]

The House of Deputies and the Senate jointly passed the law and the Regent (Crown Prince Hassan) signed it on August 23, 1992. The Political Parties Law was published as Law Number 32 for the year 1992.

LEGALIZATION AND PARTY DEVELOPMENT IN THE 1990S

The law gave final approval of political parties and their actions to the Ministry of Interior (Article 10). From December 1992 until the November 1993 elections, twenty parties obtained licenses from the Ministry of Interior (see table 4.1).

Approval by the Interior Ministry for some of the leftist and Arab nationalist parties, however, was not a smooth process. The Interior Ministry rejected the original applications of the Communist Party, the Arab Socialist Ba'ath Party, and the Jordanian People's Democratic Party. Citing references to socialism that the interior minister felt contradicted the constitution, the Interior Ministry rejected the three applications on December 3, 1991. As allowed in the law's Article 11, the three parties then filed a lawsuit with the Court of Justice to appeal the decision. However, after pressure from the Parliament and from the prime minister, the Interior Ministry worked with the three parties to change their charters and then legalized them during the second half of January 1993.[21]

With the approach of the 1993 parliamentary elections, many thought that political parties would reshape the face of the legislature. The 1993 elections were to be the first multi-party elections in Jordan since 1956. However, with the decree of a change to the Election Law to an electoral system that worked against organized political groups, parties faltered (see chapter 5). A noticeable tendency of candidates associated with parties in the 1993 election was to run as individuals, not as party associates—in some cases even to go as far as running from their political parties. Of 98 party-affiliated candidates, in 1993 only 58 ran under their party label.[22] Moreover, only 18 percent of the 534 candidates were affiliated with a political party, and only 11 percent explicitly so. Many parties—especially on the Left— revealed their factionalization, thus compounding their weakness. In some cases, the concerns of party hierarchies overrode the potential for electoral success. In general, members of a political party only took 33 of the 80 seats, 16 of which were won by the Muslim Brotherhood's political party, the Islamic Action Front (IAF). The results of the 1993 elections are discussed further in chapter 5.

The boycott of the 1997 elections further weakened the role of political parties in the House. The IAF led the boycott in response to the 1993 Election Law amendments, the 1997 Press and Publications Law amend-

Table 4.1 POLITICAL PARTIES LEGALIZED, 1992–1993

Party	Political Tendency	Leader	Legalized
Jordanian National Alliance	Centrist-Conservative; Tribalist	Mijhem al-Khreishah	December 2, 1992
Popular Unity Party	Centrist; Arab Nationalist	Talal al-Ramahi	December 7, 1992
Al-Ahd Party (Pledge)	Conservative; Jordanian Nationalist	Abd al-Hadi al-Majali	December 7, 1992
Al-Mustakbal Party (Future)	Centrist	Suleiman Arar	December 8, 1992
Islamic Action Front (IAF)	Muslim Brotherhood	Ishaq Farhan	December 8, 1992
Progressive Democratic Party of Jordan	Left of Center; pro-peace process	Ali Amer	January 16, 1993
Jordanian Communist Party	Original Communist Party	Yaqoub Zayyadin	January 17, 1993
Jordanian Ba'ath Arab Socialist Party	Arab-Nationalist	Tayseer al-Homsi	January 18, 1993
Jordanian People's Democratic Party (HASHD)	Leftist; some former DFLP members	Tayseer al-Zibri	January 24, 1993
Progress and Justice Party	Centrist; progovernment	Ali al-Sa'ad	January 27, 1993
Jordanian Democratic Socialist Party	Communist splinter	Issa Mdanat	January 27, 1993
Yaqaza Party (Vigilance)	Right of Center; progovernment	Abd al-Raouf al-Rawabdah	February 7, 1993
Jordanian Democratic Popular Unity Party	Arab Nationalist; some former PFLP members	Azmi al-Khawaja	February 9, 1993
Hurriyah Party (Freedom)	Leftist; Communist splinter	Fawaz al-Zu'bi	February 10, 1993
Democratic Arab Union Party	Arab-Nationalist; Centrist	Anis al-Mu'asher	February 17, 1993
Arab Democratic Islamic Movement (DUAA)	Islamist	Yousef Abu Bakr	April 12, 1993
Progressive Arab Ba'ath Party	Arab-Nationalist	Mahmoud al-Maitah	April 13, 1993
Jordanian Arab Popular Party	Arab-Nationalist	Abd al-Khaliq Shatat	May 27, 1993
Al-Watan Party (Homeland)	Right of Center; Tribalist	Akef al-Fayez	June 14, 1993
Jordanian Arab Democratic Party	Arab-Nationalist; Leftist	M'unis al-Razzaz	July 12, 1993

Sources: Data from "A Democratization Scorecard: Political Parties in Jordan." *Jordan Issues and Perspectives* 15 (June/July 1993), 4; Hani Hourani et al. *Jordanian Political Parties* (Amman: UJRC, 1993).

ments, and the 1994 peace treaty with Israel. A number of other opposition parties joined the boycott. However, many others did not. Chapter 7 discusses the 1997 press law amendments and the election boycott.

The 1997 elections also saw the undoing of the National Constitutional Party (NCP), which had merged nine centrist and conservative political parties in April 1997.[23] Legalized the next month, the NCP promised to challenge the IAF in parliamentary races across the country. However, the combination of the Islamists' boycott and the NCP's own contradictions resulted in the conservative party faring poorly in the 1997 elections. Only eleven of its candidates won seats in the House.

In both the 1993 and 1997 parliamentary elections, political parties failed in one of the chief objectives of political parties—gaining election. Popular attitudes of Jordanians also reflect the poor perception of parties in Jordan, as table 4.2 demonstrates.

Despite their being relegalized in 1992, by 1999 Jordan did not have a cohesive party system. A 2001 study found twenty-six political parties still active.[24] The IAF remained the only viable political party—mainly because of its roots in the Muslim Brotherhood. Leftist and Arab nationalist parties remained factionalized and marginal. Centrists and conservatives also did not organize themselves coherently through political parties. Sociocultural factors, institutional factors, and a lack of leadership among party elites combined to provide Jordan with its weak party system.[25] The effects of these factors, however, were not envisioned when the Political Parties Law was debated. The debate in the Parliament of the Political Parties Law was followed by the debate over the new press law.

THE PRESS AND PUBLICATIONS LAW OF 1993

Like the Political Parties Law of 1992, the Press and Publications Law of 1993 followed out of the National Charter. The government of Tahir al-Masri sub-

Table 4.2 OPINIONS ON THE SUCCESS OF POLITICAL WORK BY PARTIES

Degree of Success	Survey 1995	Survey 1996	Survey 1997
Great	3.9	2.3	2.9
Medium	12.0	21.8	14.8
Little	6.4	13.2	11.1
No Success	18.2	20.6	15.9
Absolutely No Success	15.2	8.2	10.9
Don't Know	44.3	24.1	43.8
Refused to Answer	—	—	0.2
Not Clear	—	—	0.4

Source: Data from University of Jordan Center for Strategic Studies, Istitla ʿa lil-Rai ʾ Howla al-Demoqratya fi al-Urdun 1997: al-Nata ʾij al-Awaliyah [Survey on Democracy in Jordan 1997—Preliminary Results], (Amman: University of Jordan Center for Strategic Studies, 1997), 15.

mitted both draft laws to the Parliament in the summer of 1991. The Press and Publications Law would follow the Political Parties Law on the Parliament's agenda. The press law, however, would not gain the approval of the legislature and receive the king's signature until March 1993. The final text of the law reflected a great deal of the government's original language. However, the Parliament made some significant changes during its deliberations.

The Jordanian constitution guarantees press freedom, but it can be limited by legislation (Article 15, Paragraph 2). Until the 1993 law was passed, the 1973 Press and Publications Law governed the press in Jordan—with provisions that reflected the martial law of the time. In the early 1990s, Jordan's media was mainly held by the state. The state fully owned and controlled the television and the radio. The printed media—mainly the daily Arabic newspapers—were also under partial state ownership. Of Jordan's two main newspapers, the state owned 60 percent of *Al-Rai*³ and 35 percent of *Al-Destour*.[26]

The Press and Publications Law can be seen as a regime institutional survival strategy because, while the law opened up greater freedoms, the law also placed clear limits on those openings. This limited the space for the opposition to publicize its dissent to the regime's politics. The 1993 Press and Publications Law can be considered a successful survival strategy for the regime since this drawing of limits was reached through negotiations with the opposition in Parliament.

The law was submitted to the Parliament in August of 1991. However, it took the Parliament until August 1992 to begin full debate on the law. The Parliament finally turned to the press law after passing the Political Parties Law during the Parliament's extraordinary session in the summer of 1992. Debate dragged on into the next ordinary session of the Parliament and the law did not pass with the approval of the Parliament until March 1993. The law was then reviewed by the Senate and signed by King Hussein on March 29, 1993.

CHANGES MADE BY THE HOUSE TO THE DRAFT LAW

The Law Committee of the House of Deputies recommended changes for many articles in the draft law. These recommendations generally kept the limits that the government had recommended; however, in some cases the Law Committee aimed to expand press freedoms. In 1992 the House's eleven-member Law Committee held many opposition-leaning deputies, including four members of the Muslim Brotherhood.

On a number of instances conservative and progovernment deputies went beyond the text proposed by the government to add further restrictions. Moreover, the Muslim Brotherhood aimed to input their view of public morality into the law. Contentious instances of debate in the House over the Press and Publications Law included: the definition of a journalist

(Article 2), journalists' ability to keep their sources secret (Article 5), the insertion of vague language which could lead to restrictive interpretations (Articles 4 and 8), explicit restrictions on the press (Article 40), and penalties for violating those restrictions (Articles 46 through 51).

DEFINING A JOURNALIST

In the debate over Article 2, which offered definitions of all the key terms of the law, the most controversial definition discussed was that of "journalist." The draft law proposed that a journalist is "any person who meets the conditions provided for in the operative Jordanian Press Association Law and adopts Journalism as his/her profession in accordance with the said law."[27] The fierce debate over terminology mirrored the debate over definitions in the Political Parties Law.

However, the Law Committee recommended that the phrase, "in accordance with the said law," be removed. The Law Committee aimed to open up the definition of the profession to include all journalists, regardless of their membership in the Jordanian Press Association (JPA). The recommendation to expand the definition of a journalist, however, did not survive the debate on the floor of the House. Progovernment deputies such as Abd al-Raouf al-Rawabdah and Abdullah al-Nsour moved to keep the definition so that it only included members of the JPA.[28]

The JPA had vigorously lobbied House deputies to keep the Association's monopoly over Jordanian journalists.[29] The JPA's governing law limits journalists to those who have certain educational and training qualifications. Having worked for certain Jordanian newspapers was a key component of such training. However, many practicing journalists in Jordan remained unrecognized by the JPA and thus faced restrictions on their work. The 1993 Press and Publications Law reinforced the JPA's monopoly over the profession of journalism. This monopoly has led its critics to call the JPA, in terms of press freedom, a "stand in for the government" and an "egregious problem."[30] With a majority of 27 of the 53 deputies present, the House confirmed the JPA's control over journalists by passing the text of the draft law's definition of a journalist.[31]

KEEPING SOURCES SECRET

In another article (Article 5, especially Paragraph D), the House imposed a more restrictive view of press freedom than that called for by either the Law Committee or the government. Article 5 lists the components of freedom of the press. Paragraph D in the draft law stated that freedom of the press included, "The right of the press publication, news agencies, editors and journalists to keep the sources of information and news they gather secret." Conservative deputies demanded the limitation of this right in cases of court proceedings. The House added the clause, "except by the court," to the text of the draft law; the motion passed with a vote of 32 of 57 deputies.[32] The addition of this restriction evoked the ire of many journalists.

The Senate, however, weakened this restriction, and the House later concurred with the upper chamber in the final version of the law. The final text of the Article read that journalists have the right to "keep the sources of information and news they gather secret, unless the Court decides otherwise when hearing criminal cases involving the security of the State, prevention of crime or realization of justice." Once again the Senate showed a somewhat more liberal view of freedom than the House.

RESTRICTIVE RED LINES

Journalists have also critiqued the vague language of a number of the articles of the draft of the 1993 Press and Publications Law. For example, according to Article 8,

> Publications shall refrain from publishing anything that contradicts the principles of freedom, national obligation, human rights, and respect of truth and values of the Arab-Islamic *Umma* and shall regard the freedom of thought, opinion, expression and access to information as a right for all citizens as much as it is a right for themselves.

According to its critics, such vague terms as "values" would leave the interpretation of this prohibition up to the government to enforce as it saw fit. A long debate ensued with the recommendation by the House's Law Committee to delete this article. Even with a number of proposed possible compromises, 49 of the 59 deputies present endorsed the text of the draft law.[33]

However, more explicit, but more restrictive limits to the freedom of the press were drafted into Article 40. This article sets a number of "red lines" for the press not to cross. According to the law, publications were prohibited from publishing:

- News which offends the king or the royal family
- Unsanctioned news of the Jordanian Armed Forces, or comments offensive to the military or security forces
- Articles or materials contemptuous to religion
- Articles which damage national unity
- Minutes of closed sessions of Parliament
- News which shakes confidence in the national currency
- Personal insults to heads of state of Arab, Islamic or friendly countries

- Articles or news which may offend the dignity or personal freedoms of individuals or damage their reputation
- News, reports, dispatches, articles and drawings which are contrary to public morals and ethics
- Advertisements for unapproved medicines

The Law Committee again recommended that the House delete the article. In the House debate over Article 40, opponents of the article focused on the duplication of these restrictions in the Press and Publications Law and the Penal Code. The government and its supporters argued that such restrictions are common not only in the Third World, but in developed democracies, like Great Britain, as well. In the end, 14 deputies of the 56 present supported the Law Committee, 37 deputies voted to keep the draft law's list of restrictions in Article 40.[34]

Penalties for Violations

One of the few successes of the Law Committee in the debate over the 1993 Press and Publications Law came when the House rejected the article that contained the penalties for Article 40. The draft law proposed that violation of any of the restrictions in Article 40 could be punished by six months imprisonment or a 2,000 to 5,000 dinar fine (5,000 to 10,000 dinars for corporations).[35] The House deleted this article from the draft law with a majority of 38 of 61 deputies.

Punishments for violating the Press and Publications Law, however, remained in the law. The most severe punishment—up to a 6,000 dinar fine—was for writers and editors receiving improper gifts (prohibited by Article 44, punished by Article 49). Publishing or distributing banned material (Article 45) could be punished by a 500 to 2,000 dinar fine (Article 50). Most other violations, including those of the prohibitions in Article 40, were punished by a 1,000 dinar fine (Article 51). However, during the House debate, it took two votes and a narrow majority to approve Article 51.[36]

The House passed the entire Press and Publications Law on December 27, 1992. The Senate made minor modifications to the law in the course of its debate (e.g., in Article 5). The House accepted the changes of the Senate on March 14, 1993. The king signed the Press and Publications Law into law on March 29, 1993.

Enforcement of the 1993 Press and Publications Law

The situation of the press in Jordan underwent a number of changes after the 1993 Press and Publications Law came into force. The major Arabic dailies, all with some form of government ownership, remained the same. However, their content began to take a slightly more open tone, with more articles on or by opposition personalities. More importantly, after the passage of the 1993 Press and Publications Law, a number of new weekly newspapers received licenses and began publishing. A number of these newspapers, known as tabloids for their format, proved to be quite controversial. Some tabloids caused controversy for their publication of material with unusual or sexually provocative content. Others challenged the official government line on matters of politics, especially on corruption and relations with Israel. Some weekly tabloids sensationalized news to boost their readership and increase their slim revenue base. The weekly press defended its right to publish the news at it saw fit. Over time, however, the tabloids began to anger social conservatives and regime officials. This led to the greater enforcement of the 1993 Press and Publications Law's many restrictions.

During the period of May 1993 to May 1997, the government, through the Department of Press and Publications, filed sixty-six lawsuits against individuals and newspapers for violations of the Press and Publications Law and the Penal Code. Table 4.3 breaks down these prosecutions by the type of newspaper. Many violations were the result of the publishing of interviews with members of the illegal Hizb al-Tahrir. Also, comments deemed as insulting to heads of other Arab states were prosecuted. Sensational material was often charged with violating public morals under Article 40 of the Press and Publications Law.

Jordan's weekly newspapers committed the vast majority of violations. The daily newspapers—generally under partial state ownership—provoked less controversy. Moreover, four weekly newspapers—as strident critics of the

Table 4.3 PROSECUTIONS FOR PRESS VIOLATIONS, 1993–1997

Year	Violation of	Jordanian Daily	Jordanian Non-Daily	Non-Jordanian	Total
1993	Press Law	1	11	0	12
(May–Dec)	Penal Code	0	1	0	1
1994	Press Law	0	7	0	7
	Penal Code	4	14	9	18
1995	Press Law	0	9	1	10
	Penal Code	0	2	0	2
1996	Press Law	0	15	0	15
	Penal Code	0	0	0	0
1997	Press Law	0	1	0	1
(Jan–May)	Penal Code	0	0	0	0
Total		5	60	1	66

Source: Data from Article 19, *Blaming the Press: Jordan's Democratization Process in Crisis* (London: Article 19, 1997), 99–104.

Table 4.4 VIOLATIONS BY SELECTED WEEKLY NEWSPAPERS, 1993–1997

Paper	1993	1994	1995	1996	Total
Al-Bilad	5	6	4	2	17
Al-Ahali	2	4	2	1	9
Al-Majd	—	3	3	0	6
Al-Haqiqa	—	—	—	6	6
Total	7	13	9	9	38

Source: Data from Article 19, *Blaming the Press: Jordan's Democratization Process in Crisis* (London: Article 19, 1997), 99–104.

government and Jordanian society—accounted for a majority of those violations, as shown in table 4.4.

The government tried to enforce the Press and Publications Law unilaterally. The courts, however, reclaimed their position as the only power that could enforce the Press and Publications Law. For example, the Higher Court of Justice ruled in April 1995 that the Department of Press and Publications had no right to suspend the weekly *Hawadith Al-Sa'ah*, despite the fact that the paper did not have a chief editor who was a member of the JPA and thus not qualified under Article 13 of the Press and Publications Law.[37] The Department of Press and Publications accused many newspapers of violating the Press and Publications Law and the Penal Code. It, however, could not generally convince the courts to convict the journalists.

The courts often argued that the government could not prove its case, even with the generally vague wording of the Press and Publications Law. In 1996, Fahd al-Rimawi, editor of *Al-Majd*, was accused of insulting the Amir of Bahrain and tried under Article 40 of the Press and Publications Law. The court found that Rimawi was innocent since he had not disrupted relations with Bahrain.[38] Thus, the courts found that with the vagueness of the Press and Publications Law there was room to protect the freedom of expression.

Another example of the government's failure to convict offenders of the Press and Publications Law came in October of 1995. Salameh Na'mat, a correspondent for the London based *Al-Hayat* newspaper, was jailed without bail for claiming that many Jordanian businessmen were on the payroll of the Iraqi government. Na'mat based his report on unnamed Jordanian officials. After two days in prison, Na'mat was released on bail. He was later cleared of all charges that he had violated the Press and Publications Law.[39]

The government, however, did obtain some convictions for violations of the Press and Publications Law. In May 1994, the *Jordan Times* was convicted of violating Articles 40 and 42 of the Press and Publications Law for publishing a report about soldiers on trial for an attempted coup.[40] The English language daily was fined three hundred dinars.

The only prison sentence handed down by the courts during this period was to Abdullah Bani Issa, editor of the weekly *Al-Hiwar*. Bani Issa was convicted for violations of Article 40 of the Press and Publications Law and for violating three other articles of the Penal Code because of his *lese-majesty* and his publishing of a statement for the illegal party Hizb al-Tahrir. Bani Issa was sentenced to six months in prison and a five hundred dinar fine. This sentence was the first time a Jordanian journalist was sentenced by the courts to a prison term.[41]

However, such convictions and sentences were rare. In general, the courts upheld the freedom of the press. In the venue of the courts, journalists could contest the government's interpretations of the law. With prosecutors failing to obtain convictions for violations of the 1993 Press and Publications Law, the government turned to tightening up the press law in 1997.

SUCCESSFULLY MANAGING THE INSTITUTIONALIZATION OF POLITICAL LIBERALIZATION

Both the Political Parties Law and the Press and Publications Law of 1993 emerged out of the discussions and decisions of the National Charter Committee. By the time the government had drafted the two laws, however, Operation Desert Storm had blown through the region and Jordan's regime was preparing for a major foreign policy turn toward the Middle East peace process. The fall of Tahir al-Masri's government had encouraged regime hardliners to point to the hazards of political liberalization and for regime liberals to ponder the trade-off between greater democratization and political stability in Jordan. Thus, while these two laws helped institutionalize political liberalization in the kingdom, they also marked its limits. Moreover, the regime did not intend to legislate complete freedom of political activity or unlimited freedom of speech. Both laws contain numerous restrictions on the freedoms of Jordanians. Nevertheless, Jordanian commentators generally found that these two laws were far better than their predecessors.

The debate over both laws passed through normal constitutional channels. Both the regime and the opposition used the constitution and the specific procedural rules of the House to pursue their agenda. The government and its supporters used their power to draft the law to their liking. The opposition deputies in the Law Committee tried to loosen the laws' restrictions.

In the debate over Article 3 of the Political Parties Law, the cohesiveness of progovernment deputies outlasted that of the opposition. Yet the definition of a political party did not result from the regime overriding the opposition. A compromise was reached by catering to the fatigue of the entire House. This, along with the rest of the Political Parties Law, demonstrated the consensus on relegalizing parties in Jordan that had been reached in the National Charter.

With the 1993 Press and Publications Law, the regime coalition did its best to lobby House deputies to support the government's draft—if not go beyond it. The JPA responded to a threat to its organizational monopoly in the debate over the definition of a journalist in Article 2.[42] In contrast, independent journalists also tried to lobby the Parliament to remove many of the restrictions of the Press and Publications Law, though not as effectively as the government.

After the debate over the definition of a party, the debate over the Political Parties Law saw little controversy. In contrast, the House spurned attempts by opposition deputies to revisit some controversial articles during the legislation of the press law. The House rejected a proposal on constitutional grounds to revisit articles that it had already passed.[43] The opposition's disunity limited its ability to contest the government's draft law within the venue of the Parliament.

Outside of Parliament, the regime used coercive tactics as well to "lobby" House deputies to temper their opposition to the Press and Publications Law as well as the regime's participation in the Middle East peace process. In late August and early September 1992, two vocal independent Islamist deputies, Yʿaqoub Qarash and Layth Shbeilat, were arrested in connection with a case of an Islamist group illegally possessing weapons. Despite the suspicious timing and the weak evidence of the prosecution, Qarash and Shbeilat were each convicted to twenty-year prison sentences. King Hussein, however, pardoned both immediately.[44] The regime had sent a message that extreme opposition by House deputies would not be tolerated—by resourcefully using the rules present in the constitution.

The various opposition deputies in the House were united in supporting the relegalization of political parties. Although many deputies from the opposition wanted an expansive definition of political parties in Article 3, as the debate deadlocked some opposition deputies sought a compromise. In general, opposition deputies wished a definition of political parties that their weak organizations could easily meet. However, some deputies may have realized that paralysis within the House would also not get their nascent parties legalized any faster. Overall, the opposition supported legalizing parties because it had the most to gain from the Law. A majority of the parties legalized after 1992 could be considered within the opposition. Moreover, the opposition had already generally acquiesced to the regime's limits on parties by signing off on the National Charter.

In contrast, the unity of the opposition trends in the Parliament was not as strong during the debate over the press law. House deputies of leftist and Arab nationalist trends were unable to converge with the Islamists to protect the freedom of the press during the debate over the Press and Publications Law. A high degree of absenteeism in House meetings also weakened the ability of the near majority of opposition deputies to gain victories.

Often a quarter of the deputies were absent during the debates of the Press and Publications Law. The House could not finish the debate of the Press and Publications Law in the extraordinary summer session of 1992 because of a lack of a quorum of deputies on the final day of the session.[45] Moreover, the ideological factionalization of the opposition in the House also prevented a consensus to defend the freedom of the press. Strong proponents for liberalizing the press law were few in the House (leftist journalist Fakhri Qʿawar was a notable exception). The factionalized opposition did not, in general, unify on the abstract issue of freedom of the press. In contrast, most factions of the opposition found it to be in their interests to quickly gain the ability to legally organize their nascent parties.

During the House debates, the progovernment deputies generally remained united in their support for the government's draft of the Political Parties Law. Eleven deputies had been members of Tahir al-Masri's cabinet (including the prime minister himself) that had drafted the law. Five deputies remained in the cabinet of Bin Shaker; they were joined by an additional five other House deputies in the new government. Thus, of the eighty-member House, sixteen had served in a cabinet with a vested interest in the draft of the Political Parties Law. While some regime liberals in the House sought to expand the definition of a party and generally loosen the regulations on parties in the law (e.g., Hosni al-Shyab), the regime supporters in the House generally stood with the government's draft.

During the Parliament debates over the 1993 Press and Publications Law, the regime coalition's unity was also generally strong. Lobbying by the government and its allies kept the demands of journalists and opposition deputies in check. Moreover, with nine deputies in Prime Minister Bin Shaker's cabinet, the government had the support of two crucial blocs of deputies in the House. However, the regime coalition's unity was challenged by the insertion of amendments to the government's draft law by conservative deputies. On a number of occasions the government's draft law was more liberal in terms of granting freedom to the press than the changes made by progovernment deputies.[46]

In light of this, the Political Parties Law of 1992, which relegalized political parties, can be seen as a negotiated success for the regime. The legalizing of political parties reduced the level of dissent from the opposition, on the one hand, by allowing the opposition a degree of organizational autonomy, but on the other hand, by reinforcing the state's ability to regulate and circumscribe the existence of political parties. The 1993 Press and Publications Law can also be seen as a successful regime survival strategy because, while the law granted greater freedom to the press, it still held strong restrictions and penalties over journalists. The Press and Publications Law faced a great deal of fierce debate in the House of Deputies. The deputies compromised on some points—on others the government relied on a conservative majority to overcome the fractured opposition. Lobbying by the regime—inside and outside of the venue—reinforced the outcome of the episode resulting in the government's favor.

The passing of the Political Parties Law and the 1993 Press and Publications Law marked the high point of political liberalization in Jordan during the 1990s. The fall of Masri's government seems to have convinced the regime that the Arab-Israeli peace process would draw a great deal of domestic opposition. As peace with Israel became more likely, domestic political liberalization became more of a liability. Thus, King Hussein decided that the opposition's role in the Parliament needed to be reduced.

FIVE

MANAGING PEACE AND ITS DISCONTENTS

By the summer of 1993, the regime had grown tired of the opposition constantly challenging the government's chosen policies in dealing with the existential issues that faced Jordan. Although the opposition in Parliament had not yet blocked any of the government's draft legislation, it had significantly delayed many parts of the economic structural adjustment program. It had also asked embarrassing questions about Jordan's participation in the Middle East peace process, questions that would become only more probing as the potential for a Jordanian-Israeli peace treaty increased. With elections for the House of Deputies slated for November 1993, the regime decided to act. In August 1993, King Hussein decreed amendments to the Election Law that dramatically altered the electoral system. The new voting formula significantly reduced the strength of the opposition in the Parliament. Yet the opposition did little to oppose the successful implementation of this survival strategy. The Parliament elected under these new rules later quickly ratified the October 1994 Jordanian-Israeli peace treaty.

PEACE ON THE HORIZON

After the 1991 Madrid peace conference, bilateral talks between the Arab states and Israel began in Washington D.C. After some controversy, the joint Palestinian-Jordanian team functionally broke up, as each half of the team pursued separate negotiations with the Israelis. The clear distance in negotiating positions between the Palestinians and the Israelis was publicly aired in the media. The difficulties between the Syrians and the Israelis also garnered a great deal of media attention.

Quietly in the background, however, the Jordanians and the Israelis moved forward in finding common ground on their bilateral differences. The distance between Jordanian and Israeli negotiating positions was relatively small with multilateral issues and, more importantly, the Palestinian question under discussion in other venues. A past record of functional cooperation between Jordan and Israel had already settled many purely bilateral issues, save for Israel's occupation of Jordanian land in Wadi Araba.[1] Jordan and Israel signed a draft agenda of peace talks in October 1992. As the Washington talks dragged through 1993 with few advances on the Palestinian-Israeli and the Syrian-Israeli tracks, negotiators on the Jordanian-Israeli track had little to do but sit and wait. By the summer of 1993 the ground was ready for final negotiations between Jordan and Israel over a peace treaty; all that was needed was a breakthrough in the other sets of negotiations. That breakthrough would come in September 1993 with the announcement of the Palestinian-Israeli agreements reached in Oslo, Norway. Yet until that happened, the Jordanian government concentrated on preparing the domestic political sphere for peace with Israel. One of the main centers of activity was the Jordanian Parliament—which would have to ratify any future peace treaty.

However, the regime questioned the likelihood of the Jordanian Parliament—with its near majority of opposition—ratifying a potential treaty. The opposition had embarrassed King Hussein in 1991 by nearly withdrawing confidence in Prime Minister Tahir al-Masri on the eve of the Madrid conference. Moreover, the opposition—especially the Muslim Brotherhood—frequently used the platform of Parliament debates to voice their discontent with the government's participation in the U.S.-led Middle East peace process. Therefore, King Hussein desired a change in the composition of the Parliament before the legislature needed to ratify a peace treaty. The elections scheduled for November 1993 offered that possibility.

THE ELECTION LAW AMENDMENTS OF 1993

In August 1993, the regime used its constitutional power to decree amendments to the Election Law during the Parliament's absence through a "provisional law." It did so in order to prepare for the eventualities of peace and the need for speedier implementation of economic structural reforms. The changes altered the electoral system to the disadvantage of the recently relegalized organized opposition parties. The new electoral system benefited regime supporters—especially those with tribal support. The change to the Election Law would make the regime's life much easier by manipulating the composition of the House of Deputies to be elected in November 1993. With a more proregime Parliament, the challenges to the government's planned legislative agenda would be reduced and the power of opposition dissent lessened. Thus, a future peace treaty would not be blocked or delayed, and economic legislation could move forward. The decree would help ensure the regime's survival by manufacturing support for the regime's preferred policies as long as the legitimacy of Parliament was not compromised in the process. The 1993 amendments to the

Jordanian Election Law provide further evidence for the voluminous literature on the potential distributive power of electoral institutions. The Election Law amendments were also a key turning point away from the use of political liberalization in the Jordanian regime's survival strategies.

GOVERNMENT ACTIONS BEFORE THE AMENDMENTS

The amendment of the Election Law was not greeted as a surprise; changing the electoral law had been publicly on the regime's agenda since the middle of 1991. Neither the government nor the opposition made any changes to the 1989 provisional amendments to the Election Law when they were brought before Parliament for ratification in March 1992. Nevertheless, both sides complained about the shortcomings of the electoral system. At that time, government officials expressed their intent to have the 1993 elections run under a new electoral law. The regime's active desire to change the Election Law resurfaced in the spring of 1993 as the term of the Parliament elected in 1989 came to a close.

In May 1993, King Hussein appointed a new prime minister, Dr. Abd al-Salam al-Majali, considered by many to be a regime hard-liner. Majali headed a caretaker government to run the 1993 elections. The king's letter of designation to Majali charged the prime minister with holding elections. The letter also asked Majali to make sure that the elections would be held in line with the constitutional guarantee of equality between citizens, hinting at a change in the Election Law. The proposed idea of a "one-person, one-vote" system—in contrast to the list voting system of the 1989 law—began to be a common sight in the Jordanian press.

Majali and his government, however, kept references to the substance of any proposed changes vague by saying, for example, that the law had "gaps" or "loopholes."[2] Moreover, the prime minister also avoided any fixed reference to how the proposed changes would be adopted. At the time, the Parliament was out of session; it did not have an extraordinary summer session scheduled. Over the summer, Majali repeatedly denied any plans for changing the Election Law without "national consultation," especially upon meeting the speaker of the House of Deputies, a Muslim Brotherhood member.[3] At times, the king even alluded to a National Charter-style royal commission for a dialogue to endorse a change in the Election Law. Through June and July 1993, debate circled over the possibility of a change in the Election Law, the proper process for amending it, and the exact meaning of one-person, one-vote.

OPPOSITION REACTION BEFORE THE AMENDMENTS

The opposition reacted to the government-induced controversy over the Election Law by expressing its desire that any change be processed through the Parliament. As the public debate began, various opposition groups aired preferences for different changes in the Election Law. However, as government resolve for a one-person, one-vote system became clearer, opposition threats of a boycott of the elections emerged. Yet these threats seemed weakened by questions about the ability of the opposition to unite its disparate ranks over the Election Law.

Many opposition groups disliked the proposed one-person, one-vote system, especially the Muslim Brotherhood. Most opposition activity in the summer of 1993, however, focused on insuring the Parliament's role in any changes. Nevertheless, the Muslim Brotherhood member and speaker of the House, Dr. Abd al-Latif al-Arabiyat, was "satisfied" with the assurances of consultation during his meeting with Prime Minister Majali on June 7. However, the government's pledge was not concrete.[4] Fifty-seven House deputies met on June 9 to discuss the Parliament's role in a change in the Election Law. The deputies issued a statement demanding that "any change or amendment to the Election Law should pass through the legislative authority in accordance with the constitution and in commitment to cooperation between the two branches of which none should ignore the other."[5]

Representatives of the Muslim Brotherhood, leftist parties, Arab nationalist groups, as well as independent Islamists, reiterated these calls at a rally on July 4. Even after King Hussein dissolved the Parliament on August 4, opposition groups still called for changes to go through the next Parliament—after the November 1993 elections. The Muslim Brotherhood stated that holding elections under the 1989 system "in spite of its many defects," would be "far better than holding them under an unknown law ... which has not been adopted in accordance with the acknowledged constitutional stages."[6]

While united on their desire to see that the Parliament authorize any changes to the Election Law, the debate over the Election Law also revealed the vast range of preferences held by different groups over the proper shape of the electoral system. On July 27, fifteen political parties agreed that any new Election Law should be "more democratic and modern." The parties also agreed that: the voting age should be lowered to eighteen years of age, the number of seats in the House should be increased, the judiciary should supervise the elections, the ban on members of illegal political parties from running should be cancelled, and the district boundaries should be redrawn to "ensure equality among all citizens."[7] However, the parties, which spanned the Jordanian political spectrum, agreed on little else—especially the specific electoral system.

Surveys by newspapers of preferences of various parties and opposition groups revealed a wide range of opinions. While most groups expressed a desire to keep the open-list electoral system, some groups, especially leftist and Arab nationalist parties, called for a proportional representation system in a single national district.[8] Yet the Islamic Action Front (IAF) did not seem to call for any changes to the electoral system, save removing the quotas for minorities.[9] Nor did the various opposition groups rally behind a single proposal for the electoral system—except (in some cases, begrudgingly) for the 1989 open-list system.

Calls for a boycott of the election grew as the government moved closer to decreeing the one-person, one-vote system. In July, independent Islamist Layth Shbeilat called for a boycott if the government acted "without acquiring appropriate constitutional backing."[10] In early August, IAF deputy Hammam Sa'id reiterated the call for a boycott, stating that, "We will seriously consider boycotting the elections if the government changes the Election Law outside the Lower House of Parliament and introduces the one-man-one-vote formula."[11]

The Muslim Brotherhood and IAF, however, reacted to the threatened change of the Election Law with mixed voices. Muslim Brotherhood deputy Abd al-Rahim Akor threatened in early June that the Brotherhood would boycott the elections if the Election Law was changed through a decreed provisional law. However, the Brotherhood's parliamentary spokesman did not publicly support him. Moreover, internal debates between Brotherhood "hawks" and "doves" moved into public view. Brotherhood hawks wished to respond to a change in the Election Law with a full-force campaign, entering as many candidates as they could in order to demonstrate their strength in the elections. The organization's doves on the other hand, sought to avoid a confrontation with the regime while keeping its support with its grassroots by boycotting the elections. By early August, the *Jordan Times* reported that the more moderate point of view had prevailed.[12]

The most critical failure for the opposition was to not request an extraordinary parliamentary session to discuss the Election Law. Constitutionally, the parliament can be called into an extraordinary session if a majority (41 deputies) requests so in a petition to the king (Article 82, Paragraph B). However, while 57 deputies requested that any changes to the Election Law be sent through the House in June, the Muslim Brotherhood bloc of deputies failed to gain the 41 required signatures on a petition demanding an extraordinary parliament session. Other deputies put "priority to other courses of action."[13] The Islamist-led opposition, which could gather a majority in the House with the support of a handful of moderates, thus failed to exert the House's full constitutional power. This failure allowed the government to dissolve the Parliament and decree a provisional law to amend the Election Law—overriding any opposition desires for the House to have a say in its own destiny.

"SAWT WAHAD"

On August 4, 1993, King Hussein dissolved the Parliament, mooting any calls for a new electoral law to go through the legislature. Moreover, with Parliament unable to be recalled into an extraordinary session, the government could more easily use its constitutional power to issue provisional laws. On August 17, King Hussein signed the decree for (Provisional) Law Number 15 for 1993, amending the Election Law. He followed the decree with a speech on television.[14] Although the changes made by the 1993 amendments to the 1986 Election Law were extremely simple, the consequences dramatically affected the way Jordanians voted. The 1993 amendments changed Article 46:B of the 1986 law which read:

> The Voter shall write the *names* of the candidates he wishes to elect on the Ballot Paper given to him by the Chairman of the Balloting Panel and shall return to the Ballot Box to deposit the Ballot Paper therein. An illiterate Voter may ask the Chairman of the Balloting Panel to write the *names* of the Candidates the Elector wishes to elect; after having written down the *names*, the Chairman shall read the names out within earshot of the Balloting Panel.[15]

The 1993 amendments changed the instances of the word "names" from the plural to the singular. The amendments also covered for this grammatical change in other parts of the 1986 Election Law.

The 1993 amendments introduced the formula known in Jordan as the "one-man, one-vote."[16] The "*sawt wahad*" (one-vote) formula eliminated the open-list system of voting. However, under the 1993 amendments all other features of the previous electoral system remained the same. The amendments kept the disproportional district boundaries, seat magnitudes, and the quotas. Regardless of the number of seats in an elector's district, he or she could only vote for one candidate as an individual. In the technical literature on election laws, Jordan's new electoral system would be classified as the rare semi-proportional system—the Single Nontransferable Vote (SNTV).[17] Lijphart et al. argue that the SNTV system tends to aid small minorities, while offering disadvantages to large parties—something that the regime hoped it would do.

GOVERNMENT JUSTIFICATIONS FOR THE 1993 AMENDMENTS

The regime proclaimed that the change in the Election Law made Jordanian elections more democratic. The defense of the amendments by King Hussein and Prime Minster Majali tended to break down into six types of justifications. First, the central justification for changing the voting system from an open-list to the one-person, one-vote system focused on the constitutional equality of Jordanians (Article 6). In this view all voters were not equal under the 1989 voting system, as some voters could cast as many as nine votes, while others only as few as two. With all voters having one vote, this inequality was remedied. Critics would later point out that this justification focused on the equality in the act of voting, not on representation (malapportionment).

A second justification for the change to the one-person, one-vote system centered on the regime's desire for a consolidation of political currents in Jordan. Since the relegalization of political parties in 1992, over twenty parties had come into existence. Both the king and the prime minister expressed a clear desire for Jordan to have four or less distinct, organized political groupings. However, as the 1993 and 1997 election results would show, this consolidation of parties would not occur. The process was even hampered by the SNTV system. By voters only being able to choose one individual candidate, the law ironically promoted party factionalization rather than consolidation—or perhaps that was the regime's true intention.

Third, the regime reiterated that the 1993 Election Law amendments had been decreed in the same manner the 1989 amendments had been—that is, as a provisional law. The regime thus attempted to undercut criticism of the 1993 decree by pointing to the process that implemented the (more preferred) 1989 electoral system. The regime's use of precedent struck many in the opposition as disingenuous, since the Parliament had been dissolved just two weeks prior to the decree. Some opposition leaders pointed out, in comparison, that in 1989 the Parliament had been dissolved over a year before and the urgency of the matter was much greater after the April 1989 riots. Yet technically, the regime was correct in using the 1989 law as a precedent.

Fourth, the regime coupled this precedent with the claim that the 1993 amendments needed to be limited in scope. To account for leaving the district boundaries and magnitudes unchanged, King Hussein argued:

> At this delicate stage, I have taken into consideration the necessity of limiting the amendment to the election law to this aspect, due to my belief that any other amendment that aims at equating the number of the electorate in a constituency with that of another would mean depriving larger parts of the country of the right to effective parliamentary representation, which is necessary to improve their conditions, and ensure equal distribution of Jordan's comprehensive development. This is in addition to the fact that the regional political situation is not yet stable, which would affect the status of Jordan and Jordanians irrespective of their origins. Therefore the electoral districts will remain unchanged during the upcoming parliamentary general elections.[18]

Thus, matters of development and national security excused the keeping of the 1989 districts and division of seats. This claim was also reiterated in 1997 for the continuation of the same electoral system.

Fifth, the regime also justified the decreeing of the amendments on the basis that "enough dialogue" had been held on the subject, despite demands from Parliament for any change of the Election Law to go through the legislature. Prime Minister Majali claimed that a national dialogue, which had been called for by the king, was "going on in the media and the press."[19] Thus, Parliament's constitutional role in deciding the manner of its own election was a closed topic.

Sixth, the regime justified the 1993 amendments by claiming that the idea of changing the Election Law was not a new idea, which was true. The regime had officially supported electoral reform since 1991. In June 1991, King Hussein, in his letter to the then-outgoing Prime Minister Mudar Badran, spoke of the need to give voters "the chance to choose one candidate."[20] The king cited this letter in his August 1993 speech.

The reasoning behind the regime's desire to change the Election Law in 1991 generally remained unchanged in 1993. Despite the other justifications given by the regime, the not-so-subtly veiled intent behind the law was to reduce the strength of the parliamentary opposition—especially the Muslim Brotherhood. Badran's cabinet had included four Brotherhood members during the Gulf War in the first half of 1991. The vocal, but fractious, near majority of opposition deputies elected in 1989 constantly challenged the regime, but never significantly overrode its policies. However, in 1993, with criticism from the opposition stinging regime hard-liners, a peace treaty with Israel on the horizon, and a general disgust at the low productivity of the Parliament, the regime decided to act.

The SNTV system was generally recognized as being aimed at the Muslim Brotherhood. In 1989, the Brotherhood greatly benefited from the open-list system, which annoyed the regime.[21] By Brotherhood members forming electoral alliances with other candidates, the Islamists took a greater percentage of seats than their percentage of actual votes. The one-person, one-vote system, however, eliminated the Muslim Brotherhood's ability to form alliances with other candidates. Brotherhood candidates in the same district would even be in competition with each other. Thus, the regime expected that the 1993 elections, under the amended system, would produce a Parliament with fewer opposition deputies—especially from the Islamist trend.

OPPOSITION REACTION TO THE 1993 AMENDMENTS

Opposition threats to boycott the elections if the regime decreed the SNTV system faded after King Hussein's speech on television. Despite a general trend of keeping references to specific individuals and groups vague in his speeches, the king took an unusual step by singling out the IAF in his speech announcing the amendments:

> I am concerned with safeguarding the unity of the country; I am also most concerned about our sons, some of whom have been chosen to belong to a front, which they have named, the Islamic front. What I wish for them, and from them, is that they truly practice their historic responsibilities in striving to live up to the name they have chosen, and to proceed, with Allah's help, towards true Islam, in fulfillment of their spiritual and worldly duties, and in the defense of that which is most precious to us against attempts to undermine and distort Islam from within the Islamic *Umma* and from without.[22]

This challenge to the IAF moved moderates in the party to abandon thoughts of a boycott of the elections.[23] The party registered loud complaints, but proceeded to campaign for the Parliament, adjusting its tactics to accommodate for the new voting system. As the major Islamist party chose to participate, parties on the left and center followed. Without the support of the IAF, leftists and Arab nationalists saw that a boycott of the 1993 elections would be futile.

EFFECTS OF THE ELECTION LAW AMENDMENTS ON THE 1993 ELECTIONS

After the IAF and other opposition groups decided to participate, the campaign began in earnest. A total of 534 candidates ran for the 80 seats. Being the first parliamentary elections since political parties had been relegalized in 1992, one would have expected political parties to dominate the 1993 campaign. However, the SNTV system forced candidates to campaign as individuals, not as part of lists—a factor that worked against political parties.

Two nonelectoral law factors also influenced the 1993 campaign: the signing of the Oslo Accords between the PLO and Israel in September 1993, and the regime's continued harassment of the Muslim Brotherhood. The prior caused some doubt in the scheduling of the elections. The elections, however, proceeded as scheduled on November 8. The latter appeared through a government-imposed ban on public rallies that was overturned late in the campaign by the courts, as well as through more subtle forms of harassment and fraud.

The amendments to the Election Law affected the results of the 1993 elections as most had expected. The Muslim Brotherhood, and the opposition in general, lost seats. In contrast, conservatives and independents, often tribally-affiliated candidates, nearly swept the elections. The IAF, however, remained the largest organized group in the House with 16 seats. The results of the 1993 elections are outlined in table 5.1.

Public turnout for the 1993 elections was slightly higher than the 1989 elections. In 1993, 55.6 percent of the registered voters participated in the elections.[24] Turnout was significantly higher in rural constituencies and lower in urban and Palestinian inhabited districts.

Incumbents fell particularly hard in the 1993 elections. Of the 62 that ran, only 25 sitting deputies were reelected. Of the 25, however, 13 saw an increase in the actual number of votes they received in 1993.[25] In many cases the new SNTV system worked against incumbents, but also a number of deputies suffered from the popular perception of the Parliament's poor performance.

The one-person, one-vote system further weakened the ability of political parties to achieve representation in Parliament. Aside from the IAF's 16 seats, the diverse new parties combined to win only 18 seats between 9 parties. The combination of the new choice situation facing voters, and the

Table 5.1 COMPARISON OF ELECTION RESULTS, 1989 AND 1993

Trend or Party	Votes for Winners 1989	Votes for Winners 1993	% of Popular Vote 1989	% of Popular Vote 1993	Seats Won 1989	Seats Won 1993	% of Seats Won 1989	% of Seats Won 1993
Islamic Action Front	292,279	90,087	14.54	11.08	22	16	27.50	20.00
Independent Islamists	105,027	17,943	5.22	2.21	11	6	13.75	7.50
Tribal or Centrist Independents	258,569	120,103	12.86	14.77	33	32	41.25	40.00
Progovernment Party Affiliates	NA	51,168	NA	6.29	NA	13	NA	16.25
Leftists	59,425	30,685	2.96	3.77	6	10	7.50	12.50
Arab Nationalists	51,118	9,968	2.54	1.23	8	3	10.00	3.75

Sources: Data from Table 2; Hani Hourani et al., *Who's Who in the Jordanian Parliament 1993–1997* (Amman: al-Urdun al-Jadid Research Center, 1995), 181–183; Iyad al-Shalibi et al., *Intikhabat 1993 Al-Urduniah: Dirasah Tahliliah Raqamiah* [Jordan's 1993 Elections: An Analytical and Quantitative Study]. (Amman: al-Urdun al-Jadid Research Center, 1995), 32–34.

opposition's general inability to accommodate the new voting formula, produced a relative disaster for the opposition.

The SNTV system strengthened the influence of identity in the election. With only one choice, voters often turned back to their core communities, a Palestinian or a tribal identity. The tribal representatives in the 1993 Parliament often owed their seats to the "politics of identity," where candidates focused on family support and alliances. Likewise, Palestinians often rallied around their community to elect one of their own, as in the case of incumbent Tahir al-Masri. The SNTV system also reinforced key issues, such as jobs and education, when voters elected the candidate who would most likely "deliver the goods." Thus, the Election Law amendments provided the structural ground for the landslide of the centrists in the 1993 election—just as the regime had intended.

THE JORDANIAN-ISRAELI PEACE TREATY OF 1994

The August 1993 amendments to the Election Law succeeded in reducing the representation of opposition deputies in the November 1993 elections. The amendments had been made just before the surprise transformation of the Middle East peace process. The September 1993 Palestinian-Israeli Joint Declaration of Principles, or the "Oslo Accords," broke the impasse that had stalled the Washington talks. The dramatic progress on the Palestinian-Israeli track allowed rapid movement on the Jordanian-Israeli track of negotiations.

With the signing of the agreement between the Palestine Liberation Organization and Israel, the Jordanian government felt it could sign a separate peace agreement with Israel. The Jordanian government had feared the consequences of breaking the "Arab consensus" by moving toward peace with Israel faster than the Palestinians and Syrians. The Palestinians' secret agreement with the Israelis first infuriated King Hussein, but he quickly realized the utility of the advance on the Palestinian-Israeli track. In Washington, the day after the signing of Oslo, Jordan and Israel signed an agenda for peace talks.[26]

By July 1994, negotiations with Israel had reached the point where the two sides were willing to formally end the state of war between the two countries. King Hussein and Israeli Prime Minister Rabin made the "Washington Declaration" on July 24 in the presence of American President Bill Clinton. Through August and September of 1994 negotiators quickly resolved issues of borders, water, and economic cooperation. By the middle of October 1994 the treaty was completed. It was signed with great international fanfare on October 26, 1994 in a ceremony at the Wadi Araba border point. The Jordanian Parliament ratified the treaty on November 6. Opposition forces in the Parliament were unable to block or delay the treaty's ratification.

As early as July 1994, the government of Jordan had begun a media campaign to sway public opinion to support the treaty. In comparison to most government policies where the prime minister appears as the main policy actor, King Hussein made it clear that the peace treaty was his. Thus, any opposition to the treaty would be interpreted by the regime as opposition to the monarchy itself—with the resultant consequences. Nevertheless, the government attempted to persuade Jordanians to support the peace treaty with four major arguments.[27]

First, the regime presented the treaty as a strategic choice for Jordan. The government argued that Jordan had little choice in joining the peace camp. Government supporters called the treaty the "best" accord the government could have reached, given what was "possible and realistic" at that time.[28] Second, in the peace treaty, Jordan—as an independent state—would get all that it wanted back from Israel. The government argued that the treaty fulfilled all of Jordan's demands on the issues of borders, land, water, and security. Central to the government's claim was that Jordan received Israeli recognition that Jordan was not the alternative Palestine homeland. In conjunction with this argument, a third argument presented by the regime pointed to the provisions in the treaty for future multilateral negotiations. Issues such as refugees and economic cooperation were scheduled for negotiations, not just between Israel and Jordan, but with Egypt and the Palestinians as well. The government argued that such problems could not just be resolved bilaterally between Jordan and Israel. Finally, the regime tried to sell the treaty for its expected economic benefits and the potential for new investments in Jordan. This message targeted both Jordanians of Palestinian and East Bank origin. Such a peace dividend would jump-start Jordan's sluggish economy and provide new jobs, especially in the tourism industry. The government pointed prominently toward the example of Egypt and the rewards it received for signing the Camp David Accords in 1978.

Most of the members of the regime coalition lined up behind the king. Tribal, military, and government elites loudly supported the "king's peace." Many business elites, despite being generally of Palestinian origin, also endorsed the choice for peace in the hope of the expected benefits it would bring. Public opinion in Jordan, however, initially remained cautious. Most Jordanians were surprised at the speed of Jordan's agreement with Israel. Yet measurable support for peace could be found. A series of public opinion polls by the University of Jordan's Center for Strategic Studies gauged the public's reactions to the peace process. After the Washington Declaration in July 1994, the Center's polls found that almost 80 percent of those sampled supported the declaration.[29] Many Jordanians expressed hopes for better economic and political times to come if peace grew. The regime based its arguments for encouraging support for the peace treaty especially on this attitude.

However, not all sectors of Jordanian society warmly greeted King Hussein's rapid moves toward peace with Israel. Some well-known faces in the regime coalition expressed their dissatisfaction with the peace treaty. Unsurprisingly, Jordan's Islamist, leftist, and Arab nationalist ideological opposition groups questioned the peace treaty. However, only a handful of politicians rejected peace with Israel in any form. Most opposition politicians rejected the treaty but not necessarily the notion of peace itself. Opposition politicians inside and outside of the Parliament rejected the treaty for four general reasons.

The first reason that opposition politicians criticized the treaty was for its abandonment of Arab coordination and for ignoring the principles of UN Security Council resolutions dealing with the Arab-Israeli conflict. Second, the opposition criticized the treaty for only dealing with the issue of Palestinian refugees in later multilateral talks. Many in the opposition saw the treaty as "depriving the refugees of the right to return to their homeland."[30] Third, they rejected the government's claim that Jordan had reclaimed its rights to land and water from Israel. They especially objected to the provision of leasing land returned to Jordanian sovereignty to Israeli farmers. Finally, opponents of the peace treaty also criticized the government for restricting political liberties. The opposition claimed that since the regime could not refute their arguments the government tried to silence them.

After a heated debate in which supporters and opponents of the peace treaty all tried to present their best and most persuasive arguments, the House of Deputies voted to ratify the Jordanian-Israeli peace treaty by a vote of 55 to 23 with one abstention and one absence.[31] IAF deputy Abdullah al-Akayilah spoke for many opponents of the peace treaty with his comment on the passage of the treaty. He "was not surprised by the result. We cannot but accept the decision of the majority in compliance with the democracy in which we live." However, he also said that the opposition's focus would shift to resisting the normalization with Israel.[32]

THE SUCCESSFUL MANAGEMENT OF THE DISCONTENTS OF PEACE

The regime used the survival strategy of amending the Election Law in 1993 in preparation for a peace treaty with Israel and to allow easier passage of economic legislation. The survival strategy aimed to reduce the voice of the opposition in Parliament so that questions about potentially unpopular policies could not be as easily raised. The amendments also aimed to insure that what parliamentary opposition remained could not block or significantly delay the regime's desired legislation. The regime was successful in its survival strategy, as the 1993 elections included the participation by the opposition—even though the opposition significantly lost seats when compared to the previous elections in 1989.

The regime successfully used the available constitutional rules in order to pass a significant reversal of political liberalization. The regime changed the institutional venue for the Election Law from the Parliament to an executive decree in order to avoid compromising with the opposition in the legislature. If amendments to the electoral system had been processed through the Parliament, there would likely have been no significant changes to the electoral system—as was the case when the Parliament reviewed the 1989 Election Law in 1992. The regime used the advantages written into the constitution to present those opposed to the SNTV electoral system with a *fait accompli*. By waiting until the Parliament's session had ended and then dismissing the legislature before it finished its term, the government was on firm constitutional ground for its ability to use a decree.

Meanwhile, the opposition failed to block the amendments because of disunity among the opposition as well as a lack of coordination with regime liberals and centrists in the Parliament. The opposition failed to challenge the Election Law amendments on three counts. First, the Parliament could have preempted any regime move to decree changes to the electoral law by requesting an extraordinary session of Parliament. The Muslim Brotherhood failed to obtain the signatures of the majority of House deputies to demand a special session to legislate changes to the Election Law. Before the fact, however, the opposition could not have known that the regime would resort to a decree to change the electoral system.

Second, the opposition once presented with the decree could have turned to the courts to overturn the provisional law that amended the Election Law. The opposition had threatened to challenge the government in a different institutional venue. However, it did not. Opponents to the changes to the Election Law have pointed out that the amendments did not meet the requirement of Article 94 of the constitution for an "urgent necessity" for decreeing a provisional law. The constitutionality of the 1993 decree could have been susceptible to overturning by the courts on this merit—as the 1997 Press and Publications Law amendments would later be.

Nor did the opposition attempt to combat the new electoral system in a third possible venue; the opposition did not boycott the November 1993 elections. The opposition could have taken the issue to the public in an attempt to delegitimize the Election Law with a low voter turnout.

The opposition did not choose to contest the decree in any of these other venues because of the weight that King Hussein had placed behind the decree. Normally in Jordan, the king would give the appearance that the prime minister was responsible for the decision making. In this instance, King Hussein made it clear that the change in the Election Law was his decision. He also expressed his desire for all political trends to participate in the elections. In this episode, the king stepped down from his normal posture of attempting to be above politics in order to increase the strength of the regime's commitment. The threatened punishment for boycotting the 1993 elections remained unstated. Faced with a head-on challenge from the regime, the Muslim Brotherhood and the other opposition groups relented to the change in the Election Law—and suffered accordingly in the elections.

Finally, the regime coalition maintained a unified stance during this episode. The decreed amendments to the Election Law produced the regime's desired effect: a reduction of opposition deputies and greater representation of progovernment candidates. The effects of the change directly benefited some sectors of the regime coalition. However, these benefits did not come at the expense of other regime supporters, but rather at the expense of the opposition. Urban regime liberals and proregime Palestinians either did not suffer from the change or maintained their previous less formal connections to the regime. Thus, the regime coalition remained united in support of the 1993 Election Law amendments.

However, as the regime pushed to deepen the process of normalization with Israel and economic reforms began to cause pain for many Jordanians, the unity of the regime coalition and the ability of the regime to successfully implement institutional survival strategies would be put to the test.

SIX

NORMALIZATION AND STRUCTURAL ADJUSTMENT

After the ratification of the Jordanian-Israeli peace treaty, the regime sought to deepen the relationship with Israel through building a "New Middle East." The regime also expected that the pain of structural economic reforms would be relieved by commercial ties with Israel and generous foreign aid from Western donors. While in the mid-1990s Jordan did become one of the IMF's prodigies, economic reforms did not benefit most Jordanians. The unexpectedly meager peace dividend only compounded their frustration. The complications of normalizing peace with Israel combined with the pain of economic reforms fed the government's growing resolve to limit the process of political liberalization. This chapter will discuss the first part of this story of domestic reactions to Jordan's foreign and economic policies. The next chapter will detail the survival strategies that the regime used to contain this discontent.

THE EXTERNAL DIFFICULTIES OF NORMALIZING PEACE WITH ISRAEL

The Jordanian regime argued that the treaty with Israel was part of the movement toward a comprehensive peace in the Middle East. King Hussein could generally argue that peace with Israel made sense as long as there was movement toward peace between Israel and Syria and toward an equitable solution to the Palestinian issue. As early as 1995, however, Israeli actions in the region began to anger the Jordanian government. Crises on the Palestinian-Israeli track of the peace process easily echoed across the Jordan Valley. As the trust between the Jordanian and Israeli governments declined, it became more difficult for the Jordanian regime to persuade its citizens that Israel had ceased to be an enemy.

In April 1995, the Israeli government led by Prime Minister Yitzhak Rabin decided to confiscate approximately five hundred dunams of land around Jerusalem. The land was intended for expanded settlements of Israelis around Jerusalem. The Jordanian government denounced Israel's decision. The foreign minister at the time, Abd al-Karim al-Kabariti, said that the decision "put the Israeli-Jordanian peace agreement under test."[1] King Hussein and his government sent messages lobbying Prime Minister Rabin to back away from the confiscation. In Jordan, the Parliament was about to debate the repeal of laws boycotting Israel. Before the session began, 60 of the 80 House deputies signed a petition calling for the suspension of the peace treaty and maintaining the boycott laws. On May 22, the Israeli government canceled the decision to confiscate the land. Domestic Israeli politics played the greatest role in causing Rabin to relent. Nevertheless, the Jordanian regime trumpeted its ability to persuade the Israelis to change their course. Yet, at the same time the regime was trying to prohibit an opposition conference dedicated to opposing normalization (see below). Thus, many Jordanians began to question the regime's commitment to peace with Israel.[2]

With the assassination of Rabin in November 1995, King Hussein greeted Shimon Peres, the new prime minister, with a more business-like relationship. During Peres's short term in office it became clear that Hussein and Peres did not "enjoy the same level of rapport and trust" as Hussein and Rabin did.[3] Peres's Operation Grapes of Wrath operation in Lebanon cooled the Jordanian regime's warmth towards Israel's Labor government. The Jordanian government tried to use its leverage with the Israelis to stop the shelling of Lebanon. On April 18, 1996, King Hussein himself denounced Israel's "treacherous . . . aggression and the criminal military operations."[4] The House of Deputies issued a statement condemning the operation, stating that it "expresses to the world the true face" of Israel.[5] Public reaction to Israel's operations in Lebanon proved as strong. Demonstrations to show solidarity with the Lebanese and to criticize Israel brought around two thousand protesters to downtown Amman. Reaction in Amman was restrained when Peres lost to Binyamin Netanyahu in Israel's May 1996 elections.

Netanyahu's grace period with the Jordanian regime quickly ran out. Relations between Israel and Jordan deteriorated even further in September 1996 with Netanyahu's decision to open a tunnel next to the foundations of the *Haram Al-Sharif*. Over seventy Palestinians were killed in protests against the Israelis. King Hussein's government condemned Netanyahu's actions. The tunnel crisis worried the Jordanian regime for three reasons. First, Netanyahu's advisor, Dore Gold, had visited Amman for talks with the king the day before the tunnel's opening. He gave Hussein no warning of the impending act. Thus, the Jordanians were not only surprised by Netanyahu, but they also "were disturbed by the fact that they could have been seen to have acquiesced" to the opening of the tunnel.[6] Second, the Jordanian regime saw the tunnel as an affront to Jordan's special status as guardian of the

Islamic holy places in Jerusalem. Third, the Jordanian regime also feared the repercussions of the Israeli-Palestinian violence ringing in Jordan. Demonstrations in Jordan had been banned since riots had broken out in the south of the kingdom in response to the lifting of bread subsidies during the previous month (see below).

Relations between King Hussein and Prime Minister Netanyahu were strained even further in early 1997 when Israel began developing a settlement on Jabal Abu Ghanim/Har Homa on the outskirts of Jerusalem. King Hussein sent two letters to Netanyahu in late February and early March. In the second letter, which was leaked to the press, King Hussein accused the Israeli Prime Minister of initiating "tragic actions" which had made peace appear "more and more like a distant elusive mirage." Hussein questioned how he could work with Netanyahu "as a partner and true friend in this confused atmosphere," when all Hussein sensed was "intent to destroy" all he had worked to build.[7]

On the heels of Hussein's letters, a Jordanian soldier, Ahmed al-Daqamisah, shot and killed seven Israeli schoolgirls at the Jordanian-Israeli border at Baqura. King Hussein condemned the attack. He then went to Israel and paid condolence visits to the girls' families. While the visit impressed Israelis with King Hussein's compassion, Jordanians saw little reason for the king's display of grief. Some Jordanians also questioned the king's actions, "arguing that had the situation been reversed Netanyahu would not have made a similar gesture."[8] In July, Daqamisah was given a life prison sentence by a military court. Through these two incidents, more and more Jordanians questioned their government's commitment to peace.

However, opponents of normalization could not have imagined a scenario that would support their cause more than the attempted assassination of Hamas leader Khalid Mashʿal by Israeli agents. On September 25, 1997, two Israeli agents disguised as Canadian tourists attacked Mashʿal near his home in western Amman. Mash'al survived the attack and the Jordanian police quickly apprehended the Israeli agents. King Hussein swapped the two Mossad agents for Israel's release of Hamas's jailed spiritual leader, Sheikh Ahmed Yassin, to Hussein's care.

The regime must have been relieved that the outcome of the episode was not worse. Moreover, the regime attempted to distinguish between Prime Minster Netanyahu, who it blamed for the affair, and Israel in general. To the public, however, the regime denied that it had tried to cover up the details of the episode. Yet some Jordanians felt misled by the government in the matter. Some questioned the utility of the treaty if Netanyahu was to so blatantly disregard his commitments.[9]

These events in the last years of King Hussein's reign undermined the trust built between the two governments by the peace treaty. The lack of progress toward a comprehensive regional peace, especially on the Israeli-Palestinian track of the peace process, lay under all of the events described above.

Jordan's rationale for normalization with Israel eroded with the loss of intimacy between Israeli and Jordanian leaders. King Hussein and his cabinet perceived Israeli actions as increasingly aggressive. The Jordanian regime blamed Israeli intransigence for the failure to make peace between Israel and the Palestinians. As its frustration with the Israelis mounted, the regime found it harder and harder to defend the process of normalization. The Jordanian public, already lukewarm toward normalization, cooled quickly toward normal relations with Israel. Israel and its behavior in the region, however, was not the only force tempering a warm peace between Jordan and Israel.

THE DOMESTIC RAMIFICATIONS OF NORMALIZATION

After the opposition's failure to block the ratification of the peace treaty in Parliament, IAF Deputy Abdullah al-Akayilah said that the opposition would shift its focus to preparing a program to resist normalization with Israel and the "coming Zionist invasion of our culture."[10] However, in general, the opposition could not mobilize public opinion. Rather, the public mostly turned apathetic. Nevertheless, the regime remained fearful of the opposition's potential for mobilization on the antinormalization issue.

Opponents of normalization began to organize themselves even before the peace treaty with Israel was signed. On May 15, 1994, the Muslim Brotherhood's political party, the IAF, and seven leftist and Arab nationalist parties formed the Committee for Resisting Submission and Normalization (CRSN). The Committee also included independent politicians, such as independent Islamist Layth Shbeilat. The diverse members of the CRSN were united by their joint ideological commitment to combating peace and normalization with Israel. The Committee issued numerous statements of condemnation of the Washington Declaration and of the peace treaty. With the signing of the peace treaty in October 1994, however, the CRSN and its members turned to action, not just words, in an attempt to rally public opinion against normalization.

The opposition attempted to mobilize their supporters through demonstrations and marches. However, most were denied permits. Nevertheless, nearly one thousand students demonstrated on the campus of the University of Jordan on October 24, 1994. On the next day, thousands of Muslim Brotherhood supporters filled Hashemiyah Square in downtown Amman. The IAF had organized the demonstration secretly and without a permit. IAF Deputy Bassam Emoush remarked to the crowd that if the party had asked for permission to hold the rally it would have been denied. The rally took place peacefully, but under the watchful eye of heavily armed security troops.[11] Opposition groups consistently complained that permits for rallies were denied in cities across the country. Security forces broke up a rally in Irbid after the governor reversed his decision to permit the demonstration.

Nevertheless, opposition groups reiterated their commitment to democracy and peaceful demonstrations while protesting the treaty signing.

After the ratification of the peace treaty, opposition forces turned to blocking normalization of relations with Israel. The opposition attempted to block laws ending the boycott of Israel from passing. In May 1995, the Parliament was beginning to consider the repeal of Jordanian laws prohibiting economic ties to Israel. During this time, the CRSN attempted to organize a conference.

Important among the scheduled speakers at the conference was the former Prime Minister, Ahmed Obeidat. The former chief of intelligence and chairman of the Royal Committee for Drafting the National Charter was perhaps the most well-known member of the regime coalition to defect to the ranks of the antinormalization forces. The king revoked Obeidat's appointment to the Senate for his vote against the peace treaty. Other former government officials were also planning on attending the opposition's conference. The regime feared such a public display of the opposition's position because it could undermine the regime's arguments for normalizing relations with Israel. It also feared showing prominent former officials, such as Obeidat, disagreeing with one of the regime's central policies. Generally, the regime had accused the "usual suspects" of rejecting the king's wise leadership. Former high-ranking government officials joining with the opposition undercut this argument. Organizers had expected six hundred attendees. However, the government banned the conference at the last minute. Police turned away conference-goers—peacefully.

The banning of the conference again allowed the opposition to question the government's commitment to democratization. Columnists queried why the government needed to monopolize the debate over normalization. Eventually the conference was held on September 29, 1995. The meeting, however, took place at the headquarters of a political party where it did not need government approval. However, only about three hundred attended the meeting. The conference issued a communiqué denouncing peace and normalization with Israel. But the event was viewed as being a much lower-key event than the event planned for May.

Jordan's professional associations joined political parties in the opposition to normalization. The twelve professional associations included syndicates for doctors, lawyers, engineers, and others. For most professions in Jordan, membership in a professional association was mandatory. During the long absence of political parties, the professional associations were home to opposition against regime policies. Their base in Amman's middle class often reflected the preferences of educated Palestinian professionals. However, Jordanians of both Palestinian and East Bank origins were active in the leadership of the professional associations. Factions of the various opposition groups generally led the professional associations during the mid-1990s. Professional associations, however, were better organized than some opposition political parties. Thus, the professional associations maintained their role at the forefront of opposition activity even though political parties had been legalized.

Opposition to normalization with Israel became one of the central concerns of the professional associations. Most associations banned their members from promoting ties with Israel. Members who visited Israel or worked with Israelis were censured. Others had their membership in their association revoked. Since membership in a professional association was mandatory for employment in certain professions, being expelled was tantamount to the loss of one's livelihood. For example, Hisham Yanis, Jordan's best-known comedian, was expelled from the Writers' Association for performing in Israel. In June 1995, the Dentists' Association barred its members from treating Israelis in nonemergency situations. In general, however, the professional associations rescinded most expulsions if the member denounced normalizing activities. The many controversies over the blacklists testify to the number of Jordanians attempting to normalize with Israel.

The regime had tolerated opposition from the professional associations in the past. The regime objected to the professional associations expelling members for following the government's foreign policy. After the treaty with Israel, successive cabinets threatened to amend the legislation controlling professional associations in order to limit activities not related to the associations' professional concerns. These threats continue to this day.

The professional associations and the opposition parties, however, had few concrete successes in blocking the process of normalization between Jordan and Israel. One notable exception occurred in January 1997 when the Jordanian antinormalization forces united to push a boycott of an Israeli trade fair in Amman. Israeli government institutions, in cooperation with some Jordanian businessmen, organized the exposition with the Jordanian government's blessing. In December 1996, however, the Amman Chamber of Industry denounced the planned expo. The CRSN also joined the boycott efforts and began coordinating work between the professional associations and opposition parties. The CRSN called for a public boycott of the fair and threatened to blacklist the Jordanian participants. A number of centrist political parties, including the conservative Al-Ahd, joined the call for a boycott of the event. The Jordanian government distanced itself from the trade fair because of the hostile reaction to it. Most opponents of normalization called for the government to cancel the expo. After being postponed, the trade fair did eventually take place on January 8, 1997. Attendance was negligible; meanwhile, more than four thousand protested in front of the gates of the fairground. The demonstrations remained peaceful despite a heavy security presence.

The boycott of the Israeli trade fair also served to energize the antinormalization forces. Leftist Deputy Toujan Faisal felt "empowered" at the trade fair protest. She recalled her amazement at being flanked on one side by the head of the IAF and on the other by former Prime Minister Ahmed Obeidat.[12] More troubling for the regime, though, was the fact that diverse ideological trends were uniting around a single issue in opposition to the government. Moreover, the opposition was beginning to show a greater sense of organization in the antinormalization endeavor. With the growing institutionalization of the antinormalization forces, the regime felt compelled to curtail political liberties by limiting popular discontent with peace with Israel. One of the main tactics included cracking down on the press, which will be discussed in chapter 7. However, active opposition to normalization with Israel remained an elite phenomenon. The vast majority of Jordanians may have objected to the regime's foreign policy moves and the actions by Israel during the slow decline of the Middle East peace process. However, most Jordanians were too busy making ends meet in a difficult economic situation. The regime placed grand hopes on the transformation of the region into a "New Middle East" and a generous peace dividend to solve Jordan's economic difficulties.

THE PUBLIC OPINION AND THE POLITICAL ECONOMY OF PEACE

Today many fault the regime for overselling the prospects for a financial windfall as a result of the peace treaty with Israel. Jordanians were led to believe that by signing a peace treaty with Israel, Jordan would receive economic assistance from the U.S. and the West on the scale of Egypt's financial benefits from Camp David. However, Jordan received much more modest rewards from the Americans for signing the peace treaty. Jordanian public opinion expressed an interest in trading peace for economic benefits. As these rewards failed to develop, it only added to the disappointment and distrust in the peace process and normalization with Israel.

At the time of the signing of the peace treaty, most public officials tried to remain restrained in their promises of the economic benefits of peace; however, a media frame expecting a large peace dividend was fostered. The semi-official daily newspaper *Al-Rai*³ editorialized that "The large-scale international welcome of the signing of the Jordanian-Israeli peace treaty is an asset which we hope will reflect positively on Jordan's security, stability, and economy."[13] The Jordanian regime publicly sought debt reduction, foreign aid, and foreign investments for Jordan as a result of the peace treaty. The receipt of these external economic inputs was promised to benefit all Jordanians.

Despite deals to refinance Jordan's debt in the early 1990s, the country remained heavily in debt. *Middle East International* saw that the regime had reached the conclusion that "the issue of scrapping or reducing the kingdom's foreign debts ($6.6 billion) could only be solved through the pro-Israel U.S. Congress."[14] Congress behaved as expected. Two days after Hussein and Rabin's Washington Declaration, the U.S. Congress agreed to reduce Jordan's $700 million debt by almost $200 million. Britain soon followed suit. Based on such early successes, in September 1994 Jordan asked for an aid package of $25 billion for the next ten years. The regime's publicity surrounding debt relief and aid inflated expectations of the ordinary Jordanian on the benefits of peace.

The regime also sold the public a diet of hopes for foreign investments. Prime Minister Majali told *Al-Dustour* that, "Peace is one of the main conditions for investments" since "the only way to eradicate unemployment and poverty is through investments."[15] Majali welcomed the ratification of the treaty by the Parliament since it would "usher in a new state whose meaning and effects are clear to the citizens."[16] In case the point was not clear enough, progovernment deputies, like Fawwaz al-Zoʿubi, remarked: "Through this treaty Jordan has opened the door for investment in the country and for economic project which means more trade with the world, more tourism and an end of sufferings for many people."[17]

Such a discourse to the public about the economic benefits of peace led Asher Susser to conclude that

> Debt relief by the U.S., it was hoped, would have a "roller coaster" effect and Jordan could therefore expect more economic and financial aid and foreign investment, not only from the U.S., but from other quarters as well. Peace with Israel added to Jordan's water supply which would have a positive impact on agricultural production and on industry. Tourism was expected to increase markedly and become a major source of foreign exchange. Transport and transit trade was also expected to rise and the West Bank market would allow for Jordanian exports to grow rapidly. In the longer term, the major factor would be new investment by Arab, foreign and local investors in what would be seen as a more secure environment.[18]

The public welcomed the regime's promises of a windfall peace dividend. Although Jordan's economy grew modestly in the early 1990s, the economic benefits were not being distributed evenly. Most of the economic development inspired by the opening to Israel either took place in Amman or near the archeological sites at Petra.

A 1994 Center for Strategic Studies poll found that a clear majority supported the Washington Declaration. Moreover, 82 percent of the people surveyed thought that Jordan's economic situation would improve as a result of the peace process, half of whom expected the economic benefits to be visible in the short run. Even among those opposed to the peace process, half thought that peace would bring economic benefits.[19] Thus, even many of those who held ideological beliefs against peace with Israel accepted the government's argument of peace leading to better livelihoods for Jordanians.

Table 6.1 Will Peace Lead to Economic Benefits for Jordan?

Sample	Yes	No	Don't Know
National Sample	50%	38%	11%
Refugee Camp Sample	43%	30%	17%
Opinion Leaders	35%	58%	6%

Source: University of Jordan Center for Strategic Studies, *Istitla'a lil-Rai' howl al-Alaqat al-Urduniyah al-Isra'iliyah: al-Nata'ij al-Awaliyah* [Poll on Jordanian-Israeli Relations: Preliminary Results] (Amman: University of Jordan Center for Strategic Studies, 1997), 13.

The public's perception that peace would lead to economic benefits continued through the 1990s. However, support for the proposition began to waver as the peace process sputtered. In December 1997, the Center for Strategic Studies conducted a poll on Jordanian-Israeli relations. The poll contained three samples: from the national population, from among residents of refugee camps, and from among "opinion leaders." Table 6.1 summarizes the responses to the question if peace will lead to economic benefits for Jordan.

This poll demonstrates a weakening belief among Jordanians in the economic benefits of peace. However, in the national sample and sample of camp dwellers, more respondents held expectations for peace to still bring economic benefits than those who did not. The noticeable divorce between the responses of the opinion leaders and those of the general public can further demonstrate the alienation of elites both within the regime coalition and the opposition to normalization. The sample of opinion leaders heavily drew from members of the professional associations, writers, and university students.

The respondents of the 1997 poll also demonstrated the difficulties of normalization with Israel reaching a popular level. Due to a lack of trust, a belief that Israel does not keep agreements, and religious reasons, Jordanians overwhelmingly saw Israelis as enemies. Table 6.2 summarizes responses to the question of "now that there is peace between Jordan and Israel, do Israelis remain enemies?"

Table 6.2 Do Israelis Remain Enemies?

Sample	Yes	No	Don't Know
National Sample	81%	11%	8%
Refugee Camp Sample	87%	9%	9%
Opinion Leaders	80%	15%	5%

Source: University of Jordan Center for Strategic Studies, *Istitla'a lil-Rai' howl al-Alaqat al-Urduniyah al-Isra'iliyah: al-Nata'ij al-Awaliyah* [Poll on Jordanian-Israeli Relations: Preliminary Results] (Amman: University of Jordan Center for Strategic Studies, 1997), 13.

Based on the responses of the Center's 1997 polls one can see that support for peace and normalization with Israel was very tenuous among Jordanians. The hope for economic benefits was fading, but perhaps it was one of the few reasons that Jordanians could support peace. A lack of trust and the belief that Israelis do not keep agreements were reasons cited by a majority of those who saw Israelis as enemies.[20] Still, in 1997, among those polled in the Jordanian public, more saw peace as leading to economic benefits than those who did not. If the economic rewards of peace had been greater, perhaps the Jordanian public would have more warmly greeted normalization with Israel. However, the enormous economic rewards of peace did not come.

From 1990 to 1997, the U.S. gave Jordan $1.65 billion in grants, loans, and loan guarantees. While sizeable, this amount did not meet Jordanian expectations or needs. Moreover, the Jordanian government was "disappointed and humiliated by the congressional hurdles it had to overcome, 'cap in hand,' before the U.S. commitment to debt relief was actually fulfilled."[21] The World Bank and the IMF also aided Jordan in rescheduling its debts in return for Jordan adhering to a program of conditional economic reform. Yet economic reforms, such as reducing the bread subsidy (see below), increased the public's perception of greater economic hardships. Thus, with the failure of peace to create massive economic benefits, the public's sour mood was only increased.

Dashed hopes were especially notable in the tourism sector. Grand visions of tourism lifting Jordan's economy where inflated by the experience of 1995. That year Jordan saw a huge increase in the number of tourists visiting Jordan. However, the trend was not sustained in later years. Regional instability caused by the faltering negotiations on the Palestinian track exacerbated this trend. A number of hotels recently built in Amman now stand almost empty. Table 6.3 details the increase in the number of tourists arriving in Jordan.

Overall, Jordan's economy grew in the 1990s; however the country did experience an economic slowdown in the second half of the 1990s. Table 6.3 offers some basic economic indicators from the 1990s. While, after the peace treaty with Israel, Jordan's economy did grow. Yet in the eyes of most Jordanians, this growth only benefited a few. The regime's promises of an economic windfall for Jordan proved empty. Peace did not deliver the most important measure of well-being to Jordanian public opinion. The opposition was able to tap into some of the public's disappointment. However, for the most part the public withdrew into political apathy as it struggled for economic survival. That apathy, however, was still subject to bouts of public displays of anger at the economic situation and the regime's handling of it.

STRUCTURAL ADJUSTMENT AND BREAD RIOTS

In the 1990s, the regime followed the recommendations of the IMF in implementing economic structural adjustment policies. The regime accepted the short-term costs of the program in order to better the chances for the long-

Table 6.3 PERCENTAGE CHANGE OF SELECT ECONOMIC INDICATORS, 1994–2000

Indicator	1994	1995	1996	1997	1998	1999	2000
Real GDP Growth	5.9	6.4	1.4	1.3	1.2	1.6	2.5
External Debt Change	1.3	3.8	2.5	1.2	3.5	–3.7	–2.5
Increase in Tourist Arrivals	12.0	20.1	2.6	2.1	10.3	7.5	NA

Sources: Data from Economist Intelligence Unit, *EIU Country Report: Jordan*, February 2001, 5; EIU, *EIU Country Report: Jordan*, 4th Quarter, 1996, 5; *Regional Surveys of the World: Middle East and North Africa 2001* (London: Europa Publications, 2000), 763.

term economic development of the country. Over the decade, the Jordanian government reduced government debt and improved the macroeconomic situation of the kingdom. By 1996, the government had raised taxes, reduced government spending, especially on public sector salaries, and begun (albeit hesitantly) a program of privatization as prescribed by the IMF program. Jordan, after 1994, had also cut military spending and ended the economic boycott of Israel. However, the government had not tackled one of the major requirements of the IMF—consumer subsidies. With the price of wheat skyrocketing in the summer of 1996, the government of Prime Minister Abd al-Karim al-Kabariti turned its attention to reducing the subsidy on bread.

The last time the Jordanian government cut a major subsidy, in 1989, riots erupted in the southern cities of the kingdom. In 1996, with the country in less dire economic straights the government gradually introduced the idea that subsidies on bread were to be cut. Thus, over the summer Prime Minister Kabariti talked of the necessity of ending the subsidy. However, the government framed the issue of "refocusing" the subsidy toward the neediest Jordanians and away from foreigners and tourists.

Also in contrast to 1989 was the amount of public discussion about the decision to cut subsidies. Over the summer, debate about the need for cutting the subsidy on bread ran through newspaper columns and in the Parliament. Prime Minister Kabiriti even felt the need to defend the decision in a news conference in July. However, while discussion of the issue in the public sphere was allowed, the government's resolve in taking the decision was not going to be weakened by the debate. During the session in Parliament on the issue, the government's inflexible determination to pursue the economic reforms angered the opposition. The opposition demanded that the subsidy cuts be replaced with higher taxes on the rich and a crackdown on corruption. The IAF bloc of deputies boycotted the Parliament sessions attended by the prime minister. However, the Parliament—in the absence of the Islamists—voted to support the government's policy. Had the Islamist deputies been in attendance, their votes may have helped pass a parliamentary alternative to the government's program. However, on August 12, 1996, the government raised the price of bread and animal fodder by decree, even before the parliamentary debate over the subsidy cuts was concluded.[22]

Within a few days of the decree, the price of bread in Jordan nearly doubled. Despite the government's efforts at softening public opinion toward the decision, the public did not turn out to be as docile as it initially appeared to be. Spontaneous riots broke out in the southern city of Kerak on August 16, 1996 after Friday prayers. Later, the rioting spread to other towns like Ma ͨan and Tafilah. The police in Kerak lost control of the demonstrations and order was imposed by a military curfew. Nearly five hundred people were arrested in relation to the rioting. In November, King Hussein eventually pardoned all those who had not been previously released.

However, instead of blaming the riots on the cabinet—as was the case in 1989—King Hussein stood firmly behind the bread subsidy cut and the government of Prime Minister Kabariti. The regime, instead, held outside agitators responsible for the riots. The Islamists, despite their parliamentary boycott, were not blamed for the riots. King Hussein used the occasion of the riots to put further distance between Jordan and Iraq by claiming that Iraqi Ba ͨath party sympathizers in Jordan had organized the riots. Many leaders and members of Arab nationalist parties—especially the Jordanian Arab Socialist Ba ͨath Party and HASHD—were rounded up. Meanwhile, in a move to split the opposition, King Hussein praised the IAF's commitment to the democratic process and absolved the Islamic movement from causing the riots. The government, however, did ban an IAF march in Amman to protest the subsidy cut in the wake of the riots.

The king's move to split the Arab nationalist opposition from the Islamists, however, did not prevent most sectors of the opposition from calling for the resignation of Prime Minister Kabariti. The IAF's deputies eventually tempered their demand for the sacking of the prime minister in the face of the king's firm confidence in Kabariti. Nevertheless, the prime minister's appetite for controversial economic policies declined during his remaining time in office. Kabariti was eventually dismissed the next spring as a result of disputes with King Hussein over foreign policy.

The king's maintaining of both the subsidy cut and the government that implemented it convinced many Jordanians that the benefits of the economic structural adjustment program would remain in the capital while the costs would be paid by the poorer sectors of the country. The pain of economic reforms and the stalling of the peace process engendered discontent among Jordanians of both East Bank and Palestinian origin. With parliamentary elections scheduled for November 1997, the regime began to fear the opposition's potential for mobilizing this popular dissatisfaction with the regime's existential policies. The regime undertook a series of survival strategies in order to prevent the opposition from mobilizing discontent with the government's foreign and economic policies. These survival strategies would seek to limit the opposition's ability to voice its opinions in the press and to utilize political parties in the parliamentary elections.

SEVEN

PRESS RESTRICTIONS AND THE 1997 ELECTIONS

In the context of slowing of the peace process, the growing institutionalization of the antinormalization forces, and bread riots in response to economic structural adjustment reforms, the regime undertook further institutional survival strategies to limit the opposition's ability to mobilize the public's discontent. The survival strategies again focused on political parties, the Parliament, and the press. By limiting the freedom of the press—especially that of the independent weekly tabloids—the regime hoped to not only limit criticism in the public sphere but also to limit the exposure of opposition party candidates for the November 1997 elections. The new press restrictions, decreed in May of 1997, coupled with concern about the effects of the 1993 electoral law, provoked a boycott of the parliamentary elections by many sectors of the opposition. The opposition's challenge to the legitimacy of the Parliament, however, backfired as the regime held the elections as scheduled. Locked out of the Parliament, the opposition was unable to capitalize on the courts overturning of the decree of the amendments to the press law. A solidly progovernment Parliament later approved many of the same changes to the Press and Publications Law through regular constitutional procedures. Thus, in King Hussein's last days, relations between the regime and the opposition had reached a nadir.

THE PRESS AND PUBLICATIONS LAW AMENDMENTS OF 1997

For many months the government had tried to persuade the Parliament to revise the 1993 Press and Publications Law, and failed. Thus, in May 1997, the regime sought to limit the "excesses" of the press by using an executive decree to amend the press law. The regime also sought to influence the November 1997 elections by denying a voice to the opposition candidates. The May 1997 decree brought not only an outcry from the opposition and international human rights observers, but from liberals within the regime coalition as well. When the newly amended law was used to shut down most of Jordan's weekly newspapers, the aggrieved asked the courts to overturn the decree. The courts concurred by saying that there was no necessity for a decreed provisional law to amend the Press and Publications Law at that time. Thus, this survival strategy did not fully work as the regime had planned.

PROLOGUE: TOWARD A NEW PRESS AND PUBLICATIONS LAW

The government made several attempts to amend the legal frameworks regulating the press because of the combination of perceived tabloid irresponsibility and a lack of success in prosecuting violations of the Press and Publications Law. First, the government sought assistance from the Jordanian Press Association (JPA) in limiting the press. Next, the regime turned back to the Press and Publications Law and began consultations on amending it in order to remedy the situation. Resistance and lack of government cooperation with the JPA, the Parliament, and journalists doomed all of these efforts to further regulate the press.

As early as August 1993, the government of Abd al-Salam al-Majali proposed amending the JPA law to include a "code of honor." The code included clauses about the respect of citizens' honor and dignity, support for higher national and humanitarian interests, and respect for human rights. According to Maʿan Abu Nuwar, the Minister of Information, in a 1993 interview with *The Star*:

> The code of ethics is a reaction to what has happened in Jordan, where certain journalists have lied and are accused of incitement to rebellion. The law is to protect the good name of journalism in this country and the freedom of the press.[1]

Reactions of journalists to the proposed code were mixed. The leadership of the JPA rejected Abu Nuwar's code because it had not been consulted on the issue. However, Nabil al-Sharif, the editor of the partially government-owned daily *Al-Dustour*, commented that the proposed code would let journalists "solve the problems within" the association. In contrast, Jamil al-Nimri, editor of the weekly *Al-Ahali*, the voice of the leftist party HASHD, argued that the code and the press law were "intimidation" on the part of the government.[2] Eventually, the controversy over a press code of honor died down without the JPA ratifying any changes to its organizing law.

The regime again tried to limit the press after the peace treaty with Israel. The November 1994 treaty had caused a rash of criticism of the agreement from the opposition press. In May 1995, the king criticized the poor standards of the press, and in December 1995, he directed the government to make the press more responsible. The government of Prime Minister Bin Shaker then drafted new amendments to the Press and Publications Law.

The amendments reportedly would have added much greater restrictions to the 1993 law, including harsher fines and prison sentences for violating the restrictions of Article 40, as well as raising the minimum capital requirements for newspapers as high as JD 100,000. The prime minister argued that the amendments were aimed at only the "irresponsible" behavior of some journalists, and tried to bring "responsible" journalists to his side in a meeting with editors of the government-owned daily newspapers.[3]

The government's amendments met with harsh criticism from the opposition and journalists. The JPA completely rejected the new Press and Publications Law amendments. Moreover, former Minister of Information, Mahmud al-Sharif, who had shepherded the 1993 Press and Publications Law through the Parliament, also publicly opposed the amendments. He argued that "press violations do not give the government the excuse to amend the current law."[4] Other editors, especially from weekly newspapers, also saw the law as muzzling the press.

Bin Shaker's government, however, did not submit the draft of the amendments to the Parliament. In February 1996, bin Shaker's government was replaced by a new cabinet led by Abd al-Karim al-Kabariti. Kabariti's government promised to lead a "white revolution" with a more liberal inclination. Early on, the new Information Minister, Marwan al-Mu'asher, announced a new information plan for the government. In Mu'asher's plan, the Ministry of Information would eventually be abolished, and the state-owned radio, television, and the government news agency would all be privatized. The plan also envisioned amending the Press and Publications Law to enhance the freedom and responsibility of the press.

The Parliament joined the government in reexamining the press regulations. In February 1996, the House Law Committee met with media representatives to investigate demands for a new JPA law and for amendments to the Press and Publications Law. In June 1996, the cabinet finalized its draft of a new law regulating the JPA. However, controversy over details of the law kept the cabinet and the JPA from agreeing on the specifics of a draft law to send to the Parliament.

During this time, the House also offered its input on changes in press regulations. In July 1996, the House met to informally discuss the situation of the weekly newspapers. House Speaker, Sa'ad Hayl al-Srour, noted that deputies agreed that Parliament might need to issue new legislation to deal with "loopholes" in the Press and Publications Law. Islamists joined progovernment conservatives in expressing their concern over press stories that had harmed national unity and social values. At that time, however, the House restricted its action to releasing a statement calling for the press to "protect national unity," since some of the practices by some newspapers were "considered offensive."[5]

In July and August 1996, however, the attention of the government, the Parliament, and the press turned toward the crisis inspired by the IMF economic reform program and the resulting bread riots. The crisis severely damaged relations between Kabariti's government and the opposition in Parliament. Many journalists in the press also criticized the subsidy cut and the cabinet's handling of the situation, which resulted in the prosecution of a number of journalists for violations of the 1993 Press and Publications Law.[6] The appetite of Kabariti's government for reforming the press laws declined in the face of parliamentary and press opposition, and instead focused on prosecuting journalists—often unsuccessfully.

RESTRICTIONS IN THE 1997 PRESS AND PUBLICATIONS LAW AMENDMENTS

When Prime Minister Kabariti was removed in March 1997 over foreign policy differences with King Hussein, he was replaced by Abd al-Salam al-Majali. Majali's previous government had decreed the change in the election law in 1993 and signed the peace treaty with Israel in 1994. Many saw the return of Majali as a harbinger of hard-line policies to come; they did not have to wait long.

On May 15, 1997, the king endorsed (Provisional) Law Number 27 for the year 1997, amending the Press and Publications Law. The Parliament had ended its last regular session in March, but it had not been dissolved for new elections yet. As in 1993, under these conditions, the cabinet could constitutionally use its power to decree temporary laws under Article 94 of the constitution—if urgency necessitated the law. The government argued that the regulation of the press was an urgent matter and proceeded with the decree. However, influencing the outcome of the upcoming parliamentary elections appeared to be the unstated urgency in decreeing the changes to the press law. By reducing the coverage of opposition candidates in the press, the regime hoped to insure that the Parliament would be an even more compliant venue. Moreover, the amendments hoped to silence public debate over peace and normalization with Israel and the economic reform programs.[7]

In many ways, the 1997 amendments were similar to those proposed by the Bin Shaker government; however, the restrictions and penalties for violations of the 1997 amendments were much stricter. The 1997 amendments limited the freedom of the press in Jordan in five main areas: restrictions on editors, reversing privatization of state owned newspapers, raising minimum capital requirements for newspapers, revising prohibitions on content, and increasing penalties for violations of the law.

The new amendments added restrictions to the necessary qualifications of an editor in chief (Article 4, amending Article 13 of the 1993 law). Before, the editor in chief only had to meet the qualifications of a journalist. Under the 1997 amendments, an editor in chief needed to have been a journalist for at least ten years. Moreover, under the new law, the proprietor, the editor in chief, and the writer of an article were all held jointly responsible for any violations of the law (Article 13, amending Article 46 of the 1993 law).

The 1997 amendments also reversed the mandate contained in the 1993 Press and Publications Law for the government to sell its shares in any state-owned newspapers. The government owned 60 percent of the company that published Al-Rai' (and The Jordan Times) and 35 percent of the company that published Al-Destour. Under Article 19, Paragraph D of the 1993 law, the state was to reduce its holdings to below 30 percent for each company. Article 7 of the 1997 amendments eliminated this mandate, allowing the state to continue to hold its stock in the two largest daily newspapers in Jordan.

The most far-reaching of the amendments contained in the 1997 law regulated the minimum amounts of capital that newspapers should have (Article 8, amending Article 24 of the 1993 law). Under the previous Press and Publications Laws newspapers were required to have a base value of capital resources or lose their license. In the 1997 amendments, minimum capital requirements for daily newspapers were raised from JD 50,000 to JD 600,000; for nondaily newspapers the minimum was raised from JD 15,000 to JD 300,000. The two government-supported and the two private dailies could all meet the new capital requirements—the privately-owned Al-Arab Al-Youm's capital holdings approached JD eight million.[8] Rather, the new capital requirements were aimed at the tabloid newspapers—which were privately owned and operated. Since most of the weekly newspapers were run on shoestring budgets, the new requirements were particularly onerous. Most of the weeklies would not be able to raise the capital to meet the new requirements. Under Article 51 of the amendments, newspapers had three months to rectify their capital holdings or face suspension. If they remained unable to meet the capital requirements after six months, the newspaper would lose its license.

The 1997 amendments to the Press and Publications Law also rewrote the list of prohibitions contained in Article 40 of the 1993 law. The general list of forbidden topics remained the same; a prohibition was added on reports containing "false information or rumors harmful to public interest" (amended Article 40, A:8). However, the revised list included stiffer restrictions than the 1993 law. For example, Article 40, Part A, Paragraph 2 from the 1993 law prohibited "any information about the number, weapons, equipment, deployment or movements of the Jordanian Armed Forces, unless such publication is sanctioned by a responsible authority." With the 1997 amendments, news was prohibited from being published if "it involves the Jordanian Armed Forces or Security Forces, unless the publication thereof is permitted by the competent authority." In other words, it became forbidden to write about the military unless authorized by the government. Under the 1997 amendments, other topics on the list of prohibitions were likewise restricted or given vaguer language.

Increased penalties for violations of the law were also included in the 1997 amendments. Although the 1997 amendments eliminated any possibility of prison time as a punishment for violations, most fines were increased.

Moreover, the related sections of the penal code, in which journalists could be tried and sentenced to prison time, remained on the books. Table 7.1 details the increase in punishments for violations of the amended Press and Publications Law.

Moreover, if a publication violated any of the articles listed in table 7.1 twice in a period of five years, the publication could be suspended for three to six months in addition to the fine. If a publication violated any of the above articles for a third time the court could revoke the paper's license—"three-strikes and you're out."

THE AFTERMATH OF THE 1997 PRESS AND PUBLICATIONS LAW AMENDMENTS

Needless to say, most journalists and political opposition figures were outraged by the decreed amendments. The writers and editors of the weekly newspapers were especially offended.[9] On May 20, the police broke up a protest by journalists at the residence of the prime minister, leading to the arrest of at least eight journalists.[10] The board of the JPA, with the exception of President Seif al-Sharif, resigned in protest of the amendments. After a few days, however, the board reversed their resignations in order to engage in a "dialogue with the government."[11] Editors of a number of the weekly newspapers formed a committee to protect their interests and to foster collective action against the Press and Publications Law amendments. Later, the press law amendments added to the list of the opposition's grievances when boycotting the November 1997 parliamentary elections. Opposition groups

Table 7.1 Maximum Fines for Violations of Press Laws, 1993 versus 1997

Violation of (Amended) Article	1993: JD Fine for: Individuals	Corporations	1997: JD Fine for: Individuals	Corporations
No foreign funding (10)	1,000	1,000	50,000	50,000
Providing government a copy of publishers budget (11)	1,000	1,000	5,000	5,000
Publishing outside of specialty (15:C)	NA	NA	5,000	5,000
List of prohibitions (40:A)	1,000	1,000	25,000	25,000
Publishing proceedings of court cases (42)	1,000	1,000	25,000	25,000
Receiving gifts (44)	6,000	6,000	25,000	25,000
Printing banned publications (45)	2,000	2,000	2,000	5,000

Source: Data from *The Press and Publications Law of 1993: Law Number 10 for the Year 1993, with All Amendments*. Amman: Press and Publications Department, 1997.

and international human rights organizations expressed their concern about the decline of democracy and the apparent willingness of the government to use the Press and Publications Law amendments to help determine the outcome of the 1997 elections in advance.[12]

After the expiration of the three-month grace period given by the 1997 Press and Publications Law, the government demanded that the weekly newspapers comply with the new minimum capital requirements. On September 23, 1997, the government suspended seven weekly newspapers—*Al-Majd, Al-Mithaq, Al-Hadath, Al-Bilad, Sawt Al-Mar'a, Al-Sayad,* and *Hawadeth Al-Sa'a* for not complying with the JD 300,000 minimum capital requirement. Six more newspapers, *Al-Urdun, Tareq Al-Mustaqbal, Fares, Al-Najoum Al-Arabi, Al-Ummah,* and *Al-Hadaf,* were suspended a few days later.[13] *Al-Majd* would reappear in December 1997 after having obtained additional funding to meet the JD 300,000 requirement.

In order to fight the 1997 Press and Publications Law amendments, as well as to stave off suspension, five weekly newspapers filed a lawsuit against the government charging that the amendments were unconstitutional.[14] After the September suspensions, the same five newspapers, with the addition of three more, filed a second suit.[15] The court's decision, however, was postponed until after the November 1997 elections.

In January 1998, in reaction to the second lawsuit, the High Court of Justice ruled that the 1997 Press and Publications Law amendments were unconstitutional. The ruling of the ten-judge panel focused on the issue of necessity for the amendments to be issued through a provisional law. The Jordanian constitution allows provisional laws to be issued when there is an urgent need for such a law. However, the court ruled that "the law was issued when Parliament was in recess at the time, there were no necessitating circumstances. The necessitating circumstances arise only in times of war, catastrophes or internal strife."[16]

Therefore, the court found that the provisional law was in contradiction with the constitution and that all decisions based on the law should be canceled. Thus, the suspended newspapers could resume publishing. On February 8, the government issued an order allowing the newspapers to do so, but only after the weeklies had accused the government of delaying the implementation of the court's order. The Law Committee of the House of Deputies sent the provisional law, which had been given to the Parliament for ratification, back to the government after the High Court invalidated the law.

Again the Jordanian judicial system showed its independence from the executive authority.[17] However, the short-run effects of the decree may have been sufficient for the needs of the regime in implementing such a survival strategy. In 1997, the regime had intended the press law amendments to help stack the Parliament with more progovernment deputies. This was the outcome of the 1997 elections. Yet the regime had not foreseen a boycott of the elections by the opposition. In the end, the opposition miscalculated and the boycott failed. The boycott, however, nearly eroded the legitimacy of the electoral process in Jordan.

THE BOYCOTT OF THE 1997 ELECTIONS

After the 1993 decree of the SNTV electoral system, which had reduced the opposition's power in Parliament, and the 1994 peace treaty with Israel, which most of the opposition rejected, the 1997 decree of the press law amendments broke the proverbial camel's back for the Jordanian opposition. As the two decrees—to the Election Law and to the Press and Publications Law—were designed to limit the opposition's chances in being elected to Parliament, many sectors of the opposition chose to boycott the November 1997 parliamentary elections rather than face electoral defeat.

The opposition's boycott of the 1997 elections moved elite frustrations to the arena of public opinion. The boycott was a challenge to the regime for the loyalty of the public by some of the opposition forces. If the opposition could gather enough support for its cause then the legitimacy of the Parliament elected in 1997—and thus the regime—would be damaged. Regime liberals who joined the boycott would aid the opposition.

The regime sought to counter this challenge with a counter-mobilization of its own. The challenge of the boycott was sufficient for the regime to perceive it as a severe threat to its legitimacy. The accumulation of institutional survival strategies, notably the 1993 Electoral Law change and the 1997 Press and Publications Law restrictions, had been designed to insure the regime's survival by minimizing the opposition while still keeping regime opponents within political society. The results of these earlier episodes aided the regime's counter-mobilization by weakening and silencing the opposition. The elections proceeded on schedule without the boycotters. The dip in participation in the elections was significant, but turnout was high enough for the elections to be seen as legitimate. The boycotting members of the opposition were locked out of Parliament. The Parliament elected in 1997 consisted almost entirely of regime supporters. The regime survived the boycott by overriding the opposition.

In contrast, the opposition saw the boycott as a failure. The boycott did not wring concessions from the government. Nor did the boycott result in a massive voter absence from the polls. Thus, the 1997 elections provided a landslide for progovernment deputies. A rump opposition, however, remained in the Parliament.

PROLOGUE I: OPPOSITION PREFERENCES FOR ELECTORAL REFORM

The opposition had demanded a change to the electoral system since the decree of the 1993 amendments to the Election Law. By participating in the

1993 elections the opposition had proven that the SNTV system worked to their disadvantage. Between the 1993 and 1997 elections, however, the opposition never succeeded in uniting around an acceptable alternative to the SNTV system. During this period, various groups proposed different preferred substitutes for the SNTV system. Yet none of the alternative electoral systems garnered the support of all the groups. In preparation for the 1997 elections, the opposition, therefore, could not present the regime with a strong front to demand a change to the Election Law.

As the main target of the change in the electoral system, the Muslim Brotherhood lost the most because of the SNTV system in the 1993 elections. The Muslim Brotherhood obviously preferred 1989's open-list system where it took a much greater number of seats than its percentage of the vote. However, other than a desire to go back to the previous system, neither the Muslim Brotherhood nor the IAF presented a concrete proposal for a change from the SNTV system.[18] At a 1995 conference on the Election Law, deputy Abdullah al-Akaylah presented the IAF's point of view on the Election Law. According to Akaylah, the IAF sought "a contemporary, civilized Election Law that produces deputies of the nation not deputies of the neighborhood or tribe." In this view, national representatives needed to be drawn from a single national district, or at least from the governate level. Other than rejecting the one-person, one-vote system Akaylah does not, however, detail how such elections should be held. For example, he did not demand a proportional representation (PR) electoral system. He wanted an equal distribution of seats. Moreover, he called for eliminating the quotas for minorities, since they denied "equality to all Jordanians under the law." The IAF did not rule out a single-member district (SMD) system, or a mixed electoral system. However, it did not explicitly endorse any single alternative to the SNTV.[19]

The various groups of leftists and Arab nationalists likewise did not unify over a single proposal to combat the SNTV system. In general, however, these groups tended toward supporting PR systems. Since these parties tended to be small and fractious, a PR system would help to insure their representation. Under the open-list system, leftists and Arab nationalists needed to team up with a larger organization or a strong local tribe. They faired even more poorly under the SNTV. Thus, even before the decree of the SNTV system, some groups supported a PR system in place of the open-list system. Long-time leftist Issa Mdanat remained constant in his support of a PR system in a national district.[20] Moreover, leftists and Arab nationalists tended to be stronger in their criticism of the malapportionment of seats since their constituencies tended to be in urban areas. In contrast, they often remained silent on issues of minority quotas, or even defended them, since their leadership frequently was drawn from the Christian minority (e.g., Mdanat and Haddadin).

One proposal that seemed to gain currency over time was the call by HASHD for an Additional Member District (AMD, or mixed) electoral system. Although originally listed as a secondary but more realistic preference, HASHD proposed a combination of local and national districts.[21] Voters would have two votes: one vote for a local representative and one for a national representative. 60 percent of the seats would be given to national representatives in a list PR system, while local seats would be distributed to individuals. Over time, variations on this "German style" AMD system would gain support among sectors of the opposition—though not necessarily as the preferred option. After the imposition of the SNTV, opposition representatives proposed the keeping of the 80 seats assigned under the 1989/1993 system, but the addition of 20 to 40 seats to be distributed on a list PR formula—often called a "quota" for parties.[22]

Opinions and primary preferences for the various opposition groups, however, remained far from unified. In a 1995 survey of the twenty-three political parties at the time (including those that would normally support the government), al-Urdun al-Jadid Research Center found that of the eighteen parties wanting changes in the Election Law:

- Eight preferred a national electoral district with a list PR system
- Four preferred a SMD system with 80 deputies in 80 districts
- Three preferred an AMD system
- Two preferred 40 to 50 two seat districts
- One preferred three-seat districts with voters holding three votes.[23]

Moreover, twelve of the parties wished for a division of seats based upon population. This survey reveals the diversity of opinion and preference held across the Jordanian political spectrum in 1995. By 1997, the situation had changed little.

A number of factors worked toward keeping the opposition fragmented on the issue of electoral reform. Most critical was the lack of a concrete agenda by the opposition groups—especially the Muslim Brotherhood. Most groups made general or vague proposals for amendments to the electoral law. The opposition did not present detailed maps for boundaries of SMD's or for aligning the current districts to their proportion of the population. Also, many groups saw that they had retained at least some of their parliamentary seats despite the change to the SNTV system. Moreover, with the breadth of ideological positions among Jordan's opposition, consensus on many issues has been difficult. With each group promoting its own interests in electoral reform, a common position remained out of reach.

In addition, electoral reform was a difficult issue for the opposition to keep in the public's attention. After the opposition groups participated in the elections of 1993, popular interest in electoral law amendments faded. Other issues with much greater popular appeal and interest emerged—

especially the 1994 peace treaty with Israel, the lifting of bread subsidies in 1996, and the amendments to the Press and Publications Law in 1997. Finally, the distinction between the SNTV system and the fact that it took place in malapportioned districts often confused the presentation of alternatives to the system decreed in 1993. It is the combination of the electoral system and malapportionment that has discriminated against the opposition in Jordan. However, the fact that the latter has been more detrimental to opposition representation is often overlooked.[24]

PROLOGUE II: THE RATIFICATION OF THE 1993 AMENDMENTS

In January 1997, the decreed 1993 amendments to the Election Law came up for review by the Parliament. As in March 1992, the Parliament had the possibility of accepting, rejecting, or amending the terms of the provisional law. However, the opposition was determined to not let the provisional law that created the SNTV system pass as the 1989 amendments had in 1992. Yet, despite their attempts, the opposition did not have enough votes to prevent the government from relying on its supporters in the Parliament to override the opposition and to ratify the provisional law.

Before the decision of the whole House of Deputies, the House's Law Committee studied the provisional law and made recommendations upon it. During the 1996–1997 session, the Law Committee held a majority of opposition deputies and was chaired by IAF member Ibrahim Zeid al-Kilani. The majority of the members of the Law Committee recommended that the provisional law be rejected and sent back to the government.[25] Moreover, the committee demanded that the government draft a new Election Law with an equal number of districts as deputies (a SMD system). The majority decision argued that the provisional law "does not meet the demands put on it,"[26] namely, that the law amended the voting style but did not alter the voting age, quotas for minorities, or the districting of seats. Moreover, the committee argued that public opinion did not support the provisional amendments in their content or in the process of their approval by decree. Finally, the committee rejected the provisional amendments on the grounds that the inequality in the number of votes—cited by the regime as the necessity for the change to the SNTV system—was not covered by the constitution's protection of equal rights. Thus, the opposition set the terms of the debate on the floor of the house with the Law Committee's recommendation that the provisional amendments to the Election Law be rejected and the SNTV system be replaced with a new SMD system.

However, a minority of the Law Committee dissented to the majority's decision. The dissenters responded to the decision of the Law Committee by saying that the 1993 amendments to the Election Law did equalize citizens under the constitution. Therefore, the dissenters argued that the House should approve the provisional law and keep the amendments.[27] On January 26,

1997, the full House debated whether it should follow the recommendation of the Law Committee and reject the provisional amendments, or approve them. During the debate on the floor of the House, progovernment supporters of amendments generally echoed the dissenting opinion offered by the minority of the Law Committee. They argued that the 1993 amendments to the Election Law remedied a constitutional deficiency in the 1989 election system—the inequality in the number of votes cast by different voters.

Independent conservative Farah al-Rabadhi's presentation can be seen as a typical presentation of the progovernment position. Rabadhi argued that the one-person, one-vote system represented Jordanians equally because each Jordanian under the system "has a representative" in the Parliament, regardless of place, religion, or gender. Moreover, according to Rabadhi, all "developed democracies" rely on a one-person, one-vote system. Rabadhi noted that if there are electoral lists in such democracies, the lists are under the control of the candidates, not the voters. Thus, Rabadhi implied that Jordan's SNTV style of voting for individuals was superior. Rabadhi also reiterated the claim that the 1993 elections resulted in a more proportional translation of votes into seats. Finally, Rabadhi claimed that contrary to the opposition's charges, the 1993 elections were less "tribal" than the 1989 elections because there were fewer tribal candidates in 1993. Most presentations of supporters of the SNTV system incorporated Rabadhi's themes. In this manner, progovernment deputies argued their position to keep the 1993 amendments to the Election Law.[28]

The opposition deputies' grievances also centered on a specific point during most of their presentations—malapportionment. The opposition agreed that the SNTV system might constitutionally equalize Jordanians in terms of the number of votes they have. However, they noted that under the Election Law, the number of citizens represented by each deputy varied from district to district. In most opposition presentations, deputies also claimed that the SNTV system encouraged deputies to represent a "tribe or neighborhood," not the nation. Moreover, the opposition argued that the 1993 amendments should be rejected because the process of their decree by Prime Minister Majali and his government violated the spirit of the constitution.[29]

In the debate on the floor of the House, however, the opposition deputies continued to lack unity on presenting any alternative to the one-person, one-vote system. Under the Jordanian constitution, if the opposition succeeded in rejecting the 1993 provisional amendments to the Election Law, then the electoral law would revert to its 1989 form. If the government then wanted a different system, it would need to draft and have the Parliament approve, a new Election Law before the next election. Some deputies demanded a return to the 1989 open-list system.[30] However, most other deputies, seeing the resolve of the government and its supporters, instead seconded the Law Committee's recommendation that the government draft a new SMD-style electoral system.[31] The compromise would be one-person, one-vote but for one deputy per district. In contrast to previous expressions of preferences for electoral systems, the PR and AMD systems did not receive much support during the debate.

At the conclusion of the House debate, Prime Minister Kabariti spoke to encourage the deputies to accept the provisional law's amendments. Kabariti welcomed the deputies' suggestions made during the debate. He promised that his government would look into drafting a new "modern" electoral law. He stated, however, that under no conditions would the one-person, one-vote system be abandoned. Yet division of electoral constituencies, the number of seats in Parliament, quotas for minorities, and the voting age would be open for discussion—later.[32]

The Law Committee proposed that the House send the 1993 provisional amendments to the Election Law back to the government and that the government draft a new Election Law with a SMD system. The House voted and rejected both of the Law Committee's proposals. The House then voted and ratified the provisional law without amendments with the support of 51 of the 76 deputies present. Although the Islamists, leftists, and Arab nationalists in the opposition joined forces and gained the support of a handful of independents, the opposition could not override the support of the SNTV system among the progovernment deputies.

Thus, unlike Parliament's 1992 review of the 1989 Election Law amendments to the 1986 law, the opposition in the Parliament in 1997 used its constitutional power to attack and offer an alternative to the provisional law. The opposition in January 1997 was again reminded that the Election Law predetermined many political outcomes. Thus, the intention of the government to reduce the size of the opposition by changing the Election Law in 1993 again showed its utility. The change in the institution of the Election Law held within itself its own reinforcement mechanism—a more quiescent Parliament. A majority of deputies that were elected under the 1993 electoral system refused to change the way they had been elected.

ANNOUNCEMENT OF THE BOYCOTT OF THE 1997 ELECTIONS: WHO AND WHY?

On July 8, 1997, to the surprise of many, the Muslim Brotherhood announced that the organization would boycott the November elections. Other individuals and parties would join the boycott to protest, among other things, the SNTV electoral system. The boycott would become the focal issue of the 1997 parliamentary election campaign. Moreover, it would be the first time in the 1990s that the opposition led a serious challenge to the regime's management of institutions in political society.

The Muslim Brotherhood justified its boycott of the 1997 elections as a protest against three controversial policies of the regime. The one-person, one-vote electoral system provided the Islamists four years of grievances with the regime. The organization's reduced parliamentary strength did not eliminate its voice in Parliament, but it did weaken the Brotherhood's ability to block or delay legislation. Notable in the Muslim Brotherhood's legislative failures was the Parliament's ratification of the 1994 peace treaty with Israel. The regime's continued normalization of ties with Israel was a second major justification of the Muslim Brotherhood's decision to boycott the 1997 elections. Finally, when the government of Abd al-Salam al-Majali returned to power and decreed the amendments to the Press and Publications Law, the Islamists finalized their decision to boycott. The Brotherhood made their participation in the elections contingent on the reversal of the one-person, one-vote election formula, revocation of the Press and Publications Law amendments, and a suspension of normalization with Israel.[33]

A number of prominent individuals and groups joined the Muslim Brotherhood in the boycott. After some controversy within the party, the IAF followed its parent organization in the boycott.[34] Jordanian offshoots of the PFLP and the DFLP—the Jordanian People's Unity Party and HASHD respectively—joined the IAF. Smaller parties, like the Constitutional Front Party, the Jordanian Arab Partisans Party, and the Nationalist Action Party (Haqq) also joined in the boycott. However, more important additions to the boycott came from Suleiman Arar (former House speaker and minister of interior) and his Mustaqbal Party, and independents Tahir al-Masri (former prime minister and House speaker) and Ahmed Obeidat (former prime minister and security chief).

While the Election Law, the peace process, and the amendments to the Press and Publications Law all drove the Muslim Brotherhood's decision to boycott the 1997 elections, two additional factors were present in the group's decision. The consolidation of the progovernment section of the political spectrum in 1997 fueled the Muslim Brotherhood's unstated fear of continued electoral losses. The formation of the National Constitutional Party (NCP) out of nine centrist and conservative parties finally presented the IAF with a major competitor. The NCP threatened to reshape the Jordanian political landscape with its array of former ministers and government officials, including the prime minister's brother Abd al-Hadi al-Majali. The regime's long-desired consolidation of political parties seemed at hand. The IAF greeted these developments with fear as informal preelection surveys predicted the Islamists winning as few as ten seats in the 1997 elections.[35] These fears, while not publicly used as a justification, nevertheless influenced the Muslim Brotherhood's decision to boycott the elections.

Second among the unstated reasons for the Muslim Brotherhood's boycott of the 1997 elections was the simmering tension between the Muslim Brotherhood and its political party, the IAF. Adding to this tension was the underlying philosophical and tactical differences between the hawkish and dovish wings of the Islamist trend. Underneath the apparently seamless facade of the Islamist trend in Jordan lies a profound split over the tactics of contesting power, the relationship with the regime, and even the basic goals of the Islamist movement.[36] The debate over whether to boycott the 1997 elections brought these distinctions to the surface.

In contrast to the immediate reaction to the change to the Election Law in 1993, where doves sought a boycott of the elections and hawks argued for campaigning for a parliamentary majority in the elections, in 1997, the doves sought continued dialogue with the regime while hawks argued for a boycott.[37] Before the announcement in May 1997 of the provisional amendments to the Press and Publications law, the IAF had announced that it would be campaigning with "full force" in the November elections. Even after the amendment of the Press and Publications Law, the IAF held primaries to select the Front's candidates. The IAF was prepared to present 40–45 candidates in the hope of winning at least 20 seats, in spite of the SNTV electoral system. A month later, however, the leadership of the Muslim Brotherhood declared that the organization would be boycotting the November 1997 elections. The leadership of the IAF reacted somewhat coolly to this announcement. While the IAF eventually followed the lead of the Muslim Brotherhood, IAF leaders predicted that not all of its members would adhere to the boycott. The decision to boycott the 1997 election helped reveal the underlying organizational distinctions between the Muslim Brotherhood and the IAF. This lack of Islamist unity was put on full display when six IAF and Muslim Brotherhood members broke the boycott. They were later ejected from the Muslim Brotherhood.

OPPOSITION DEFECTORS FROM THE BOYCOTT

The boycott, moreover, was not supported unanimously among the various other opposition groups. Five opposition political parties joined the race for the thirteenth Parliament in 1997. The Arab Socialist Ba'ath Party, the Democratic Unionist Party (an extended offshoot of the DFLP), the Jordanian Communist Party, and the Arab Land Party presented a total of nine candidates. A total of thirty-two independent Islamists and twenty-eight leftists and Arab nationalists ran in spite of the boycott. Not all, however, would be considered as hard-core opposition.[38]

Opposition candidates who did not join the boycott in 1997 tended to fall into three categories. First, many prominent boycott breakers were incumbents from the 1993 Parliament. Some deputies had an incentive to not boycott because they did not wish to lose the power and perks that the office provided. When questioned, however, these incumbents pointed more to their role as critics of the government and the need for their Parliament seats to keep their "oppositional" voice in the public eye.[39] Yet these reasons did not stop incumbents like Tahir al-Masri and most of the IAF parliamentary delegation from boycotting the election. Secondly, many nonboycotting candidates were running for either the Christian or Circassian minority seats. In

Amman's third district, for example, the former head of the Communist Party, a Communist Party politburo member, and the incumbent Baʿathist, all competed for the same Christian seat in west Amman. Moreover, many leftists or Arab nationalists did not follow the Muslim Brotherhood's political line and refused to back the boycott. Finally, in less urban areas of the country, tribal support figured in the candidacies of nonboycotting opposition members. Abdullah al-Akayleh, a prominent IAF member, combined strong tribal support with his dovish Islamist ideology to win easily in 1989, 1993, and in 1997. The SNTV system in Jordan rewarded candidates that could combine tribal and ideological constituencies. Some candidates saw this opportunity in the 1997 elections, with or without the boycott.

A council called the "High Coordinating Committee of Opposition Parties" organized the opposition boycott. The committee had originally formed to support protests against normalization with Israel. On August 17 the committee released a statement supporting the boycott with the signatures of over eighty prominent Jordanians. In late September the committee published a "National Salvation Program" highlighting the justifications and demands of the boycotters.[40] While the committee helped forge a rare degree of unity among the opposition groups supporting the boycott, it did not manage to persuade the government to accede to any of the boycotters' demands.

REGIME RESPONSE TO THE BOYCOTT.

Despite calls by both the government and opposition for a "dialogue" to bring the boycotters back into the election process, such dialogue proved superficial and ineffective. The opposition hoped that their announcement of the boycott would spur the government to change its stance on the Election Law and the new Press and Publications Law. Although leaders from the Muslim Brotherhood and other boycotting opposition groups did meet with Prime Minister Majali, such negotiations never got beyond the "talks about talks" stage. The government sought to include "all groups" in discussions about the demands of the opposition and did meet with a number of groups not participating in the boycott. However, the boycotting opposition eventually concluded that the government was "not serious" about the dialogue.[41] Eventually, King Hussein closed any of the opposition's hopes of electoral reform when he announced that there would be no changes in Jordan's Election Law until the "Palestine question" was resolved.[42] Thus, both the government and opposition went into the campaign for the 1997 elections resolute in their positions.

ELECTION 1997: THE CAMPAIGN

The issue of the boycott crosscut the 1997 campaign. The boycott, however, did not prevent 524 candidates from running for Parliament in 1997. Yet, by most accounts, the 1997 campaign was lackluster and mostly devoid of serious political content, save for the issue of the boycott.

Without the threat of the opposition in the campaign to unite its disparate ranks, the NCP alliance began to unravel even before the elections. In September, a number of NCP supporters resigned to protest the lack of democracy in the party. In addition to nominating an official list of twelve party candidates in the 1997 elections, the NCP also ran an unofficial list of approximately fifteen "stealth" candidates. These candidates did not hold any public link to the party—for some candidates feared that a party label would cost them votes or that it would put two party candidates in direct competition with one another in the same district.[43] The revelation of the stealth list prompted even more resignations. The NCP limped rather than ran in the 1997 election campaign.

Accusations of electoral fraud also plagued the 1997 elections. Controversies over duplicated voting lists and disappearing voter cards prompted arrests and investigations. To many observers such heavy-handed manipulations seemed redundant, given that most candidates were strong regime supporters.[44] Yet the fraud also sought to alter races between various individual proregime candidates as well.

Finally, to improve turnout for the elections and to drown out the calls of the boycotters, the regime engaged in a media offensive over the state-owned Jordan Television and Radio. But most importantly, the amendments to the Press and Publications Law were in effect during the campaign. Journalists feared giving the boycott too much flattering attention lest the newspaper be punished. Observers, internal and external, saw the restrictive new press law as aiding the proregime candidates who tended to rely on tribal networks rather than news publicity.[45]

ELECTION 1997: THE RESULTS

A rainy day seemed to reflect the general apathy to the November 4, 1997 elections. Not surprisingly, independent and progovernment candidates won in a landslide. The opposition boycott did lower voter participation somewhat. However, boycotters were locked out of the Parliament. A token opposition was elected to the Parliament, but it was as fractious as it was small. Women, despite support from the regime, also fared poorly.[46] Nor did the NCP perform up to expectations; only three official NCP candidates were elected. Table 7.2 details the results of the 1997 elections.

The boycott of the election by the opposition did reduce public participation in the elections. In 1997, 822,318 voters cast their ballots. With a turnout of 44.7 percent of registered voters, the 1997 elections saw an approximately 10 percent lower participation rate than 1989 or 1993. Participation in heavily urbanized and Palestinian inhabited areas was quite low. In Amman's second district and in the district of Zarqa, both home to

Table 7.2 RESULTS OF THE 1997 ELECTION

Trend	Votes for Winners	% of Popular Vote	Seats Won	% of Seats Won
Former IAF members	17,332	2.11	4	5.00
Independent Islamists	8,459	1.03	4	5.00
Tribal or Centrist Independents	196,293	23.87	51	63.75
NCP Affiliates	13,583	1.65	3	3.75
NCP Stealth Candidates	39,486	4.80	8	10.00
Leftists	15,335	1.86	5	6.25
Arab Nationalists	15,761	1.92	5	6.25

Source: Hussein Abu Rumman, Results of 1997 Elections: Facts and Figures (Amman: al-Urdun al-Jadid Research Center, 1998).

impoverished residents and a number of Palestinian refugee camps, turnout stood at 26 percent and 29 percent respectively. In contrast, 72 percent of registered voters participated in the rural district of Tafilah.[47] However, the drop in voter turnout in 1997 cannot be attributed to the boycott alone. A great deal of voter apathy, and—as all the newspapers noted—heavy rains, also contributed to decreased public participation in the 1997 elections.

Enough opposition candidates broke ranks to run (and to win), and voter turnout rates were not significantly lowered to demonstrate to the opposition that their boycott had failed. Since the government had refused to cede to any of the opposition's demands and had pushed as hard as it could to boost voter turnout, the opposition's boycott did not deliver any compensating benefits for being excluded from the Parliament. The exclusion of the boycotters was complete when no Muslim Brotherhood figures or independents that boycotted (like Arar or Masri) were appointed to the forty-seat Senate later in November.

Moreover, the 1997 election proved not to be the year for the consolidation of the Jordanian right wing. The NCP, hoping for a sweep of the elections, proved that without the threat of the IAF, regime supporters would remain as factionalized as the opposition. The SNTV system also worked against the NCP (as it does against any large organized group) by pitting allied candidates against one another for votes. Thus, the necessity for the stealth list of candidates was proven—a greater number of stealth candidates succeeded than those on the official NCP list.

Thus, what the regime's SNTV electoral system began, the opposition boycott completed: the near "tribalization" of the Jordanian Parliament and the exclusion of the opposition from the legislature. The Parliament elected in 1997, aside from a quarrelsome handful of opposition deputies, focused its activities on patronage as much as on legislation.

THE PRESS AND PUBLICATIONS LAW OF 1998

Through the 1998 Press and Publications Law, the regime would finally obtain the restrictions on the press that it had desired. Moreover, by overriding the opposition, the regime would shore up its control of the public sphere, some of which was lost in the previous year. Despite the failure in January 1998 of the 1997 press law amendments, the November 1997 elections did produce a Parliament almost exclusively composed of regime supporters. Thus, with the draft of the 1998 Press and Publications Law, the government proposed restrictions and penalties that were even stronger than the failed 1997 amendments. What few opposition deputies remained could not effectively delay, let alone block legislation. In contrast, the government knew it could rely on the vast majority of deputies to support draft laws the cabinet submitted for approval.

DRAFTING THE LAW

The government of Abd al-Salam al-Majali drafted the 1998 Press and Publications Law under a great deal of secrecy. The virtual news blackout during the writing of the law created an avalanche of media speculation by anxious journalists. While government spokesmen would not provide any details on the cabinet discussions of the draft law, they felt free to criticize the media's prognostication about the coming Press and Publications Law. Rumors reported in the press included the possibility that the draft law would raise minimum capital requirements for daily newspapers to JD 1 million. The cabinet did eventually consult with the JPA over the content of the new Press and Publications Law, but reportedly only after the draft had been completed.

On June 15, 1998, the text draft of the Press and Publications Law was released to the public and another wave of media fear and indignation crested.[48] Although some writers did find something positive to say about the draft law, most journalists and opposition columnists sought to bury the draft law with resentful newsprint. A common feeling among journalists and editors was that Jordan, at least in terms of press freedom, had come "full circle . . . to martial law."[49] The journalists' fate, however, was in the hands of the Parliament.

RECOMMENDATIONS OF THE HOUSE'S NATIONAL GUIDANCE COMMITTEE

The draft Press and Publications Law was submitted to the Parliament for review during its extraordinary session during the summer of 1998. While journalists advised the Parliament to think carefully about the draft law, opponents of the law had little confidence that the Parliament would reject, or even water down, the draft law.[50] On June 22 the House began to review the Press and Publications draft law. In the initial debate, over forty House deputies expressed opposition to at least part of the draft law. However, only eighteen deputies of sixty-four present supported a motion that would reject the draft outright. Instead, the draft law was sent to the National Guidance Committee with the support of forty-eight deputies.[51]

Through the month of July 1998, the National Guidance Committee met to research elite and public opinion and offer recommendations on the draft law. The committee members, and other interested deputies, met with a number of newspaper editors and former ministers of information who engaged in a point-by-point critique of the draft law for the committee. Moreover, after a long delay, the newly-elected leadership of the JPA issued a statement urging the Parliament to reject the draft law in its entirety. In a preliminary vote, however, a majority of the National Guidance Committee refused to concur with the JPA. After a heated debate, which included some fisticuffs, six of the nine committee members voted to keep the draft Press and Publications Law in the House in order to amend it; three committee members dissented.[52]

While not rejecting the law, the National Guidance Committee did make a number of important amendments that weakened the severity of the draft Press and Publications Law. These amendments, however, only changed the form, not the substance of the law. Important committee amendments included:

- Deleting "in their specific domains of activities" from the end of Article 6:B which defines freedom of the press as including "allowing citizens, political parties, professional associations, cultural, social and economic societies to express their opinions, thoughts and achievements in their specific domains of activities"

- Limiting revealing of journalist's sources in court cases (Article 6:D) to lawsuits involving "state security," the prevention of crime, or to "enforce justice"

- Reducing the minimum capital required of a nondaily newspaper to JD 50,000 from JD 150,000 (Article 13:B). Under the 1993 law a minimum capital of JD 15,000 was required. The 1997 decree had set the figure at JD 300,000

- Eliminating the requirement for newspapers to deposit a bond out of which fines would be paid (Article 14). Daily newspapers would have been required to deposit a JD 100,000 bond and nondaily newspapers a JD 50,000 bond

- Reducing the penalty for violating the long list of prohibitions (Article 53) from JD 15,000–JD 20,000 to JD 5,000–JD 10,000. The list of prohibitions was similar to the list in the 1993 law, however, a number of points were added by the draft of the 1998

Press and Publications Law that the National Guidance Committee did not amend

- Eliminating Article 56, which would allow punishment of a violation of the Press and Publications Law and any other law (most likely the penal code), to be punished with the higher of the two penalties. By eliminating this clause, the National Guidance Committee reduced the likelihood that a journalist would be punished with imprisonment.[53]

THE HOUSE DEBATE

On August 2, 1998, the House began its debate over the draft Press and Publications Law based on the recommendations of the National Guidance Committee. On a number of occasions, the House approved the amendments made by the committee. On many others, however, the House kept the government's language of the original draft. For example, the House accepted the committee's recommendations to delete the sections from Article 6:B (noted above) and to delete the requirement for "accuracy" in reporting in the journalists' code of conduct (Article 7). The House also agreed with the committee to delete the requirement for the bonding of newspapers (Article 14).[54]

On Article 11, the House also agreed with the National Guidance Committee's recommendation. The original article allowed foreign investors to hold 25 percent equity in a Jordanian press company to encourage privatization. The National Guidance Committee changed this clause to restrict investments in press companies only to Jordanians. Many deputies from tribal or conservative backgrounds generally opposed the government's attempts at privatizing Jordanian industries, fearing that vital sources of patronage would be sold off. According to committee member Mahmoud Kharabsheh, the decision "protects our press's national identity." The House concurred with the committee on this matter.[55]

The House also agreed with the committee on keeping the original draft's requirement of a JD 500,000 minimum capital for daily newspapers (Article 13). The House, after over an hour of stock market-like haggling, raised the minimum capital required of a nondaily paper from JD 50,000, as recommended by the committee, to JD 100,000. This figure still fell below the JD 150,000 envisioned in the original draft law.[56]

The House disagreed with the National Guidance Committee on Article 5, which stated:

> Publications should respect the truth and are prohibited from publishing anything that contradicts the principles of freedom and national responsibility, human rights, and the values of the Arab Islamic Nation.

This article contains the restrictions of Article 8 of the 1993 Press and Publications Law. In the 1993 law, however, the article also added that publications should:

> Regard the freedom of thought, opinion, expression and access to information as a right for all citizens as much as it is a right for themselves.

The National Guidance Committee recommended that Article 5 of the 1998 draft law be deleted, because the article was "too broad and opens the way for negative speculation."[57] The House, with the support of former Muslim Brotherhood members Abdullah al-Akaileh and Mohammad Azaidah, rejected the committee's recommendation and kept the language of the government's draft law. In the end, 30 of 58 deputies present supported keeping Article 5.[58]

The National Guidance Committee also recommended that the House delete from Article 37 the clause that prohibits:

> Articles or reports containing personal insult to the heads of Arab, Islamic, or friendly states, or the heads and members of diplomatic missions accredited to the kingdom provided that the principle of reciprocity is observed. (Article 37:A:7)

Again, this article had its predecessor in the 1993 Press and Publications Law (Article 40:A:7). A number of journalists had been tried for violating this clause of the 1993 Press and Publications Law. On the first vote, 27 of the 50 deputies present voted to delete the paragraph. However, upon a second vote on the same article, the original draft was left intact. This caused 14 deputies to walk out of the session.[59] The controversial clause remained in the final version of the law.

The entire law was approved by a vote of 38 to 10 (without the votes of the 14 protesting deputies).[60] The Press and Publications Law then moved on to the Senate where on August 19, it passed without any additional amendments. The Senate approved the Press and Publications Law by a majority of 27 of 35 senators present (out of a total of 40).[61] Crown Prince Hassan (in King Hussein's absence) signed the 1998 Press and Publications Law on August 31, 1998.

The government had succeeded in the parliamentary venue where it had failed by decree. Prime Minister Majali finally had the hard-line ability to restrict the press. Majali's victory, however, was short-lived as a crisis over polluted water, unease over King Hussein's illness, and popular dissatisfaction with the new Press and Publications Law caused his government to fall before Prince Hassan's signature of the law. Majali was replaced on August 20, 1998 by the more moderate Fayiz al-Tarawnah.

Tarawnah's government promised that, despite the new law's harsh conditions, his government would offer a "soft implementation" of the Press and Publications Law.[62] In October, the government even dropped all the prosecutions of the 1993 law still pending in the courts. To further demonstrate its good will toward the press, Tarawnah's government later ordered that violators of the 1998 Press and Publications Law not be prosecuted in court. Rather, the violating journalists should be punished under the JPA's own code of conduct. From September 1998, when the 1998 Press and Publications Law took effect, until the death of King Hussein in February 1999, the government did not prosecute any journalists for violating the new Press and Publications Law. However, the 1998 Press and Publications Law was in force with its threats of heavy sanctions for violators during the succession crisis in January 1998 and King Hussein's death the next month.

SURVIVAL STRATEGIES AND THE REVERSAL OF POLITICAL LIBERALIZATION

In response to the growing public discontent from the regime's foreign and economic policies, the regime cracked down on political liberties. When the Parliament did not cooperate in muzzling the press by amending the 1993 Press and Publications Law, the regime did it by decree. The restrictive 1997 amendments to the press law can be considered a short-run success for the regime because they helped reduce the voice of the opposition. However, over the longer term, this survival strategy seemed to backfire. Not only did the courts eventually overturn the decree, but also the manner of the amendments and their content alienated a number of leading regime liberals. The amendments also helped push the opposition into boycotting the November 1997 elections. In the end, the regime received an overwhelmingly progovernment Parliament, but at the expense of nearly delegitimizing the electoral process. Thanks to the new pliant Parliament the press restrictions overturned by the courts were successfully legislated through the Parliament in 1998.

The resourceful use of constitutional rules had a strong effect on the outcome of the fate of the 1997 amendments to the Press and Publications Law for both the regime coalition and the opposition. Attempts by the regime to restrict the weekly tabloids by prosecuting them under the 1993 Press and Publications Law had generally failed to silence the regime's critics in the press. The drive by the Bin Shaker and Kabariti governments to convince the Parliament to amend the press law also came to little avail. Thus, the regime changed the venue from the Parliament to an executive decree by using an interpretation of the executive's constitutional power (which the courts later invalidated).

Unlike the 1993 Election Law episode, however, the opposition also attempted to make different institutional venues work to its advantage. The opposition attempted to mobilize the public against the Press and Publications Law amendments through the boycott of the elections. However, the crucial venue for the opposition was the courts. With the regime coalition split, the united opposition overturned the regime's decree with the help of the judiciary. By acting with unity and having learned to change the venue to the courts, the opposition limited the success of the regime's decree.

At its core, the boycott of the 1997 elections was a contest for the loyalty of Jordanians. Some sectors of the opposition sought to challenge the regime's manipulation of the electoral arena. By changing from the venue of the biased electoral system to making participation in the elections a referendum on the regime's policies, the opposition sought to mobilize public opinion in a measure of the legitimacy of the elections. This challenge by itself proved a significant threat to the regime. The reduced public participation in the 1997 elections demonstrated the effect of the boycott. The boycott tarnished the perception of the legitimacy of the Parliament elected in 1997 both inside and outside of Jordan.[63] The decline in participation in the 1997 elections, however, varied across constituencies. Opposition strongholds, such as eastern Amman, saw minimal pubic participation in the electoral process. Rural districts, in contrast, saw record voter turnout. Since the latter types of constituencies are well over-represented in the Parliament, the effects on generally lower voter turnout were mitigated.

Before the elections, however, the regime did feel threatened by the boycott. Thus, it made sure that regime supporters were mobilized to vote through the mass media and tribal patronage networks. A tour of the country by the king in October 1997 helped rally support for the elections—especially in the traditionally loyalist rural regions.

In the normally no-holds-barred arena of public mobilization, in contrast, the opposition also had to face the 1997 amendments to the Press and Publications Law. The press restrictions reduced the coverage of the boycotters' demands. Thus, the boycotters' attempts to mobilize public opinion were hampered. Even opposition candidates running for Parliament, such as Toujan Faisal, told Human Rights Watch that the press law had hurt her ability to present her message.[64]

In conclusion, in the contest for the public's loyalties in the boycott, the opposition faced obstacles in its attempt to delegitimize the 1997 elections. Again, a lack of opposition unity allowed the regime to claim that the opposition was represented in the new P arliament—by over a dozen boycott breakers. Moreover, the two previous episodes of executive decrees—in 1993 and in 1997—helped cause the boycott. The two decrees also significantly influenced the strategies of all actors involved in the episode. Thus, the Parliament elected in 1997 was delegitimized to a certain extent. However, the opposition could not declare the boycott a success because of the final results of the election and because voter turnout was only partially reduced. The regime successfully overrode the opposition in this case.

With the 1998 Press and Publications Law the composition of the Parliament was stacked in the regime's favor. There was little that the opposition could do to combat this overriding force. Journalists opposed to the draft law tried to lobby the House. The result was the watering down of the draft law, but not the law's defeat. Opposition activists failed to provide an alternative to the government's draft law.[65] The handful of opposition deputies in the House also tried to rally support for press freedom.[66] However, their numbers had been reduced to the point where they could not even delay legislation. They had no hope of blocking the 1998 Press and Publications Law.

Finally, after the law had been passed, some opposition personalities proposed turning back to the courts by asking for the 1998 Press and Publications Law to be ruled unconstitutional since it violated the constitution's guarantee of free speech.[67] However, the idea was not pursued. The precedent set by the courts, in relation to the 1997 amendments to the Press and Publications Law, dealt only with the procedures of the decree. The 1998 law had been passed through the regular constitutional channels. Moreover, the court's verdict on the 1997 amendments said nothing about the decree's content. The issue of the restrictions in a Press and Publications Law violating the constitution's Article 15 was not part of the January 1998 ruling. Thus, the regime resourcefully turned defeat into victory by using the newly-elected Parliament to pass what the courts had invalidated.

The addition of the 1997 Press and Publications Law amendments added to a growing list of grievances regime liberals held against the regime's hard-line policies of the time. In contrast to previous episodes of institutional manipulation, the unity of the regime coalition in this episode was fractured. The limitation of press freedom was perceived as a loss not only to the opposition, but also to reform-minded supporters of the regime. For example, Mahmoud al-Sharif, who had defended the 1993 Press and Publications Law in the Parliament during his tenure as information minister, was outraged by the 1997 amendments.[68] Regime liberals, such as Senator Layla Sharaf and former Royal Court Chief Adnan Abu Odeh also questioned the necessity of such restrictions on the press.[69] Former Prime Ministers Tahir al-Masri and Ahmed Obeidat even joined the opposition's boycott of the parliamentary elections in protest of the Press and Publications Law amendments. Liberals and soft-liners in the regime coalition saw the 1997 amendments to the Press and Publications Law as a reversal of the process of political liberalization in Jordan. Coupled with the hard-liners' relatively small gain by silencing the press, their push for reshaping this institution of civil society eventually ran out of steam. The opposition found allies against the amendments inside the regime—in the form of the courts—to fight the hard-line policy.

In contrast to the splits within the regime coalition, the opposition unified its ranks in support of the press. Even though the Islamists did not object to limiting the more sensational and erotic stories of the weekly press, the Muslim Brotherhood came out strongly against the circumventing of the Parliament. To protest the Press and Publications Law amendments, a number of opposition groups joined the boycott of the 1997 parliamentary elections. Opponents of the amendments joined with regime liberals in protesting the decree. In this way the opposition exploited the splits within the regime coalition. Moreover, the most aggrieved by the new restrictions, the owners of the weekly newspapers, acted collectively to challenge the decree in the courts—and won.

The boycott of the 1997 parliamentary elections also caused splits within both the opposition and the regime coalition. For a variety of reasons, a number of opposition groups and personalities did not support the boycott. A number of leftists and Arab nationalists opposed the peace process, the Election Law, and the Press and Publications Law amendments as strongly as the Muslim Brotherhood. Nevertheless, they participated in the elections. Ideological differences between opposition trends sometimes proved stronger than anger at the regime in alienating opposition groups from each other. Moreover, splits within the Islamist movement also revealed different strategies on how to deal with the regime. Finally, the power of patronage and incumbency in the Parliament pulled regime opponents away from the boycott.

The differences within the regime coalition centered along the fault between regime hard-liners and regime liberals. Grievances against the SNTV system among regime liberals were muted. However, with the regime signing a peace treaty with Israel in 1994, regime coalition unity began to fray. Ahmed Obeidat, former prime minister and president of the National Charter's Royal Committee, began to voice the frustrations of some regime coalition members with the king and his policies. After the decree of the amendments to the Press and Publications Law in 1997, a number of regime liberals, such as former Prime Minister Masri and former Minister of Interior Arar, questioned the necessity of Prime Minister Majali's rush to silence the press. The accumulation of these policy differences drove a number of prominent regime liberals to join the election boycott. Aside from these individuals, however, the regime coalition was generally able to mobilize support for the November 1997 elections. The possibility of a lower-ranking regime supporter winning election to parliament—with all of its perks—increased with much of the opposition sitting out of the race.

In the debate over the 1998 Press and Publications Law, the degrees of unity of the regime coalition and opposition remained about the same as during the episode of the press law amendments of the previous year. The opposition still stood united against the attack on press freedom. The deep divisions within the regime coalition over the limiting of the press also changed little from 1997. The king, however, took ill in July 1998 and left for the United States for cancer treatment. Thus, during this episode he could not intervene to support the prime minister on the press law. The degrees of unity of the opposition and the regime coalition were not the major factors in the regime's ability to override the opposition in this episode.

King Hussein's fight with cancer would bring an end to an era in Jordanian politics. When Crown Prince Hassan took over the reigns of government in July 1998, however, he did not know that it would be his last few months in power as well. Jordan entered this short transition time between monarchs with relations between the government and the opposition at their lowest point since the disengagement from the West Bank in 1998. This situation offered to potentially complicate the succession of Jordan's new king and the consolidation of his rule. But more threatening to the stabilization of the rule of King Abdullah II was the end of the Middle East peace process and a new Palestinian intifada.

EIGHT

A NEW KING AND A NEW INTIFADA

In February 1999, King Hussein passed away from cancer. He was succeeded by his son, Abdullah, a former military officer. When taking the throne, King Abdullah II seemed inclined to pursue both economic reform and political liberalization. However, Jordan's fourth monarch was faced with severe external challenges in his first years of rule. The final status talks between Palestinians and Israelis collapsed into a new intifada, the United States was struck by international terrorists on September 11, 2001, and the United States prepared for an invasion of Iraq that eventually occurred in early 2003. The combination of these events pushed Jordan's new king to implement restrictive survival strategies and curtail political liberties.

In a televised message in July 1998, King Hussein announced that he needed to continue his battle against cancer and left for treatment at the Mayo Clinic. Upon leaving for the U.S., the king expressed full confidence in his brother and his ability to carry the regency—Hassan had been appointed for over thirty years to succeed Hussein to the throne. Most elites interviewed by the author before the king's illness had expressed their certainty that Hassan would be Jordan's next king. Politics in Jordan during Hassan's brief regency, however, seemed to be in a holding pattern awaiting the outcome of King Hussein's fight with cancer. Jordanians were correct in their caution as, just days before his death, King Hussein stripped Hassan of the regency and his place in the succession and appointed Hussein's oldest son, Abdullah, as crown prince.

From his hospital bed in the U.S., King Hussein appointed a new government headed by Fayiz al-Tarawnah in August 1998. Prime Minister Tarawnah promised to be less adversarial with the opposition than his predecessor Abd al-Salam al-Majali. Tarawnah demonstrated his government's good will by offering to softly implement the new Press and Publications Law of 1998. He, however, ruled out any further changes to the press law. The government held dialogue meetings with the heads of the professional associations. The crown prince also met opposition figures in an attempt to better relations between the regime and the opposition. Like most attempts at dialogue during the late 1990s, however, these meetings did not lead to a thaw in the chilly Jordanian political climate.

In October 1998, U.S. President Clinton called King Hussein out of his treatment to help negotiate the Wye River accord between Israel and the Palestinian Authority. The diplomatic breakthrough promised to put the faltering Middle East peace process back on track. However, the failure to implement the Wye agreement led to further recriminations between the Israelis and the Palestinians over the next year. The king's reappearance in international diplomacy again displayed Prince Hassan's role as a mere caretaker.

THE SUCCESSION

King Hussein returned to Jordan briefly in January 1999 after having supposedly recovered from his cancer. It appears, however, that he came to wrap up loose ends before he passed away. After a few days of hints—first in the press, and then from the king himself in an interview on CNN—King Hussein stripped his brother of the regency and gave it to his son. Only a couple of days after reorganizing the succession, King Hussein left again for the U.S. for more cancer treatment. King Hussein returned to Jordan about a week later and died on February 7, 1999. The recently-appointed Abdullah became king.

Explanations abound for King Hussein's sudden decision. However, three major themes dominate theories of Jordan's succession battle. The first type of explanation focuses on the policy tendencies of the potential heirs. Some East Bankers viewed Prince Hassan as lacking support among the tribes and the military. In contrast, Abdullah had spent his career in the Special Forces—a critical component of Jordan's army. Yet many Palestinians viewed Hassan as biased against their interests as well. In contrast, as Abdullah's wife was of Palestinian origins, some saw the couple as metaphorically reunifying the two Banks. Moreover, Lamis Andoni found that former officials and opposition leaders believed that "Hassan was attempting to restore the national consensus that had been fractured by the peace treaty, the lack of economic growth, and the pro-American policies."[1] In contrast, Abdullah has not only continued Jordan's pro-American alignment, but deepened it as well—thus Abdullah was the American's preferred candidate for the succession.

A second type of explanation draws from King Hussein's letter to Prince Hassan removing him from the succession. From the letter, it seems that Hussein was disturbed by Hassan moving to consolidate power and authority even before the king's death. The letter includes reasons for shifting the succession of Hassan's tampering with appointments in the army and rumors of criticism of King Hussein's wife, Queen Noor. Prince Hassan's wife apparently was also making plans for redecorating the royal palace which confirmed "Hussein's suspicion that his brother was anticipating his demise."[2]

The letter also mentions another explanation for the change in the succession: the question of who would follow Hassan on the throne. Hassan sought to have his son, Rashid, come next in line. In contrast, many report that King Hussein—at the urging of Queen Noor—wanted his fourth son, Hamzah, to take the throne.[3] Since, in 1999, Hamzah was still finishing school, however, Hussein chose his oldest son Abdullah for the throne, with the condition that Hamzah was named crown prince—which he later was. Thus, for Andoni, "Most Jordanian politicians, including former aids to both Hussein and Hassan, believe that the late monarch was motivated simply by a father's ambition to be succeeded by his own sons."[4] Curtis Ryan's interviews concur with this point.[5]

King Abdullah quickly consolidated his rule. He treated his uncle with respect, but moved to put his own stamp on Jordanian politics. He did, however, keep a number of his father's advisors around him. Prime Minister Tarawnah was kept for Abdullah's first month in power. In March 1999, Abdullah appointed the conservative Abd al-Raouf al-Rawabdah as his first prime minister. Rawabdah's appointment was balanced by the appointment of economic reformer Abd al-Karim al-Kabariti as chief of the Royal Court. Adnan Abu Odeh, a regime liberal, was also appointed as a court advisor. Moreover, Abdullah relied heavily on General Samih Batikhi, the head of the security services—the *Mukhabarat*—for his advice. Thus, Abdullah placed an experienced cadre of advisors from the major wings of the regime coalition around him.

Where King Hussein placed a priority on foreign policy, King Abdullah made economic reform his primary concern. King Abdullah placed less importance on Jordan's relationship with Israel and refocused Amman's attention toward Washington. King Abdullah promoted himself as a champion of globalization and free-market economic reform. This, coupled with his good relationship with the younger princes of the Gulf monarchies, allowed Jordan to reopen relations with countries like Kuwait and Saudi Arabia that had been strained since King Hussein's neutrality in the Gulf War. This thaw also helped reopen the Gulf labor market for a return of Jordanian workers. King Abdullah renewed Jordan's program with the IMF and began reforms that would lead to Jordan's entry into the WTO. The privatization program, which had been frequently stalled over the decade, was speeded up, leading to the sale of part of Jordan's telecommunications system and railways. Abdullah also pushed for administrative reform of Jordan's moribund bureaucracy. In a series of undercover visits to industrial zones and hospitals, and even a stint as a taxi driver, the new king sought to hear the grievances of ordinary Jordanians while prompting officials to follow through on reforms.[6]

In the course of consolidating his reign, King Abdullah promised a return to policies of political liberalization in Jordan. In July 1999, elections for municipal councils were held in cities across Jordan. In these local elections the Islamic Action Front returned to the electoral arena after its disastrous boycott of the 1997 parliamentary elections. The IAF also felt confident in its electoral power to run without forming alliances with leftist or Arab nationalist parties. The IAF performed well in many cities in the north and center of Jordan—their traditional strongholds. The front even took a quarter of the available seats on the Amman city council. Other opposition groups fared poorly without an alliance with the Islamists, which left the remaining seats for conservatives and tribal candidates.[7] However, during the first year of Abdullah's rule, moves toward political liberalization mainly took the form of revisiting the Press and Publications Law yet again.

1999 PRESS AND PUBLICATIONS LAW AMENDMENTS

To the surprise of many, a bill to amend the 1998 Press and Publications Law was included on the agenda of the Parliament's summer 1999 extraordinary session. However, the government of Prime Minister Rawabdah did not send a draft of the amendments to the Parliament until August.

The major feature of the 1999 amendments to the Press and Publications Law was the elimination of Article 37, which had included the list of fourteen restrictions on the press (much like Article 40 of the 1993 law). The government's draft had called for reducing the fourteen prohibitions to nine. The House's National Guidance Committee called for further reducing the restrictions down to two. However, in the floor debate in the House, the deputies voted to eliminate the article altogether.[8] Yet even this move did not meet the demands of many journalists. They feared that with the elimination of these prohibitions in the Press and Publications Law, the same offence could potentially be prosecuted under the Penal Code—with penalties of up to life imprisonment.

The House also reduced the capital requirements of nondaily newspapers from JD 100,000 to JD 50,000. This move followed the government's draft amendments. Some deputies had called for reducing the capital requirement or even eliminating it entirely. By a new amendment, journalists were also given greater access to government sources of information. Penalties for reporting on court sessions without permission were also halved by the House to a maximum of JD 5,000.

However, the 1999 amendments to the Press and Publications Law did not restore the necessity for privatization of government-owned newspapers, alter the mandatory membership requirement in the Jordanian Press Association, or eliminate the ban on reporting secret sessions of Parliament. In the end, as with the 1993 Press and Publications Law, many deputies and journalists saw the new law as an improvement, but they felt that the new law did not meet their full expectations.[9]

The 1999 Press and Publications Law stands as the accumulation of the previous decade's experiment in political liberalization. King Abdullah sought to broaden his support among the public by reintroducing some of the political liberties that had been limited in the previous few years. The amending of the harsh 1998 Press and Publications Law was one part of this liberalization package. Despite the elimination of some restrictions on the press, however, many restrictions remained.

PREPARING FOR THE PALESTINIAN-ISRAELI FINAL STATUS TALKS

King Abdullah's program of political liberalization did not last for long. In 1999, the negotiations toward a final status agreement between the Palestinians and the Israelis began—especially after the election of Ehud Barak as Prime Minister of Israel. While Jordan was not a direct party to the negotiations, a final resolution of the conflict would impact Jordan in one form or another. King Abdullah began policies to lend Jordanian support for peacemaking while further limiting the opposition to the peace process. A crackdown in the autumn of 1999 on the Palestinian-Islamic resistance group, Hamas, signaled the rapid end to political liberalization under King Abdullah.

For a number of years both Israel and the Palestinian Authority had asked Jordan to limit the activities of Hamas in the kingdom. In Jordan, the group's political wing and spokesmen were allowed to operate freely, as long as they did not maintain any overt connection to the group's military activities across the Jordan River. In 1997, Israeli agents attempted to assassinate Hamas spokesman Khalid Mashʿal, leading to King Hussein's growing disappointment with Israeli Prime Minister Netanyahu.

In 1999, however, with growing pressure from, not only the Palestinian Authority and Israel, but the U.S. as well, the Jordanian regime decided that the presence of Hamas in the kingdom was a liability. On August 30, 1999, police raided the offices of Hamas in Amman and issued arrest warrants for the organization's four main leaders: Ibrahim Ghoshah, Khaled Mashʿal, Musa Abu Marzuq, and Khalid Nazzal. At the time, only Nazzal was present in Jordan, and he immediately fled into hiding. Ghoshah, Mashʿal and Abu Marzuq were in Iran and they delayed their return. While the Jordanian government insisted that the crackdown was purely a security matter and that Hamas had engaged in weapons trafficking and military training in the kingdom, many observers noted that the move coincided with a visit by U.S. Secretary of State Madeleine Albright.[10]

In late September, when Ghoshah, Mashʿal, and Abu Marzuq attempted to return to Jordan they were detained at the airport. Abu Marzuq, who had earlier been deported from the U.S., was expelled because he did not hold Jordanian citizenship. Ghoshah and Mashʿal, who were Jordanian nationals, were arrested. The Jordanian Muslim Brotherhood attempted to negotiate with the government on Hamas's behalf. A series of meetings between the Brotherhood's spiritual guide, Abd al-Majid Theneibat, and Prime Minister Rawabdah failed to resolve the crisis. Moreover, the government insisted that the issue was a "legal matter" and that no political solutions would be reached. King Abdullah refused to intervene, stating that the "law would take its course."[11] Moreover, Hamas supporters in the Muslim Brotherhood, like former deputies Abd al-Munʿam Abu Zant and Dhib Anis, were arrested for their criticism of the government during mosque sermons.

The prosecution's case against the organization, however, appeared weak. Ghoshah and Mashʿal insisted that they would prefer to stand trial rather than leave Jordan. But on November 21, 1999, the two Hamas leaders, as well as two other members of the organization, were deported to Qatar. The government ignored criticisms by the Muslim Brotherhood and others that the deportation of Jordanian citizens violated the Jordanian constitution. The charges against twenty other Hamas members, however, were dropped. Ghoshah unexpectedly tried to return to Jordan in June 2001. After nearly a month of being stranded in the airport, he froze his membership in Hamas and was allowed entry into Jordan. Thus, by the end of 1999, Hamas's presence in Jordan had essentially been removed. The opposition also saw that the brief political opening instigated by King Abdullah as he consolidated power had been closed.

The crackdown on Hamas in Jordan was caused by a number of external pressures on Jordan stemming from the impending "final status" negotiations between the Palestinians and Israel. The Palestinian Authority, Israel, and the U.S. had all been calling on Jordan to curtail the Palestinian-Islamic group since the arrival of the Palestinian Authority in the occupied territories and the rise of Hamas as a popular alternative to Arafat's leadership. King Hussein, however, had ignored the calls. In 1999, the government claimed that it had planned to shut the offices of Hamas in 1997, but that Israel's attempted assassination of Mashʿal had spoiled those plans. King Abdullah, moreover, had been gradually shedding Jordan's commitments in the West Bank made by his father. At the same time, Hamas's offices in Amman were being shuttered, the government announced that Jordan was turning over the control of Jerusalem's holy places to the Palestinian Authority.[12] The crackdown on Hamas also sent a message to the domestic opposition that the regime's tolerance of dissent to peace and normalization had reached a limit. The regime especially wished to send this message since a major point of the final status negotiations would be the Palestinian refugees. Jordan desired a voice in the negotiations on this issue, but the Palestinians, the Israelis, and the Americans often rebuffed it. The regime feared that an agreement would be reached where refugees in Jordan would be settled in the kingdom. And if this happened, Jordan's share of the compensation would not be sufficient for the task. Thus, with the Middle East peace process seemingly on the verge of a final settlement of the Palestinian-Israeli conflict in late 1999, Jordan's regime feared being both marginalized from the process and from the potential domestic ramifications of such a settlement. Cracking down on the Palestinian-Islamist group in Jordan was an attempt to demonstrate both Jordan's relevance to the negotiators and the regime's resolve to its domestic discontents.

ECHOES OF A NEW INTIFADA

In the summer of 2000, the final status negotiations of the Middle East peace process were pushed to their breaking point. In order to secure his place in history, U.S. President Clinton invited Israeli Prime Minister Barak and Palestinian Authority President Arafat to Camp David. Instead of reaching a breakthrough, the talks collapsed after two and a half weeks. Palestinians and Israelis attempted to restart negotiations over the next couple of months, but they made little progress in bridging the gaps remaining after the summit. As Barak's governing coalition collapsed, Arafat delayed a declaration of a Palestinian state in September 2000. The disappointment of Palestinians in the occupied territories with the continuing Israeli occupation, the growing Israeli settlements, economic hardship, and ineffectual leadership was ignited by Israeli hard-liner Ariel Sharon's visit to the *Haram al-Sharif* on September 28, 2000. The Al-Aqsa intifada began, and the uprising threatened to engulf the region in conflict.

The new intifada did not drag neighboring countries into a war with Israel. Both Jordan and Egypt maintained their peace treaties with Israel. Yet the conflict in the West Bank echoed across the Jordan Valley into the domestic politics of Jordan as it did with the first intifada. The regime perceived the new intifada as threatening, not only Jordan's peace agreement with Israel, but also the survival of the regime itself. As with the prior Palestinian uprising, the Jordanian regime treaded cautiously between placating domestic anger at Israeli repression and a spillover of the rage of Palestinians in Jordan. Externally, Jordan tried to square this circle by chilling relations with Israel. When Jordan's ambassador to Israel finished his term in November 2000, he was not replaced. Jordan has also joined in offering regional and international solutions to the conflict by joining in the October 2000 Sharm al-Shaikh summit, by proposing with Egypt a cease-fire initiative in April 2001, by strongly pushing for acceptance of the Saudi peace plan in the Arab League in early 2002, and by working for the implementation of the U.S.'s Middle East "road map." In contrast to his father's flashy diplomacy, however, King Abdullah has generally followed the lead of Cairo and Washington in relation to the second intifada. Moreover, Jordan's foreign minister has become the diplomatic channel of choice—as compared to King Hussein's personal diplomatic touch.

Jordan's domestic management of the fallout of the intifada shows a return to an iron fist. The regime has demonstrated a near "zero-tolerance policy" of public demonstrations in support of the uprising. A ban on demonstrations was imposed after rallies in early October led to a shooting death and property damage. The regime condemned those who have dared to demonstrate for endangering the country's "security and stability."[13] A march organized by the professional associations in the Jordan Valley in late October 2000 attracted nearly 20,000. It was violently broken up by the security forces. In May 2001, demonstrators returned to Amman's streets only to be beaten again. In response to the Israeli reoccupation of the West Bank in April 2002, massive protests erupted.

However, on the rare occasions when protests were permitted, the demonstrators generally remained calm.[14] Often at acute moments of public outrage, the regime tried to diffuse tension by permitting protests and then placing them under the leadership of a government luminary. In April 2002, for example, Queen Rania led 2,000 women in a protest march condemning Israel's Operation Defensive Shield.

Following the assassination of an American diplomat in Amman in October 2002, Abdullah's government again cracked down on political liberties, leading to the declaration of martial law over the city of Maʿan in November 2002. Ostensibly, the six-day curfew was supposed to round up criminal elements; however, most point to the fact that the occupation was sparked by the attempted arrest of an independent Islamist with links to the banned *Takfir wa al-Hijra* group and his escape from custody with aid from tribal clansmen. The operation also seemed to send the message to Jordanian supporters of Baʿathist Iraq in the town to remain quiet in the event of an American invasion of Iraq. The episode left six dead in the largest episode of domestic armed conflict since September 1970.[15]

The regime has also turned to accusing the professional associations for organizing demonstrations against Israel. In October 2000, the professional associations' blacklist of those who had normalized with Israel was leaked to the press. The president of the Council of Professional Associations and other leading members of the syndicates were arrested in January 2001 after a second list of accused normalizers was released. The arrests led for calls by conservative deputies to place restrictions on the political activities of the professional associations since they threatened to become "a state within a state."[16]

The Parliament, elected in 1997, finished its term in 2001. Although the House overwhelmingly consisted of progovernment deputies, the deputies often resisted government legislation to cut government spending and to globalize the economy. For example, the Parliament rejected government plans to raise taxes or to strengthen anti-trust laws. Thus, when the Parliament's term expired in June 2001, King Abdullah dissolved the assembly. Again in the absence of the Parliament, the government began to pass legislation by decree.

One of the first laws decreed was a new electoral law. The new law raised the number of seats in the House of Deputies from 80 to 104 and the number of constituencies from 21 to 45. Seats were distributed into mostly single-member districts with some multiple-member districts. The one-person, one-vote system, however, was kept. The law also simplified voting registration. Thus, the government claimed that the elections slated for November 2001 would be delayed for at least ten months while voters were registered into the new electoral system. The elections would not take place until June

2003, after the U.S. invasion of Iraq. For although the delay of elections was claimed to be for procedural reasons, the government's fear of holding elections while the intifada raged next door and the U.S. threatened military action against Iraq seemed quite clear. The Election Law of 2001, however was not the only law decreed after the dismissal of Parliament.

In October 2001, the government decreed amendments to the Penal Code to show Jordan's commitment to joining the U.S.'s war on terrorism. The amendments also included restrictions on the press that included stiff fines and/or prison sentences for publications that carry "false or libelous information that can undermine national unity or the country's reputation."[17] Journalists complained that the latest restrictions on press freedom undermined political liberties in Jordan. In response, the king appointed a "Higher Media Council" that was intended to eventually take the place of the Ministry of Information. However, not all journalists were impressed with the composition or the early actions of the council.

The government used its decree power not only to reshape political and civil society. Economic laws by the dozen—many stalled or blocked by the Parliament—were decreed by the government of Prime Minister Ali Abu-Ragheb. The government attempted to use greater integration into the world economy to offset economic losses—especially from tourism—caused by the intifada. Between June 2001 and May 2002 the Jordanian government decreed over eighty provisional laws and amendments.[18]

SURVIVING A CONTESTED SUCCESSION AND RENEWED REGIONAL CRISES

King Abdullah has not been offered the luxury of relaxation so far in his brief reign. Soon after he consolidated his rule from a surprise placement onto the throne Jordan faced the imminent conclusion of the Middle East peace process. However, instead of a "New Middle East" emerging from President Clinton's last days, the region was again placed into conflict between Arabs and Israelis. The intifada has threatened to spill over into Jordan and the regime has implemented a variety of survival strategies to prevent this from happening. It is too early to judge the full success or failure of these new survival strategies. In the short run, however, the Jordanian regime had managed to maintain peaceful relations with Israel while allowing very limited displays of public despair over the treatment of Arabs west of the Jordan River. While Jordan has not revoked the strategic choice of peace with Israel, attempts at "warm" relations have frozen.[19] Jordan's ambassadorship to Tel Aviv remained empty and occasional demonstrations have been permitted to relieve tension. Again the regime has attempted to manage this balancing act through resourceful use—and in some cases abuse—of constitutional rules. The opposition remains united in their dissent to peace with Israel as well as to the American invasion of Iraq. However, the regime coalition patched some of the splits that emerged in the late 1990s. Many discontented regime supporters returned to the fold in order to preserve an orderly succession for King Abdullah. Also, for many in the regime coalition, the regime has sufficiently registered disappointment with Israeli actions in the occupied territories while still maintaining Jordan's good graces with the U.S. It remains to be seen whether this is enough to keep discontented Jordanians from further mobilizing their grievances of economic hardship and feelings of angst at the treatment of Palestinians by Israel and of Muslims by the U.S.

NINE

INSTITUTIONS AND THE POLITICS OF SURVIVAL: AN APPRAISAL

Since 1998, a series of crises have buffeted Jordan's stability. The regime has attempted to reform Jordan's struggling economy by closely following the "Washington Consensus" of economic structural adjustment and opening up of the country to the forces of economic globalization. It has also had to deal with a series of foreign policy challenges presented by war and peace in the Middle East. Some of the regime's policy choices in confronting these existential challenges have been popular with Jordanians; however, most have not been. Thus, the regime has implemented a series of domestic institutional survival strategies in order to contain the domestic discontent caused by unpopular existential policy choices and the opposition's ability to mobilize. Some of these survival strategies have been more successful than others in containing the opposition. In some cases, the institutional manipulation itself has become a salient political issue in Jordanian politics. This chapter will summarize the effects of the regime's survival strategies on the three arenas they have generally aimed at: political parties, the Parliament, and the press. The factors behind the success or failure of the regime's survival strategies will then be evaluated. Finally, the Jordanian regime's experience with survival strategies will briefly be compared with other cases of authoritarianism in the Middle East.

THE IMPACT OF INSTITUTIONAL SURVIVAL STRATEGIES

Political parties, the Parliament, and the press have been regular targets of regime survival strategies in Jordan. The regime has chosen them because they are likely centers for the opposition to voice the public's discontent and to mobilize it against the regime's unpopular existential policies. An initial period of political liberalization was followed by gradually increasing restrictions in all three arenas. A dozen years after the riots of April 1989, each of the three has suffered from manipulation and restrictions imposed by the regime.

Political parties began this period with weak organizations from decades of prohibition. The National Charter and the Political Parties Law of 1992 reintroduced party life into Jordan. Today, while they have been legalized, political parties generally still have little impact on major policy decisions in Jordan. Political parties are hampered by severe factionalization. This resulted in over twenty-five political parties in 2001, most of which hold no representation in the Parliament. Only the Muslim Brotherhood's Islamic Action Front holds a mass base among Jordanians. Even loyalist parties like the National Constitutional Party have found it difficult to maintain organizational unity and public support. Factionalization has thus prompted some nostalgia for the political party life of the 1950s, especially among Arab nationalists. However, as Ellen Lust-Okar points out, "The common observation that the Jordanian party system is significantly weaker today than it was in the 1950s is simply wrong. Unfortunately, the party system was weak in the 1950s and remains so today."[1]

A number of the regime's survival strategies have compounded the fractious and marginal condition of Jordanian political parties. The Political Parties Law legalizes the establishment of parties in Jordan. However, the law also restricts parties from ties to non-Jordanian political organizations. This condition limits the ability of leftists, Arab nationalists, and even Islamists to create natural links across the artificial borders of the Middle East. It has also forced the Jordanian Muslim Brotherhood to weaken its links to natural partners like the Palestinian organization Hamas. The Election Law amendments of 1993 further weakened political parties from obtaining representation in Parliament—one of the most important activities of political parties anywhere. The SNTV electoral system works against organized groups winning Parliament seats. It also encourages the localization of electoral contests, which has prevented Jordan's many parties from consolidating into broader blocs. Press restrictions also present further difficulties for political parties when communicating their political message.

Despite the regime's claims that it wishes to see a consolidation of parties in Jordan into three or four cohesive blocs, the regime benefits from the factionalization of the political party system in the kingdom. For the regime, the greater number of political actors in the political arena, the greater the demand for royal favor and thus a lower cost for forming ruling coalitions. Therefore, the monarchy has an interest in maintaining the factionalization, of political actors in Jordan—even among its strongest supporters. Moreover, with factionalization, especially acute among opposition parties, the regime can limit the ability of any particular group to mobilize in an organized manner. Thus, the regime has used survival strategies to weaken political parties and keep them factionalized. Nevertheless, the mere act of legalization has allowed political parties a role in Jordanian politics in the 1990s that they did not hold in the decades before.

Like political parties in 1988, Jordan's Parliament had been absent from the political scene for a number of years. The return of elections and parliamentary activity in 1989 was one of the regime's first liberalizing survival strategies. The 1989, 1993, and 2001 electoral laws have attempted to balance the regime's desire to control the political makeup of the House of Deputies with the need to keep the electoral process legitimate in the eyes of voters and the international community. The surprising success of the opposition in the 1989 elections persuaded the regime to fine tune the electoral rules in 1993. The new one-person, one-vote system did that job. However, the bias of the electoral system coupled with the fallout of other survival strategies, like the 1997 amendments to the Press and Publications Law, pushed the opposition into a boycott of the elections in 1997. The 1997 elections resulted in an overwhelmingly progovernment Parliament. However, the support for the regime by the mostly tribal and conservative deputies, did not translate into the uncritical support of every government proposal. The Parliament elected in 1997 gave the governments of Prime Ministers Tarawnah, Rawabdah, and Abu Ragheb numerous difficulties in passing economic legislation that would hurt the deputies' constituents. The House even rejected some government bills. Thus, in 2001, with the dissolution of Parliament, the government resorted to not just decreeing provisional laws for institutional survival strategies, but for many mundane laws as well.

Between June 2001 and June 2003, the Parliament was suspended. The holding of elections while the second Palestinian intifada raged and the U.S. prepared for its invasion of Iraq convinced the regime that rising frustration from a delay in elections was less risky than the holding of elections with an opposition that could mobilize discontent with the regime's unpopular foreign policy choices. Even though many Jordanians hold the Parliament and their deputies in low regard, the Parliament has become an institution in the Jordanian political system that most citizens prefer not to do without.

In contrast to the public outcry over the suspension of parliamentary life, the recent reaction of Jordanians to reduced press freedom has been fairly passive. The National Charter and the Press and Publications Law of 1993 greatly expanded the bounds of freedom of expression in the kingdom. Since the decree of amendments to the press law in 1997, however, the progression of press freedom could be described as "one step forward, two steps backwards." The 1997 amendments, which the courts later overturned, and the 1998 press law legislated by the Parliament were both roundly criticized by journalists. The 1999 amendments to the press law, which removed some of the restrictions found in the 1998 law, were welcomed by the press, albeit lukewarmly. The decree of amendments to the Penal Code in 2001 introduced additional vague but harsh restrictions on the press.

Some journalists would claim that the state of the freedom of the press in Jordan today might be even worse than that of the martial law era that preceded the April 1989 riots. However, there are more newspapers publishing today than before 1989. Moreover, these newspapers, especially the weekly tabloids, provide a voice to those outside of the official channels. Nevertheless, journalists seem to have had more freedom of expression during the mid-1990s than they do today—a result of the regime's series of survival strategies that have kept moving the ceiling of press freedom in Jordan.

Thus, as a whole, the regime's survival strategies have succeeded in limiting the ability of the opposition to mobilize and voice discontent with the regime's existential policies. However, not all of the particular survival strategies the regime has implemented have fully met the regime's apparent intentions.

EXPLAINING THE SUCCESS OR FAILURE OF REGIME SURVIVAL STRATEGIES

Most of the survival strategies introduced by the Jordanian regime in recent years have been successful. The only true failure for the regime among the institutional manipulations discussed in this book was the 1997 decree of amendments to the Press and Publications Law. The courts overturned the provisional law within a year of its decree. Moreover, the press restrictions pushed much of the opposition to boycott the 1997 elections. This challenge—one of the few organized moves by the opposition to mobilize protest against the regime—cannot properly be considered a *regime* survival strategy. However, it demonstrated the frustration felt by the opposition to the regime's management of domestic politics. The boycott, coupled with the effects of the decreed press restrictions, backfired on the opposition; the elections went ahead as scheduled and the opposition was, for the most part, locked out of the Parliament. Thus, the failure of the decree was mitigated—but nearly at the expense of losing the legitimacy of the Parliament.

It is still too early to tell if the decrees introduced in the 2001 changing of the Election Law and the Penal Code will provoke intervention by the courts or other circumstances that could result in a failure for the regime. However, early indications point toward the continued run of success for the regime in implementing its domestic survival strategies. Other survival strategies discussed in this book can be generally considered successful for the regime in managing the opposition. This success stems from the regime's resourceful use of constitutional rules to reinforce the disunity of the opposition while maintaining the unity of the regime coalition.

In all of the cases of regime survival strategies investigated in this book the regime resourcefully used the rules in the constitution to manipulate political parties, the Parliament, and the press. In many cases the regime used the standard method of legislation through the Parliament to introduce the survival strategy. This method was used in the cases of the Political Parties Law and the Press and Publications Laws of 1993, 1998, and 1999. However, if the regime expected the Parliament would not produce the regime's desired outcome then the regime used its constitutional ability to decree laws. This was the case with the Election Law of 1993 and the Press and Publications Law amendments of 1997. The National Charter and the Royal Committee that wrote it stood outside of the procedures dictated by the Jordanian constitution. Yet the idea of a national conference and pact had existed in the past in Jordan—notably in the 1928 National Pact. The regime's choice of venues for making the institutional change generally prepared the ground for the successful implementation of the survival strategy. However, the regime's resourceful use of constitutional rules did not alone make a survival strategy successful. It was how the institutional manipulation was used which made the difference.

Most survival strategies aimed to keep the fractious opposition from unifying their ranks. The opposition forces in Jordan are divided between the Islamists on the one hand, and leftists and Arab nationalists on the other. This ideological gap often prevented the various opposition groups from acting collectively against the regime coalition. Moreover, each trend is also generally subdivided into competing groups. The opposition may disagree with the regime on policy and institutional issues; however, opposition groups may disagree with each other even more strongly. This pattern prominently occurred during the debates over the National Charter and the 1997 election boycott.

Thus, from these cases, one can conclude that a lack of opposition unity tends to reduce the influence the opposition has on the outcome of regime survival strategies. Selective incentives from the regime to specific opposition groups (and even to specific members within opposition groups) provide grounds for regime successes in reshaping institutions in political society. Electoral gains by minority candidates, for example, have made leftists and Arab nationalists less likely to cooperate with Islamists on proposing a unified opposition alternative to the SNTV electoral system. These types of incentives also weakened the universality of the 1997 election boycott. In contrast to such carrots, the regime may also wield sticks to divide the opposition—in other words, selective disincentives. By King Hussein singling out the IAF in his speech announcing the amendments to the Election Law in 1993, he deterred the Islamists from boycotting the 1993 election. Without the largest opposition party supporting a boycott to protest the new electoral system, opposition threats were vaporous.

Often a barrier to collective action among the opposition is a lack of clear policy and institutional preferences. Without detailed proposed alternatives to the SNTV electoral system or the 1998 Press and Publications Law, the opposition was liable to having groups shaved off by the regime's selective incentives. Ideological and organizational cleavages among the opposition have led to a lack of initiative in proposing both policies and institutional reforms. Often the only factor uniting Jordanian opposition groups is their shared dislike for regime actions, such as the 1997 Press and Publications Law amendments. Without presenting viable alternatives, the opposition generally does not act, it only reacts.

Moreover, the structure of institutional venues also influences the ability of the opposition to unite its disparate ranks. The composition of the Parliament highlights existing ideological gaps between opposition trends. Leftists, Arab nationalists, and Islamists all may oppose the regime's policies, but for different reasons. Within the Parliament, regime supporters may turn to their left or right to forge winning coalitions. Such a pattern is not uncommon in other regimes as well. Minority governments in many democracies, such as Norway, have relied on the same tactic of forming legislative electoral majorities in each policy area. Jordan's Islamists occasionally joined with proregime deputies to limit press freedoms in the legislation of the 1993 Press and Publications Law. In the Parliament, however, the opposition still may achieve some of its goals through negotiations—as attested by the Political Parties Law and the 1993 Press and Publications Law cases.

However, one should not write off the opposition in Jordan too quickly. During many cases under study, the opposition made a difference—but only under certain conditions. When the opposition can lay claim to the center of the political arena, the opposition may at least force the regime to resort to overriding the opposition (as with the 1998 Press and Publications Law). In the case of the 1997 Press and Publications Law amendments, a unified opposition even brought about the failure of a regime survival strategy. The unified opposition must also exploit splits within the regime coalition. When regime liberals are alienated from regime hard-liners over a policy or survival strategy, the opposition and regime liberals can claim the center space of the political spectrum, thus marginalizing the regime hard-liners. The transitions literature has already noted this point. However, the opposition—regime liberal alliance must also act on their collective unity. The alliance must try to circumvent the venue the regime hard-liners have chosen. Thus, in the case of the 1997 Press and Publications Law amendments, this type of alliance challenged the regime's executive decree in the courts where regime liberals held a greater sway. In 1998, this alliance was not able to challenge the legislation of a similar press law in the Parliament. The opposition makes a difference depending on its ability not only to unify its ranks, but to mobilize dissatisfied regime coalition members to act as well.

The contingent choice model of transitions has also argued that weakened regime coalition unity is one of the precipitating factors of political liberalization. When soft-liners defect from hard-liners and align with opposition moderates, a regime transition often results.[2] In Jordan, the regime's use of survival strategies supports a related position: strong regime coalition unity seems to be correlated with successful institutional survival strategies achieved through political liberalization. However, the causation of this pattern seems unclear. Did strong regime coalition unity lead the regime to pursue liberalizing negotiations with a clear agenda? The case of the National Charter seems to support this thesis. Or did the regime not pursue negotiations when it was unclear that all the coalition's members would support the action? The case of the decree of the amendments to the Election Law in 1993 offers greater support to the latter explanation. More investigation is needed to tease out the factors involved in this variation.

In contrast, the relationship between weak regime coalition unity and the failure of survival strategies seems clearer. In fact, the pattern complements the unity of the opposition as discussed in relation to the 1997 amendments to the Press and Publications Law. The institutional reform is likely to lead to failure if regime coalition unity is weak, the opposition strongly contests the survival strategy while using the rules of a venue to its advantage, and the regime fails to respond in kind. During the 1997 Press and Publications Law amendments episode, hard-liners of the regime coalition only weakly defended the decree in the venue of the courts. A similar pattern occurred with the opposition boycott of the 1997 elections. The opposition exploited the regime coalition's disunity by taking the initiative. The regime nearly failed to simultaneously limit the inclusion of the opposition in the Parliament while keeping a legitimate public perception of the elections.

The resourceful use of constitutional rules by the Jordanian regime, the weakness of the unity of the opposition, and the unity of the regime coalition each contributed to the success of many of the regime's domestic institutional survival strategies. Each of these factors was facilitated by their taking place within a context of regime-led state building. Yet this historical process alone did not guarantee the stability of the regime. It did, however, lead to the monarchy holding a central place in the Jordanian political arena. But in the late 1990s this central point of the monarchy was threatened by King Hussein's policies of peace with Israel and economic structural adjustment. With growing opposition unity and faltering regime coalition support for the regime's existential policies and institutional survival strategies, like the 1993 Election Law amendments and the 1997 Press and Publications Law amendments, Jordan faced a potentially serious political crisis in 1998. The poor relations between the regime and the opposition were temporarily abated with the surprise ascension of King Abdullah to the throne in 1999. The regime coalition rallied around the new king, putting aside differences over policy until he consolidated his rule. The opposition, likewise, offered its support for Abdullah. The succession owed part of its stability to the fact that domestic and foreign policy differences seemed to not get mixed into the internal politics of the Hashemite family.

King Abdullah, however, quickly found that the bandwagoning around his succession did not last for long. The second Palestinian intifada brought back disagreements over both foreign policy and the regime's institutional manipulations to limit the discontent caused by external events. As the existential threats to Abdullah's reign compounded, the regime responded with greater deliberalization and coercion. In contrast, a dozen years earlier King Hussein had chosen the course of political liberalization in a similar situtation. However, use of deliberalization as a survival strategy had already begun before Abdullah took the throne. As the Hashemites' attempt to maintain their rule over Jordan in the context of existential crises, the use of survival strategies of both the liberalizing and deliberalizing varieties will continue.

INSTITUTIONS AND THE POLITICS OF SURVIVAL IN A REGIONAL PERSPECTIVE

Jordan shares a number of attributes with other authoritarian regimes in the Middle East. In Morocco, Kuwait, Egypt, and Iran under the Shah, an authoritarian regime used domestic institutional survival strategies to cope with public discontent. The Moroccan, Kuwaiti, and Egyptian regimes have more or less successfully managed their country's opposition. In contrast, the Shah of Iran failed to contain opposition to his rule and fell to the 1979 Islamic Revolution. These four cases offer a point of comparison with Jordan's use of survival strategies to help show how rulers can resourcefully divide the opposition and unify their supporters.

MOROCCO

Perhaps the case closest to Jordan in terms of its regime structure is Morocco. In both Jordan and Morocco, the king rules but uses the cabinet to present the façade of commoner control over politics. Both the Hashemite and Alawite royal families are small in comparison to their Gulf counterparts. In this variant of monarchical authoritarianism—a subtype that can be labeled a "linchpin monarchy"—the ruling family generally only participates in the political institutions of the monarchy and not the state bureaucracy (the military excepted). The linchpin monarch stands above and away from routine politics to a greater degree than dynastic monarchs. Finally, linchpin monarchies encourage social pluralism and mobilize it along vertical lines in order to participate in the governing of the state—underneath the leadership of the monarchy.

The regime coalition in Morocco, as in Jordan, is a broad and diverse spectrum of social forces. The monarchy's supporters draw especially from landed and business elites. Regime supporters in Morocco participate formally in politics through a number of competing royalist parties as well as informally through personal connections to the royal family and the state bureaucracy.

The opposition in Morocco, in contrast to Jordan, is highly focused on the activity of political parties. Although opposition political parties in

Morocco were not historically banned as opposition parties were in Jordan from 1957 to 1992, they have been highly controlled and repressed. Moreover, opposition parties frequently charge that elections for Morocco's Parliament have been marred by fraud. Traditionally, the opposition in Morocco derived from the nationalist trend—notably the Istiqlal party and the Left—with the major party today being the Socialist Union of Popular Forces. Islamist parties in Morocco have not been as prevalent in opposition politics until recent years and Islamist organizations have split over participating in a political process that is stacked against the opposition.

In the late 1980s and 1990s Morocco's political sphere was reshaped by a number of institutional changes that can be viewed as survival strategies. The need for the Moroccan monarchy to undertake survival strategies derived from the country's persistent economic crisis. Morocco, like Jordan, recently turned to international lenders to rescue the economy. Along with these bailouts, economic structural adjustment policies follow. Abdeslam Maghraoui argues that the scope of economic reforms has far outpaced political reforms in Morocco.[3]

In the 1990s Morocco's King Hassan II did reshape a number of domestic political institutions. Through these reforms, he intended to preserve his rule in the face of public discontent caused by difficulties imposed by the structural adjustment policies. King Hassan twice amended the Moroccan constitution in the 1990s in order to capture the opposition while still preserving the monarchy's power. These survival strategies have delegated some of King Hassan's many powers, but the reforms have not devolved them. His successful manipulation of domestic institutions paved the way for the calm succession of Hassan's son, Mohammed, in 1999.

Under the 1972 constitution, King Hassan's rule was virtually unchecked by the indirectly elected legislature. During the early 1990s, however, pressure on the king mounted with internal economic crises and European criticisms of the condition of human rights in Morocco. In response, Hassan promulgated a new constitution in 1992. The new constitution contained many changes, however, the most important being the increased power of unicameral legislature. Under the 1992 constitution, the prime minister would be jointly responsible to the king and to the Parliament. Previously, all cabinet ministers served solely with the confidence of the king. The Parliament also gained greater powers of oversight and interrogation over the cabinet. The legislature and even the cabinet, however, remained subsidiary to the king with his extensive reserved domains of power.[4]

The new constitutional changes, however, did not meet the opposition's demands for a fully directly elected legislature. Most of the various opposition parties in Morocco urged a boycott of the referendum that was to ratify the 1992 constitution. The regime, through a combination of mobilization and fraud, gathered a supposed 97.4 percent of voters to participate in the referendum. Of these voters, 99.98 percent reportedly voted "yes." The regime overrode the opposition and imposed the new constitution, as it had in past referenda.

In the 1993 elections, the opposition groups were nearly able to win a majority of the directly elected seats in Parliament. Only with the "correction" of the indirect second round of elections was the regime able to reach a majority with 195 of the 333 seats in the Parliament. The results alienated many voters. Moreover, it worsened relations with European human rights activists who influenced European Union trade policy toward Morocco. Thus, King Hassan undertook a number of steps toward greater political liberalization in Morocco. Political prisoners were released, political exiles allowed to return, and additional amendments to the constitution were offered.[5]

The 1996 constitutional amendments represent "yet another manifestation of Hassan II's attempt to consolidate royal authority just as he also seeks to facilitate a genuine democratization of the political system."[6] The amendments created a bicameral Parliament. The Lower House would be completely directly elected. The new upper house would be indirectly elected by various methods. The amendments represented a major compromise with the opposition's demands.

Thus, it was no surprise that the vast majority of opposition groups urged the public to vote "yes" in the 1996 referendum to ratify the amendments. Nevertheless, the 99.56 percent support for the amendments still appeared fraudulent.[7] The 1996 amendments to the constitution can be seen as a negotiated success for the regime. The regime made some concessions to the opposition, but still held on to a number of reserved centers of power for the king and his conservative allies. The 1997 elections, however, gave the largest share of seats to the opposition. This opened the door to the appointment of socialist Abd al-Rahman Yousufi as prime minister in 1998. Morocco now has a period of *"alternance"* of political parties. Yet it is the opposition figures in the government who have had to implement Morocco's structural adjustment policies. Meanwhile, Kings Hassan II and Mohammed VI have maintained their ability to appease disgruntled citizens while maintaining their veto power over all policy decisions.

KUWAIT

Kuwait also shares with Jordan and Morocco a ruling monarchy that has delegated some of its power to the cabinet and an elected Parliament. Nevertheless, the Kuwaiti ruling al-Sabah family maintains a central place in the policy-making process. A key difference between linchpin monarchies (like Jordan or Morocco) and Kuwait is that in the latter the monarch and his family rule as a corporate unit.

This variant of monarchical authoritarianism has been called a "dynastic monarchy." Michael Herb highlights the distinction between dynastic monarchies and others.[8] Herb defines dynastic monarchies as regimes where the ruling family monopolizes the highest state offices, controls the institutions of the state by distributing family members throughout the bureaucracy, and develops mechanisms for settling family disputes—especially over succession. Social pluralism is encouraged in dynastic monarchies, but commoners generally have less say in policy decisions than in linchpin monarchies. Kuwait, along with Saudi Arabia, stands as the paradigmatic example of this subtype of monarchical authoritarianism.

The amir, Jabir Ahmad al-Sabah, is the central figure within the Kuwaiti ruling family; however, he does not have unlimited power to go against the wishes of the rest of the family. Rather, the amir is *primus inter pares*. Other members of the ruling family participate in the executive branch of government, and in Kuwait the crown prince also serves as prime minister. Other members of the ruling family are regularly appointed as ministers—especially for the crucial ministries of defense, foreign affairs, interior, oil, and finance. Members of the ruling family also often fill the high ranks of the military. Commoners, however, are also appointed to high government posts. The ruling family relies on a narrower coalition of supporters than in the linchpin monarchies of Jordan and Morocco. Nevertheless, the patronage of the ruling family enables it to buy support from a wide range of social groups. Oil revenues facilitate this cooptation through patronage—in fact Kuwait is often cited as a paradigmatic case of a rentier state.

The opposition in Kuwait, like in Jordan and in Morocco, draws from a diverse set of ideological trends. In Kuwait, political parties are not legal, but the opposition has organized through many different formal social organizations. In contrast to Jordan and Morocco, in the past Kuwait has relied less on repressing opposition groups and more on coopting them. Kuwaiti amirs over recent decades have played a delicate balancing game with the various opposition forces—especially in relation to elections for the National Assembly, Kuwait's unicameral Parliament. When opposition forces began to team up against the ruling family, the Amir suspended the Parliament. This happened in 1976 and again in 1986.[9] In the wake of the 1990 Iraqi invasion and the U.S.-led Operation Desert Storm that liberated Kuwait, Amir Jabir was forced to allow a return of the National Assembly. The 1990s have only exacerbated the long relationship between the Kuwaiti ruling family and opposition forces in the National Assembly.[10]

To honor promises made to preserve national unity during the Iraqi occupation, Amir Jabir reinstated the National Assembly in 1992. The October 1992 elections sent thirty-five representatives of the various opposition trends to the fifty-seat parliament. However, the Kuwaiti opposition is far from homogeneous. There are a number of cleavages that separate the established merchant families from the Arab nationalists and from the rising but fractious Islamists.[11] The opposition-led Parliament attempted to strengthen its power vis-à-vis the Al-Sabah controlled cabinet in a number of different issue areas. Since 1992, the Parliament has played an important role in Kuwaiti debates over the budget and privatization, debt repayment, and corruption.

In 1994, these debates became linked over the issue of ministerial accountability. During the Parliament's suspension, the amir used his power under Article 71 of the Kuwaiti constitution to decree laws in the absence of a Parliament. This power is similar to the executive power of decreeing provisional laws in Jordan. One of the most controversial decrees was known as the "Don't Try the Minister" Law. The 1990 law restricted putting cabinet ministers on trial for actions taken in the course of their job, an institutional change that would enable the Kuwaiti regime to weaken the National Assembly's oversight powers. In 1986, parliamentary investigations into the finances of Sheikh Ali Khalifa al-Sabah, the Minister of Oil, had helped bring about the suspension of the National Assembly. The decreed law was to prevent the reoccurrence of National Assembly investigations of corruption in the royal family. In 1994, when the National Assembly reviewed the decree it repealed the decree, of the "Don't Try the Minister" Law.

The bringing of criminal charges against Sheikh Ali in July 1994 again brought the ruling family and the Parliament to loggerheads. In April 1995, the regime asked the constitutional court to review the assembly's revoking of the 1990 law—basing its request on Article 71 of the Kuwaiti constitution. This affront to the constitutional privileges of the assembly infuriated the opposition. Most opposition deputies felt that the regime was using the court to rewrite the constitution. A serious row developed and rumors abounded that the amir would once again suspend the assembly. However, by late May 1995, a compromise was reached between the regime and the assembly where the regime withdrew its request for constitutional court review and the assembly dropped the repeal of the "Don't Try the Minister" Law. However, later in the summer—this time with regime support—the opposition passed a law modifying key sections of the law that were objectionable to the opposition. In the end a compromise was reached, thereby avoiding a possibly thorny crisis.[12] Despite the negotiated outcome, the regime had generally failed to prohibit investigations into the finances of the al-Sabah family. When liberals and Islamists unified their disparate ranks and cooperated in the Kuwaiti National Assembly, they could command a majority. This opposition unity and action weakened the ruling family's ability to implement survival strategies.

However, later in the 1990s, the ruling family used the issue of women's suffrage to help split the two opposition strands. Elections in Kuwait in 1996 produced a more proregime National Assembly with the growth of deputies from tribal backgrounds. This did not, however, prevent the game of parliamentary inquisition into the affairs of the cabinet. In May 1999, the National Assembly was about to remove the Minister of Islamic Affairs for incompetence when the amir dissolved the Parliament to prevent the vote of no-confidence.[13] During the brief interlude between the dissolution of the assembly and the elections in July 1999, the amir again used his constitutional power to decree almost sixty laws.

The most controversial of the decrees gave women the right to vote for the National Assembly in later elections.[14] Of course, this expanded suffrage applied only to those women who can meet the electoral law's strict citizenship and residency requirements. Previously, the male-only electorate had comprised 15 percent of the citizen population. The decree of women's suffrage became a hot campaign issue. The decree facilitated the election of a greater number of liberals, who generally supported the decree, and Islamists, who generally opposed it.[15]

When the new National Assembly reviewed the decree in November 1999, it led to fierce debate between liberals and a few government supporters on the one hand, and Islamists and traditional tribal deputies on the other. Some liberals, however, voted to reject the suffrage law, not for its content, but for its method of legislation. The decree was overturned. A few weeks later, however, the liberals were unable to gather enough support to pass a bill drafted by the Parliament to grant women the same rights as the decree.[16] The regime's attempt to offer greater political liberties can be seen as an attempt to draw greater support for the government from educated middle and upper class women. The regime's attempt failed to broaden its support base by expanding suffrage.

Both the opposition and the regime coalition split over the issue. However, the Islamists were joined by a great number of traditionalist regime supporters, giving them the overwhelming edge in the Parliament. Both sides attempted to contest the issue using the rules of the National Assembly. However, with previous victories by the Parliament over the regime's decrees, the Islamists and their tribal allies defeated the granting of women's suffrage. Thus, even if a regime survival strategy aims to increase political liberalization, it may be rejected by sectors of the opposition acting to block the regime's power.

In Kuwait, the liberal and Islamist opposition groups have occasionally joined to assert the power of the National Assembly. However, ideological disputes between the two trends have fractured their alliance over recent years. The ruling family has thus preserved its place at the center of the Kuwaiti political spectrum. Yet the National Assembly has had a growing role in determining the country's policy priorities.

IRAN

Unlike the Jordanian or Moroccan kings or the Kuwaiti amirs, the Pahlavi shahs of Iran no longer rule. The last shah of Iran, Mohammed Reza Shah, was overthrown by a social revolution in 1979. The Persian shah had narrowed his regime coalition to the point that he practically ruled alone. Social discontent stemmed from a growing economic crisis caused by, on the one hand, an embarrassment of riches from the 1973 oil boom, and on the other hand, the bottlenecks of rapid and distorted development. However, the shah failed to implement institutional survival strategies to capture the opposition and to rebuild a regime coalition to support his rule.

With his 1963 "White Revolution" the shah removed rural landlords as a pillar of his regime through land redistribution. Growing oil revenues bought the loyalties of some individuals, but not of whole sectors of society. According to Nikki R. Keddie, "It was hard for many to give the shah credit for any achievements when so much more could have been done with his oil billions . . . and when there was little freedom of speech or press and opposition was so ruthlessly suppressed."[17] Thus, unlike in Kuwait, Iran's spectacular oil revenues were not partly redistributed to co-opt potential opposition forces. Rather, the shah spent billions on military equipment and white-elephant development projects.

The shah, however, did try to implement some survival strategies. The shah tried to manufacture the consent of society by instituting a single mass party, the Rastakhiz party, in 1975. The shah demanded the participation of all Iranians in his new party. However, "The Rastakhiz party inadvertently politicized a vast segment of the population and intensified the spirit of contumacy against the incumbent regime."[18] Given the failure of his political party, the shah's secret police, SAVAK, repressed any form of opposition instead.

As society's discontent boiled into the late 1970s, newly-elected U.S. President Carter called on the shah to give greater respect for human rights. Despite fearing that the U.S. administration was trying to subvert his rule, the shah complied. The shah's program of granting greater freedom of speech and releasing jailed opponents, however, did not attempt to channel the greater liberties into an institutional venue. The shah dragged his feet in offering elections for the Parliament. The shah's liberalizing moves did not aim to split the secular opposition—mainly based in the modern middle classes—from the religious opposition—which relied on support from traditional bazaar merchants and the mass lumpen proletariat. Some middle-class groups, it seems, would have been content to cooperate with the shah and exclude the Shiᶜite religious activists.[19] The shah, however, refused to share power. Falling into indecision, the shah also oscillated between repression and liberalization, thus pushing the various opposition groups to unite into a front that toppled the regime in 1979. The shah's half-hearted survival strategies failed to resourcefully use his immense political and economic power to magnify the disunity of the opposition or to build the support of a broader unified regime coalition. He and his regime failed to survive.

EGYPT

Egypt, like Jordan, has used institutional survival strategies to manage popular discontent stemming from unpopular foreign and economic policies—especially in the areas of laws regulating political parties, elections to Parliament, and the press. The Egyptian regime, however, derives its power from a different regime coalition structure and a presidential-republican system. In contrast to Jordan's linchpin monarchy, Egypt can be considered a postpopulist republic. Despite the fact that the power personalized in the office of the president in Egypt seems similar to that of Jordan's king, the Egyptian political system offers a contrasting environment for the pursuit of regime survival strategies.

For Robert Springborg, "the key factor that explains the ebb and flow of Egypt's dominant parties over the past three decades has been presidential attitudes toward them."[20] In the 1950s and 1960s, Gamal Abd al-Nasser set up a populist authoritarian regime that catered to a broad and varied regime coalition and institutionalized it in the Arab Socialist Union party. After Anwar Sadat consolidated his power in the mid-1970s, he sought to dilute the power of Nasser's party by breaking it up into a number of competing progovernment parties. The core of the Arab Socialist Union became the National Democratic Party (NDP) in 1978, but the party had to face limited competition from both the right and left wings of the former Arab Socialist Union. The government's party base among the peasants and workers was severely eroded by the shifts in party apparatus which reflected Sadat's turn toward free market economic policies.

After Sadat's assassination in 1981 and Hosni Mubarak's rise to the presidency, the NDP remained at the center of the president's base. Thus, unlike Jordan where the king has encouraged a proliferation of social groups that the monarch stands above, in Egypt, the president has explicitly identified himself as the leader first of a political party and then of the nation.[21] The greater social heterogeneity found in monarchies, especially of the linchpin variety, may have given the kings of Jordan and Morocco greater latitude in pursuing unpopular foreign policy changes and economic reforms than the Egyptian presidential system where Mubarak has had to balance competing demands first within the NDP and then between the NDP and the opposition. In other words, "paradoxically, a legacy of relative pluralism makes its easier for elites to use survival strategies."[22]

Power flows from the president down to the party through the Parliament in Egypt, despite the fact that the president owes his position to a nomination vote from Parliament followed by a referendum. Since there are no limits to presidential terms, Mubarak was reelected for his fourth term in 1999. The unicameral People's Assembly constitutionally holds legislative powers. However, the decree power of the president, as well as the fact that the president's Cabinet presents all but a miniscule number of bills that are passed into law, undercuts the separation of legislative and executive power in Egypt.[23]

In addition to the NDP, a number of smaller opposition parties have been allowed to operate legally in Egypt under Mubarak. During Sadat's rule, three political parties—besides the NDP—received licenses because they were chosen by Sadat to operate loyal opposition platforms. In addition, the New Wafd party gained its license independently. Following 1990, nine other political parties gained licenses through the court system, which recognized the parties' right to form despite being denied a license by executive authorities.[24] Nevertheless, these opposition parties represent a spectrum of political ideologies and interests and have not been able to gain more than a foothold in the People's Assembly. Their lack of representation can be traced both to their inability to mobilize voters and Mubarak's use of institutional survival strategies to marginalize opposition forces while reinforcing the dominance of himself and the NDP.

A clear intention of laws regulating political parties in Egypt has been to limit the ability of the Muslim Brotherhood to organize politically. The Muslim Brotherhood, as the dominant opposition group in Egyptian politics for most of the twentieth century, has had a troubled relationship with Egypt's republican governments. Nasser suppressed the movement. The organization was revitalized under Sadat, who used the Islamists to counterbalance his Nasserite rivals. The repression of the Brotherhood under Nasser, however, caused the organization to splinter, producing more radical groups that were eventually responsible for Sadat's assassination. Under Mubarak, the Muslim Brotherhood has been tolerated as an organization, but not legalized as a political party. The basis for keeping the Brotherhood banned from organizing a political party stems from Law Number 40 of 1977 which denies a license to any party that forms on the basis of "class, religion, geographical, or on gender, ethnic or religious basis."[25] Since the Brotherhood is a "religious organization" it has been consistently denied a political party license. Nevertheless, the Muslim Brotherhood has managed to participate in most elections during Mubarak's era by forming electoral alliances with legalized political parties. These alliances have prompted the regime to also manipulate the electoral rules for the People's Assembly.

Since 1981, Egypt has held five parliamentary elections under three different electoral systems. The failure of the regime to have its manipulations of electoral laws survive challenges in the court system has shortened terms of two parliaments and forced new elections. The 1983 electoral law called for an entirely party-list proportional representation system for the 448 elected seats in the People's Assembly within forty-eight electoral districts. The only opposition party that succeeded under this system in the 1984 elections was the electoral alliance of the New Wafd party and the Muslim Brotherhood, which earned 58 seats to the NDP's 390. The courts invalidated the 1984 elections, forcing another amendment to the election law in 1986. Because the courts rejected the 1983 electoral law on the basis that it did not allow individuals to run for office, the 1986 election law mixed a proportional representation system for 400 seats with one individual seat awarded on a plurality basis for each of the 48 districts. In elections held under the new amendments in 1987, 39 of the plurality seats were won by the NDP. The NDP also won 348 of the proportional representation seats. However, most opposition parties did gain some representation in the 1987 elections: the Neo-Wafd—running alone—won 35 seats, the Muslim Brotherhood—this time teamed with the Labor party—won 57, and the Liberal party won 3. Although the opposition fared better in the 1987 elections, they still protested to the courts. Again the courts invalidated the electoral law for continued bias against individual candidates.[26]

Thus, with the 1990 election law, the proportional representation system was scrapped in favor of a system where 444 seats are allocated to the top two majority winners in 222 constituencies, with runoff elections held if necessary to achieve a majority vote for a seat. Nearly all opposition parties boycotted the 1990 elections in response to the changes, which clearly favored the NDP. In addition, the opposition demanded judicial supervision of the elections. Mubarak's government remained resolute in its holding of the elections and the opposition—save for the Tagammuᶜ (Nationalist Unionist Progressive Party) which joined the elections at the last minute—was locked out of the Parliament for its full five year term. Independent candidates earned 79 seats in the election, the Tagammuᶜ 6, and the NDP won the rest.[27]

Unembarrassed by the boycott, the early 1990s witnessed a general crackdown on civil liberties in Egypt. This crackdown came partly because of the failure of opposition groups to articulate demands for reforms, and because popular discontent was channeled less through the legal opposition parties and more through militant Islamist groups. The regime's response to the militant Islamist challenge entailed a severe restriction of rights and a violent showdown with Islamist groups which the government ultimately won—but not without its costs.[28]

At the height of this repression, the 1995 elections were held. The legal opposition parties decided to participate rather than again prove their marginality to Egyptian politics. Thus, they ran in the electoral system that was weighted in the NDP's favor. Unsurprisingly, the NDP took 417 of the 444 seats. The opposition parties combined won only 14 seats and independent candidates earned nearly as many. The Muslim Brotherhood ran its candidates without legal party allies but managed to earn only one of the opposition's seats due to the severe repression against the group.[29]

In 2000, the courts again entered the electoral process by demanding judicial supervision of elections. While judicial supervision did prevent some electoral irregularities from occurring, most harassment was only moved outside the voting station door. While the secular opposition combined to win 16 seats, the Muslim Brotherhood, operating independently, earned 17. The NDP earned 388 seats.[30]

Thus, while the legal opposition has become a regular participant in the NDP's electoral successes after nearly losing all of its parliamentary voice in 1990, its ability to successfully challenge the government party remains weak. The Muslim Brotherhood, as the most viable of the opposition trends, also still suffers from acute repression and the inability to organize legally as a political party. The secular parties are generally severely out of touch with the lives of everyday Egyptians and thus limited in expanding their social bases of support. Through electoral manipulation, the Egyptian regime has guaranteed a super-majority of seats for the NDP in the Parliament, which insures Mubarak's continued nomination as president and his continued distribution of patronage through the party in Parliament.

Parties and the Parliament are not the only venues for the institutional survival strategies undertaken by Mubarak's regime. In 1995, the Egyptian Parliament passed a new press law in order to stem reports of corruption that had been emerging in the opposition newspapers. The law was hastily passed by the National Assembly on a day when most of its members were absent. Although the government had been threatening the press with restrictions for a number of years, the urgency in passing the law stemmed from the growing reports of corruption involving members of Mubarak's family—most likely his son. May Kassem notes dryly that "it is curious that the decision to take direct action after such a long time coincided with a widespread corruption scandal affecting members of his (Mubarak's) immediate family."[31] In 1996, the government reached a compromise on the press restrictions after negotiations with the furious Union of Journalists, and a new press law was passed by the People's Assembly.

Underlying all of these institutional survival strategies is the "state of emergency" which has been in effect in Egypt since 1967 for all but two years before Sadat's assassination. The consequences of military rule have produced a weak official opposition and radicalized militant Islamists. By marginalizing most political voices other than that of the regime, the Egyptian state has often pushed opposition into more radical and violent directions. The institutional changes designed to manage political parties, the Parliament, and the press, have not helped the regime coopt its strongest opponents, but rather alienated Islamists who then sought to vent their grievances through violence. Thus, the Egyptian presidential regime has had to rely much more heavily on coercion than the monarchies of Jordan, Morocco, or Kuwait. Moreover, the fact that the office of the president is clearly identified with the ruling party—and not standing above politics as a monarch does—has brought the legitimacy of not only the leader, but the system as a whole into question by radicals. That the Egyptian regime could survive a head-on collision with the radical Islamists is not surprising given the enormous coercive resources available to the state. However, coercive policies threaten to radicalize the opposition in the long term. Repression and institutional means to reduce the power of the opposition have been resourcefully used and have prevented President Mubarak from falling in the same manner as Mohammed Reza Shah—at least in the short run.

INSTITUTIONS AND THE POLITICS OF SURVIVAL: AN APPRAISAL   155

JORDAN IN A COMPARATIVE PERSPECTIVE

These four cases support the argument that institutional survival strategies can help regimes to overcome external crises. The Moroccan monarchy has perhaps been more successful in capturing the opposition than the Jordanian regime. King Hassan's institutional manipulations have been aided by the comparative lack of a divisive foreign policy issue—in contrast to King Hussein's controversial hope for a warm peace with Israel. The Kuwaiti regime rests on a narrower social base than the Hashemite monarchy. However, oil revenues provide the state with greater resources to co-opt discontented social groups. Nevertheless, when the regime unites rather than divides the opposition, it has to eventually begin sharing more power with representative institutions. In Egypt, the marginalization of the secular opposition and the harsh repression of the Muslim Brotherhood have forced dissident groups down the path of violence. Had the presidential republican regime been more tolerant of dissent within the representative institutions, the regime may not have needed to tarnish its legitimacy with such massive coercion. However, the republican nature of the regime has limited tolerance for pluralism outside of the ruling party. In Iran, the shah failed to decisively act to split the opposition and to rally significant support in order to save a regime woefully divorced from society. The result for his regime was catastrophic. Jordan faces both economic and foreign policy crises that have spurred the regime to use institutional survival strategies. The regime, however, has managed to successfully insure its survival while not totally marginalizing or radicalizing the opposition. The regime has also incorporated the opposition into representative institutions without ceding too much power to its ideologically-driven opponents. And when the opposition threatened to mobilize public discontent with the regime's existential policies, this process of political liberalization was reversed while still rewarding members of the regime coalition.

    The Jordan monarchy still rules, and most likely will continue to do so, despite persistent existential crises. In the 1990s, economic structural adjustment and major foreign policy shifts caused many Jordanians a great deal of discontent. However, through a series of institutional manipulations, the regime has managed this discontent and prohibited the opposition from mobilizing it against the monarchy. For the most part the regime's survival strategies have been successful because of the monarchy's resourceful use of constitutional rules that have divided the opposition and reinforced regime coalition unity. In this manner the Hashemite monarchy has endured in the face of existential crises that have overturned regimes in other countries. The first decade of the twenty-first century has already witnessed major regional crises not covered in this book. Yet early indications are that King Abdullah II will continue to use survival strategies to maintain the tautness of the strand of power binding the Hashemite monarchy with the people of

Jordan. The prudent use of survival strategies in a context of regime-led state building can help us account for the past, present, and probable future durability of authoritarian regimes in Jordan as well as in many other countries in the Arab world.

NOTES

CHAPTER ONE

1. See among many others, Elie Kedourie, *Democracy and Arab Political Culture* (Washington D.C.: Washington Institute for Near East Policy, 1992); Samir Amin, *The Arab Nation* (London: Zed Press, 1978); Bernard Lewis, "What Went Wrong?" *The Atlantic Monthly*, January 2002, 43–45.

2. Jill Crystal, "Authoritarianism and its Adversaries in the Arab World," *World Politics* 46, no. 2 (January 1994): 262–289.

3. John Higley and Richard Gunther, eds., *Elites and Democratic Consolidation in Latin America and Southern Europe* (New York: Cambridge University Press, 1993).

4. Guillermo O'Donnell and Philippe Schmitter, *Transition from Authoritarian Rule: Tentative Conclusions about Uncertain Democracies* (Baltimore: Johns Hopkins University Press, 1986), 7.

5. See Rex Brynen, Bahgat Korany, and Paule Noble, "Trends, Trajectories or Interesting Possibilities? Some Conclusions on Arab Democratization and Its Study," in *Political Liberalization and Democratization in the Arab World, Volume 1: Theoretical Perspectives*, ed. Brynen, Korany, and Noble (Boulder: Lynne Rienner, 1995), 336.

6. O'Donnell and Schmitter, 48–56.

7. Adam Przeworski, *Democracy and the Market: Political and Economic Reforms in Eastern Europe and Latin America* (Cambridge: Cambridge University Press, 1991), 59–63. He assumes, however, that all political actors have "perfect knowledge."

8. Ibid., 58.

9. See Frances Hagopian, "Traditional Politics Against State Transformation in Brazil," in *State Power and Social Forces: Domination and Transformation in the Third World*, ed. Joel S. Migdal et al., (Cambridge: Cambridge University Press, 1994).

10. Karen L. Remmer, "New Theoretical Perspectives on Democratization," *Comparative Politics* 28, no. 1 (October 1995): 105–108; Francis Fukuyama, *The End of History and the Last Man* (New York: Free Press, 1992).

11. Remmer, 105–107.

12. Ibid., 118.

13. Amatzia Baram, "Baathi Iraq and Hashemite Jordan: From Hostility to Alignment," *Middle East Journal* 45, no. 1 (1991): 51–70; Yehuda Lukacs, *Israel, Jordan, and the Middle East Peace Process* (Syracuse: Syracuse University Press, 1997); Laurie Brand, *Jordan's Inter-Arab Relations: The Political Economy of Alliance Making* (New York: Columbia University Press, 1994).

14. Giacomo Luciani, "Allocation vs. Production States: A Theoretical Framework," in *The Arab State*, ed. Giacomo Luciani (Berkeley and Los Angeles: University of California Press, 1990), 65–84; Hazem Beblawi, "The Rentier State in the Arab World," in Luciani, 85–98.

15. See Rex Brynen, "Economic Crisis and Post-Rentier Democratization in the Arab World: The Case of Jordan," *Canadian Journal of Political Science* 25, no. 1 (March 1992): 69–97.

16. Michael Bratton and Nicholas van de Walle, *Democratic Experiments in Africa: Regime Transitions in Comparative Perspective* (New York: Cambridge University Press, 1997). This point is also made in reference to the growth of political liberalization and democratization in the Middle East by F. Gregory Gause III, "Regional Influences on Experiments in Political Liberalization in the Arab World," in *Political Liberalization and Democratization in the Arab World, Volume 1: Theoretical Perspectives*, ed. Rex Brynen et al. (Boulder: Lynne Rienner, 1995), 283–306.

17. Steven Heydemann, ed., *War, Institutions, and Social Change in the Middle East* (Berkeley and Los Angeles: University of California Press, 2000).

18. Jeffrey A. VanDenBerg, "Democratization and Foreign Policy in the Middle East: A Case Study of Jordan and Egypt" (Ph.D. Dissertation, University of Cincinnati, 2000); Marc Lynch, *State Interests and Public Spheres* (New York: Columbia University Press, 1999).

19. Adam Przeworski, "The Games of Transitions," in *Issues in Democratic Consolidation: The New South American Democracies in Comparative Perspective*, ed. Scott Mainwaring et al. (Notre Dame: University of Notre Dame Press, 1992), 136.

20. Richard Snyder and James Mahoney, "The Missing Variable: Institutions and the Study of Regime Change," *Comparative Politics* 32, no. 1 (October 1999): 103. Bratton and van de Walle, 47, also note that it is "clear that scholars favor contingent explanations for *regime transitions* and structural explanations for *regime consolidation*." Snyder and Mahoney, 103, amplify this point by specifying that much of the literature studying the performance of recently democratized regimes has focused "extensively on political institutions, such as electoral laws, constitutional rules, and party systems." Studies of transitions, in comparison, have relied on voluntarist analyses. For earlier critiques see, Daniel Levine, "Paradigm Lost: Dependency to Democracy," *World Politics* 40, no. 3 (April 1988): 377–394; Gerardo L. Munck, "Democratic Transitions in Comparative Perspective," *Comparative Politics* 26, no. 3 (April 1994): 355–376.

21. Snyder and Mahoney, 103.

22. Juan Linz and Alfred Stepan, *Problems of Democratic Transition and Consolidation: Southern Europe, South America, and Post-Communist Europe* (Baltimore: Johns Hopkins University Press, 1996), 55. Emphasis in the original.

23. Barbara Geddes, "What Do We Know About Democratization After Twenty Years?" *Annual Reviews: Political Science* 2 (1999): 116.

24. Russell E. Lucas, "Monarchical Authoritarianism: Survival and Political Liberalization in a Middle Eastern Regime Type," *International Journal of Middle East Studies* 36, no. 1 (February 2004): 108.

25. Daniel Brumberg, "Authoritarian Legacies and Reform Strategies in the Arab World," in Brynen et al., 229–260.

26. Claus Offe, "Designing Institutions for East European Transitions," in *Strategic Choice and Path-Dependency in Post-Socialism: Institutional Dynamics in the Transformation Process*, ed. Jerzy Hausner et al., (Brookfield: Elgar, 1995), 53.

27. Ellen Lust-Okar, "Divided They Fall: The Management and Manipulation of Political Opposition" (Ph.D. dissertation, University of Michigan, 1997).

CHAPTER TWO

1. See Eugene L. Rogan, "Bringing the State Back: The Limits of Ottoman Rule in Transjordan 1840–1910," in *Village, Steppe and State: The Social Origins of Modern Jordan*, ed. Eugene L. Rogan and Tariq Tell (New York: St. Martin's Press, 1994), 32–57.

2. Mary C. Wilson, *King Abdullah, Britain and the Making of Jordan* (New York: Cambridge University Press, 1987), 2.

3. See Ma'an Abu Nowar, *The History of the Hashemite Kingdom of Jordan: Volume 1: The Creation and Development of Transjordan; 1920–1929* (Ithaca: Ithaca Press, 1989), 58, 104–109; Naseer H. Aruri, *Jordan: A Study in Political Development (1921–1965)* (The Hague: Martinus Nijhoff, 1972), 31–32; see also, John Bagot Glubb, *A Soldier with the Arabs* (London: Hodder and Stoughton, 1957), and James Lunt, *Glubb Pasha: A Biography* (London: Harvill Press, 1984). For a more critical view of Glubb and the nation-making process see Joseph A. Massad, *Colonial Effects: The Making of National Identity in Jordan* (New York: Columbia University Press, 2001).

4. Michael R. Fischbach, "British Land Policy in Transjordan," in Rogan and Tell, 80–107; Abdo Baaklini et al., *Legislative Politics in the Arab World: The Resurgence of Democratic Institutions* (Boulder: Lynne Rienner Publishers, 1999), 134–135; Abu Nowar, 161–200; Aruri, 28.

5. See Andrew Shryock, *Nationalism and the Genealogical Imagination: Oral History and Textual Authority in Tribal Jordan* (Berkeley and Los Angeles: University of California Press, 1997).

6. Ali Mahafzah, interview by author, Amman, 16 May 1998; Abla Amawi, "State and Class in Transjordan: A Study of State Autonomy" (Ph.D. dissertation, Georgetown University, 1992).

7. See Joseph Nevo, *King Abdallah and Palestine* (New York: St. Martin's Press, 1996), 84–94; Wilson, 168–186.

8. Adnan Abu Odeh, *Jordanians, Palestinians and the Hashemite Kingdom in the Middle East Peace Process* (Washington D.C.: U.S. Institute of Peace, 1999).

9. Robert Satloff, *From Abdullah to Hussein: Jordan in Transition* (New York: Oxford University Press, 1994), 36–57; Aruri, 101–109.

10. Uriel Dann, *King Hussein and the Challenge of Arab Radicalism: Jordan, 1955–1967* (New York: Oxford University Press, 1989), 21–30; Satloff, 108–125.

11. Glubb, 419–446; Dann, 33.

12. Dann, 40–85; Satloff, 144–175; Aruri, 134–150.

13. Dann, 154–164.

14. See Clinton Bailey, *Jordan's Palestinian Challenge, 1948–1983: A Political History* (Boulder: Westview Press, 1984), 30–48.

15. Bailey, 57.

16. Although later the Islamists would be seen as the most prominent opposition group, the Muslim Brotherhood organization has never opposed the structure of the Jordanian regime as it has in Syria or Egypt. This position, however, is not taken for granted by the regime.

17. See Robert Satloff, *Troubles on the East Bank: Challenges to the Domestic Stability of Jordan* (New York: Praeger Press, 1986).

18. For its text see Hashemite Kingdom of Jordan, *Constitution of the Hashemite Kingdom of Jordan* (with amendments) (Amman: Department of Press and Publications, n.d.). The 1952 Constitution has been amended many times in the intervening years, however, the basic political structure remains.

CHAPTER THREE

1. King Hussein ibn Talal, "Address to the Nation, July 31, 1988," in *Selected Speeches by His Majesty King Hussein I: 1989–1994* (Amman: International Press Office, Royal Hashemite Court, 1994), 9.

2. See John Roberts, "Prospects for Democracy in Jordan," *Arab Studies Quarterly* 13, no. 3/4 (Summer/Fall 1991): 119–138; Marc Lynch, *State Interests and Public Spheres: The International Politics of Jordan's Identity* (New York: Columbia University Press, 1999), 71–139; Joseph A. Massad, *Colonial Effects: The Making of National Identity in Jordan* (New York: Columbia University Press, 2001), 258–263.

3. Rex Brynen, "Economic Crisis and Post-Rentier Democratization in the Arab World: The Case of Jordan," *Canadian Journal of Political Science* 25, no. 1 (March 1992): 90.

4. Malik Mufti, "Elite Bargains and the Onset of Political Liberalization in Jordan," *Comparative Political Studies* 32, no. 1 (February 1999): 105–107.

5. See the demands of various groups during the 1989 riots reprinted in "Watha'iq al-Intifadhah" [Documents of the (Jordanian) Intifada], *Al-Urdun Al-Jadid* [New Jordan Review] 14 (Summer 1989): 56–84.

6. For an overview see Mohammed Muhasanah, "Tatawwur al-Tashry'at al-Intkhabyah al-Urduniyah" [Development of Jordanian Electoral Legislation], in *Nadwat Tashry'at al-Intikhab Hajar al-Asas fi al-Nidham al-Dymuqraty* [Conference on Electoral Legislation, the Cornerstone of the Democratic Regime], ed. Hussein Abu Rumman (Amman: Al-Urdun Al-Jadid Research Center (hereafter UJRC), 1995), 16–20.

7. See Ma'an Abu Nowar, *The History of the Hashemite Kingdom of Jordan, Volume 1: The Creation and Development of Transjordan; 1920–1929* (London: Ithaca Press, 1989), 232–233; for the text of the law see 303–307.

8. Aside from brief emergency sessions to pass constitutional amendments in 1974 and 1976.

9. See Philip J. Robins, "Politics and the 1986 Electoral Law in Jordan," in *Politics and the Economy in Jordan*, ed. Rodney Wilson (New York: Routledge, 1991), 184–207.

10. UJRC, *Intikhabat 1989: Haqa'iq wa-Arqam* [Election 1989: Facts and Figures] (Amman: UJRC, 1993), 6.

11. This system is similar to the classic Lebanese electoral system. See Arend Lijphart, "Proportionality by Non-PR methods: Ethnic Representation in Belgium,

Cyprus, Lebanon, New Zealand, West Germany and Zimbabwe," in *Electoral Laws and Their Political Consequences*, ed. Bernard Grofman and Arend Lijphart (New York: Agathon Press, 1986), 113–123. The author thanks Ilyia Harik for pointing out this comparison.

12. With an average district magnitude of four, this plurality system tends to violate the assumption that plurality electoral systems require either single member districts or perhaps dual member districts. See Arend Lijphart, *Electoral Systems and Party Systems: A Study of Twenty-Seven Democracies 1945–1990* (New York: Oxford University Press, 1994), 16–18. However, it should be noted that Cyprus and Lebanon also have had average district magnitudes exceeding 2.0; see Lijphart, "Proportionality by non-PR Methods," in Grofman and Lijphart, 115.

13. *Middle East International*, 3 November 1989.

14. Kamel Abu Jaber and Schirin Fathi, "The 1989 Jordanian Parliamentary Elections," *Orient* 31, no.1 (March 1990): 76.

15. See, for example, Terry Karl, "Petroleum and Political Pacts: The Transition to Democracy in Venezulea," in *Transitions from Authoritarian Rule: Latin America*, ed. Guillermo O'Donnell, Philippe Schmitter, and Laurence Whitehead (Baltimore: Johns Hopkins University Press, 1986); Guillermo O'Donnell and Philippe Schmitter, *Transitions from Authoritarian Rule: Tentative Conclusions about Uncertain Democracies* (Baltimore: Johns Hopkins University Press, 1986).

16. Lisa Anderson, "Political Pacts, Liberalism, and Democracy: The Tunisian National Pact of 1988," *Government and Opposition* 26, no. 2 (Spring 1991): 244–260.

17. Adnan Abu Odeh, interview by author, Amman, 9 March 1998. Some individuals, such as Labib Kamhawi, confirmed that they had "talked about talks" with Abu Odeh; Labib Kamhawi, interview by author, Amman, 11 June 1998.

18. Abd al-Latif al-Arabiyat, interview by author, Amman, 20 May 1998; Ishaq Farhan, interview by author, Amman, 22 July 1998.

19. Hani Hourani, interview by author, Amman, 22 May 1998; Ibrahim Izzadin, interview by author, Amman, 6 May 1998.

20. See Abu Odeh's "requirements for democratic dialogue" in *Jordan Times*, 8 March 1990.

21. Iyad Qattan, interview by author, Amman, 19 May 1998; remarks by Iyad Qattan in Hashemite Kingdom of Jordan, Royal Committee for Drafting the National Charter, "Proceedings of the Royal Committee for Drafting the National Charter," Session 4, unpublished documents in Arabic, 14 May 1990, 8.

22. Remarks in Royal Committee for Drafting the National Charter, Session 4, 9.

23. Ibid., 8–9.

24. Qattan, interview.

25. Remarks in Hashemite Kingdom of Jordan, Royal Committee for Drafting the National Charter, "Proceedings of the Royal Committee for Drafting the National Charter," Session 5, unpublished documents in Arabic, 16 May 1990, 30.

26. Ibid., 33.

27. Ibid., 33, 34, 36.

28. Remarks in Royal Committee for Drafting the National Charter, Session 4, 20; Farhan, interview.

29. Remarks in Royal Committee for Drafting the National Charter, Session 4, 21.

30. Farhan, interview.
31. Remarks in Royal Committee for Drafting the National Charter, Session 4, 21.
32. Kamhawi, interview.
33. Remarks by Kamhawi in Royal Committee for Drafting the National Charter, Session 4, 17; Kamhawi, interview.
34. Remarks in Royal Committee for Drafting the National Charter, Session 4, 16–19.
35. Kamhawi, interview.
36. Remarks in Hashemite Kingdom of Jordan, Royal Committee for Drafting the National Charter, "Proceedings of the Royal Committee for Drafting the National Charter," Session 1, unpublished documents in Arabic, 21 April 1990, 7; Kamhawi, interview.
37. Issa Mdanat, opinion article in *Al-Rai'*, 27 May 1990, 18.
38. Remarks in Hashemite Kingdom of Jordan, Royal Committee for Drafting the National Charter, "Proceedings of the Royal Committee for Drafting the National Charter," Session 3, unpublished documents in Arabic, 12 May 1990, 74.
39. *Al-Rai'*, 27 May 1990, 18.
40. Ibid.
41. Issa Mdanat, interview by author, Amman, 14 July 1998.
42. FBIS, 11 April 1990, 40.
43. See various speakers in Hashemite Kingdom of Jordan, Royal Committee for Drafting the National Charter, "Proceedings of the Royal Committee for Drafting the National Charter," Sessions 1–3, unpublished documents in Arabic, 21 April 1990–12 May 1990, various.
44. See Royal Committee member Ibrahim Bakr in *Al-Rai'*, 7 May 1990, 18, versus Mohamad Ibrahim Awad, *Al-Rai'*, 13 May 1990, 17.
45. Kamhawi, interview; Royal Committee for Drafting the National Charter, Session 1, 11.
46. Royal Committee for Drafting the National Charter, Session 1, 8.
47. Tahir Hikmat, *Al-Rai'*, 24 April 1990, 16; FBIS, 7 May 1990, 33–35; Kamhawi, interview.
48. The chapters were titled: "The Charter: Rationale and Aims," "The State of Law and Political Pluralism," and "Jordan's National Security," "The Economy," "The Social Aspect," "Culture, Education, Science and Information," "The Jordanian-Palestinian Relationship," and "Jordanian, Arab, Islamic and International Relations." A "Historical Introduction" opened the document.
49. Hashemite Kingdom of Jordan, *The Jordanian National Charter* [English Text] (Amman: n.p., 1990), 14. The original Arabic text can be found in *Al-Mithaq al-Watani al-Urduni* (Amman: Directorate of the Military Press, 1990).
50. *National Charter*, 15.
51. Ibid., 15.
52. Ibid., 18.
53. Ibid., 21.
54. Ibid., 22.
55. Ibid., 22.
56. Qattan, interview.
57. *National Charter*, 22.

58. Ibid., 23.
59. Ibid., 23.
60. Farhan, interview; Kamhawi, interview; *National Charter*, 14.
61. Laurie Brand, "Liberalization and Changing Political Coalitions: The Bases of Jordan's 1990–1991 Gulf Crisis Policy," *The Jerusalem Journal of International Relations* 13, no. 4 (December 1991): 26.
62. Ibid., 26–28.
63. FBIS, 2 January 1991, 43–46; FBIS, 3 January 1991, 45–46.
64. Brand, 30–31, 36.
65. Kamhawi, interview; Mdanat, interview.

CHAPTER FOUR

1. *Jordan Times*, 19 June 1991.
2. *Middle East International*, 28 June 1991, 11.
3. FBIS, 5 July 1991, 30; FBIS, 25 July 1991, 33–34.
4. FBIS, 19 July 1991, 23.
5. *Middle East International*, 22 November 1991, 8; *Jordan Times*, 17 November 1991.
6. Hashemite Kingdom of Jordan, *Majlis al-Nuwab, Mulhaq al-Jaridah al-Rasmiyyah, Muhdr al-Jalasah* [Supplement to the Official Gazette, House of Deputies, Minutes of the Session], 21 June 1992, 28–29. Hereafter, *Mulhaq*.
7. As quoted in *Jordan Times*, 22 June 1992.
8. *Mulhaq*, 21 June 1992, 31.
9. *Mulhaq*, 21 June 1992, 31.
10. *Mulhaq*, 21 June 1992, 33–34 (Abd al-Raouf al-Rawabdah), 36 (Abd al-Majid al-Shreidah), 42 (Ahmed Anab).
11. *Mulhaq*, 21 June 1992, 36–38 (Bassam Haddadin); 24 June 1992, 14 (Yʿaqoub Qarash); 21 June 1992, 4; 21 June 1992, 44–46 (Hussein Majali).
12. *Mulhaq*, 24 June 1992, 6–7.
13. *Mulhaq*, 24 June 1992, 5–7, 22–23 (Abd al-Rahim al-Akor), 23 (Yousef Khasawnah), 25 (Kamal Omari).
14. *Mulhaq*, 24 June 1992, 37–38.
15. *Mulhaq*, 29 June 1992, 12.
16. *Mulhaq*, 29 June 1992, 26–31.
17. *Mulhaq*, 5 July 1992, 29–30.
18. *Jordan Times*, 6 July 1992.
19. *Jordan Times*, 25 July 1992; 1 August 1992; 8 August 1992.
20. Hashemite Kingdom of Jordan, *Majlis al-Ummah, Mulhaq al-Jaridah al-Rasmiyyah, Muhdr al-Jalasah al-Awali (Mushtarakah) li-Majlisi al-Ayan wa-al-Nuwab* [Supplement to the Official Gazette, National Assembly, Minutes of the first (joint) session of the Senate and House of Deputies], 20 August 1992, 19–38.
21. FBIS, 4 December 1992, 43; FBIS, 22 January 1993, 38–39; FBIS, 26 January 1993, 51–52.
22. Iyad al-Shalibi et al., *Intikhabat 1993 Al-Urdaniah: Dirasah Thliliah Raqamiah* [Jordan's 1993 Elections: An Analytical and Statistical Study] (Amman: UJRC, 1995), 28–30.

23. The nine parties were al-Ahd, the Progress and Justice Party, al-Waʿed, the Jordanian National Alliance, al-Watan, the Jordanian Arab Masses Party, the Reawakening Party, the Popular Unity Party, and the Jordanian Popular Movement. See *Jordan Times*, 8 April 1997; 6 May 1997.

24. Hani Hourani et al., *Directory of Civil Society Organizations in Jordan: 2001* (Amman: UJRC, 2001).

25. Ellen M. Lust-Okar, "The Decline of Jordanian Political Parties: Myth of Reality?" *International Journal of Middle East Studies* 33, no.4 (November 2001): 545–569.

26. See George Hawatmeh, ed., *The Role of the Media in a Democracy—The Case of Jordan* (Amman: University of Jordan Center for Strategic Studies, 1995).

27. *Mulhaq*, 9 August 1992, 24. Note that *Naqabah al-Sahafiiyyin al-Urdaniyyin* is translated using the term common in the Jordanian English-language press, the Jordanian Press Association (JPA). The operative law of the JPA is Provisional Law Number 1 for the year 1983 and is reprinted in Hussein al-Awdat, ed., *al-Muwsuʿah al-Sahfiyah al-Arabiyah: Buldan al-Mashraq al-Arabi* [Encyclopedia of the Arab Press: Countries of the Arab East] (Tunis: Arab Organization for Education, Culture and Sciences, 1990), 313–322.

28. *Mulhaq*, 9 August 1992, 25–27, 31–21.

29. *Jordan Times*, 24 August 1992.

30. *Mulhaq*, 9 August 1992, 29–30 (Fakhri Qʿawar); Article 19, *Blaming the Press: Jordan's Democratization Process in Crisis* (London: Article 19, 1997), 39.

31. *Mulhaq*, 9 August 1992, 42. Eighteen of the fifty-three deputies had supported a vote on following the Law Committee's recommendation to widen the definition of a journalist.

32. *Mulhaq*, 12 August 1992, 26, 33.

33. *Mulhaq*, 12 August 1992, 41–52.

34. *Mulhaq*, 9 December 1992, 61 (Ali al-Faqir), 61–62 (Minister of Information, Mahmoud al-Sharif), 73 (vote).

35. *Mulhaq*, 27 December 1992, 34. 1 JD = 1.41 USD.

36. *Mulhaq*, 27 December 1992, 39–49.

37. *Jordan Times*, 26 April 1995.

38. *Jordan Times*, 9 May 1995; 19 March 1996; 20 July 1996.

39. Salameh Naʿmat, interview by author, Amman, 14 July 1998; Committee to Protect Journalists, *Attacks on the Press in 1995* (New York: Committee to Protect Journalists, 1996), 217.

40. Committee to Protect Journalists, *Attacks on the Press in 1994* (New York: Committee to Protect Journalists, 1995), 277.

41. FBIS, 20 January 1997; the Committee to Protect Journalists database of attacks against journalists is on the Internet at http://www.cpj.org.

42. See Article 19, 36.

43. *Mulhaq*, 27 December 1992, 32–38.

44. *Middle East International*, 20 November 1992, 13–14.

45. *Jordan Times*, 26 August 1992.

46. Information Minister at the time, Mahmoud al-Sharif, expressed his dismay about attacks by the Right; Mahmoud al-Sharif, interview by author, Amman, 30 June 1998.

CHAPTER FIVE

1. Yehuda Lukacs, *Israel, Jordan and the Peace Process* (Syracuse: Syracuse University Press, 1997); Munther J. Haddadin, *Diplomacy on the Jordan: International Conflict and Negotiated Resolution* (Boston: Kluwer Academic Publishers, 2002).
2. Jordan Times, 28 July 1993.
3. *Jordan Times*, 9 June 1993.
4. Ibid.
5. *Jordan Times*, 10 June 1993.
6. *Al-Rai*ʾ, 9 August 1993.
7. Signatories included the conservative al-Ahd party (run by PM Majali's brother) and the Jordanian National Alliance, the IAF, the Jordanian Socialist Arab Baʿath Party, the Popular Unity Party, the Arab Democratic Party, the Jordanian Democratic Popular Unity Party, the Democratic Arab Islamist Movement, the Freedom Party, the Jordanian People's Democratic Party, al-Mustaqbal Party, the Jordanian Progressive Party, the Justice and Progress Party, and the Democratic Arab Unionist Party. *Jordan Times*, 29 July 1993.
8. See *Al-Rai*ʾ, (exact date unknown, Summer 1993). The JPDUP and the Democratic Socialist parties both called for a PR system. See also *Al-Rai*ʾ, 10 June 1993, and *Akhbar al-Usbowʿa*, 10 June 1993.
9. *Jordan Times*, 29 July 1993.
10. *Jordan Times*, 6 July 1993.
11. *Jordan Times*, 1 August 1993.
12. *Jordan Times*, 5 August 1993. A point also communicated to the author in an interview by Ishaq Farhan, Amman, 22 July 1998.
13. *Jordan Times*, 11 June 1993.
14. For the text of that speech see King Hussein ibn Talal, "Address on Election Law Amendments," in *Selected Speeches by His Majesty King Hussein I: 1989–1994* (Amman: International Press Office, Royal Hashemite Court, 1994), 87–93.
15. Emphasis added by the author.
16. Despite the fact that women's suffrage was introduced in 1974.
17. On the rarity of applications of the SNTV see Arend Lijphart et al., "The Limited Vote and the Single Nontransferable Vote: Lessons from the Japanese and Spanish Examples," in *Electoral Laws and Their Political Consequences*, ed. Bernard Grofman and Arend Lijphart, 154–169.
18. "Address on Election Law Amendments," 91.
19. *Jordan Times*, 28 July 1993.
20. FBIS, 28 June 1991, 29.
21. See the king's letter to Badran, FBIS, 28 June 1991, 29; a cabinet minister at the time confirmed this with Glenn E. Robinson, "Defensive Democratization in Jordan," *International Journal of Middle East Studies* 30, no. 3 (August 1998): 409ff.
22. "Address on Election Law Amendments," 91.
23. *Jordan Times*, 28 August 1993; Farhan, interview.
24. Iyad al-Shalibi et al., *Intikhabat 1993 Al-Urduniah: Dirasah Tahliliah Raqamiah* [Jordan's 1993 Elections: An Analytical and Quantitative Study] (Amman: UJRC, 1995), 22.

25. No small feat considering that voters could only cast one vote in 1993 as compared to the two to nine votes they had in 1989; Nidham Assaf, *Al-Intikhabat Al-Niyabiah wa Al-Mujtama ͨ Al-Madani: Arqam wa Dalalat Intikhabat 1993* [Parliamentary Elections and Civil Society: Figures and Indicators of the 1993 Election] (Amman: Al-Riada Center for Sciences and Studies, 1997), 60–64.

26. Paul L. Scham and Russell E. Lucas, " 'Normalization' and 'Anti-Normalization' in Jordan: The Public Debate," *Middle East Review of International Affairs* 5, no. 3 (September 2001): 55–56.

27. Ibid., 58–60.

28. *Jordan Times*, 6 November 1994.

29. *Jordan Times*, 25 August 1994.

30. *Jordan Times*, 7 November 1994.

31. See *Jordan Times*, 6 November 1994 and 7 November 1994 for coverage of the debate in the House of Deputies over the ratification of the peace treaty.

32. *Jordan Times*, 7 November 1994.

CHAPTER SIX

1. FBIS, 11 May 1995.

2. *Christian Science Monitor*, 24 May 1995; Asher Susser, "Jordan," *Middle East Contemporary Survey 1995* (Boulder: Westview Press, 1996), 408.

3. Asher Susser, "The Jordanian-Israeli Peace Negotiations: The Geopolitical Rationale of a Bilateral Relationship," *The Leonard Davis Institute Occasional Papers* 73 (1999): 27.

4. FBIS, 19 April 1996.

5. *Jordan Times*, 18 April 1996.

6. Asher Susser, "Jordan," *Middle East Contemporary Survey 1996* (Boulder: Westview Press, 1997), 439.

7. *Jordan Times*, 12 March 1997.

8. Asher Susser, "Jordan," *Middle East Contemporary Survey 1997* (Boulder: Westview Press, 1998), 478.

9. *Jordan Times*, 5 October 1997; *The Star*, 2 October 1997; *The Star*, 9 October 1997; *The Jerusalem Post*, 10 October 1997. See also, P. R. Kuwaraswamy, "Israel, Jordan and the Masha ͨ al Affair," *Israel Affairs*, 9, no. 3 (Spring 2003): 111–128.

10. *Jordan Times*, 7 November 1994.

11. *Middle East Mirror*, 26 October 1994.

12. Toujan Faisal, interview by author, Amman, 22 June 1998. Faisal accuses the Islamists and the government for her loss in the 1989 elections. In 2002 she was jailed for criticizing the government of Prime Minister Ali Abu-Ragheb.

13. FBIS, 31 October 1994.

14. *Middle East International*, 22 July 1994.

15. FBIS, 4 November 1994.

16. FBIS, 10 November 1994.

17. *Jordan Times*, 6 November 1994.

18. Asher Susser, "Jordan," *Middle East Contemporary Survey 1994* (Boulder: Westview Press, 1995), 418.

19. *Jordan Times*, 25 August 1994.

20. University of Jordan Center for Strategic Studies, *Istitla' lil-Rai' howl al-Alaqat al-Urduniyah al-Isra'iliyah: al-Nata'ij al-Awaliyah* [Poll on Jordanian-Israeli Relations: First Results] (Amman: University of Jordan Center for Strategic Studies), 13.

21. Asher Susser, "Jordan," *Middle East Contemporary Survey 1995* (Boulder: Westview Press, 1996), 421.

22. Curtis R. Ryan, "Peace, Bread and Riots: Jordan and the International Monetary Fund," *Middle East Policy* 6, no. 2 (October 1998): 54–66.

CHAPTER SEVEN

1. *The Star*, 19 August 1993.
2. Ibid.
3. *Jordan Times*, 11 December 1995.
4. *The Star*, 7 December 1995.
5. *Jordan Times*, 16 July 1996.
6. *Jordan Times*, 18 July 1996, 4 August 1996; and 21 August 1996.
7. Human Rights Watch, "Jordan: Clamping Down on Critics: Human Rights Violations in Advance of the Parliamentary Elections," *Human Right Watch Report* 9, no. 12E (October 1997).
8. Article 19, *Blaming the Press: Jordan's Democratization Process in Crisis* (London: Article 19, 1997), 25.
9. See for example, *Al-Destour*, 19 May 1997, for interviews with a spectrum of Jordanian elites on the new Press and Publications Law.
10. *Jordan Times*, 19 May 1997; FBIS-NES, 20 May 1997.
11. *Jordan Times*, 21 May 1997.
12. Human Rights Watch; Article 19; Hani Hourani et al., eds., *Press and Media Freedom in Jordan* (Amman: UJRC, 1998) details the proceedings of a conference held in Jordan on October 28–29, 1997 in reaction to the Article 19 report.
13. *Jordan Times*, 25 September 1997; *Jordan Times*, 27 September 1997.
14. Article 19, 34. The newspapers were: *Al-Hadath*, *Al-Bilad*, *Al-Sabeel*, *Al-Majd*, and *Sawt Al-Mar'a*.
15. *Jordan Times*, 30 September 1997. The three additional papers were *Al-Sayyad*, *Al-Ummah*, and *Hawadeth Al-Sa'a*.
16. *Jordan Times*, 27 January 1998.
17. Later in February 1998, High Court Judge Farouq Kilani accused the government of retaliating for the verdict by pushing him into retirement. See *The Star*, 26 February 1998.
18. Abd Al-Latif Al-Arabiyat, interview by author, Amman, 20 May 1998; Ishaq Farhan, interview by author, Amman, 22 July 1998.
19. Abdullah al-Akaylah, "Wujhat Nadhar Hizb Jabhat al-Amal al-Islami" [Theoretical point of view of the Islamic Action Front Party], in Hussein Abu Rumman, ed., *Nadwat Tashriy'at al-Intikhab Hajar al-Asas fi al-Nidham al-Demoqrati* [Conference on Electoral Legislation, the Cornerstone of the Democratic Order] (Amman: UJRC, 1995), 35–38.
20. Issa Mdanat, "Wujhat Nadhar Hizb al-Tiyyar al-Dimoqrati al-Mowahhad" [Theoretical point of view of the Democratic Unity Movement Party], in Abu Ruman, ed., 42–45; Issa Mdanat, interview by author, Amman, 14 July 1998.
21. *Al-Rai'*, 10 June 1993.

22. Farhan, interview; Bassam Haddadin, interview by author, Zarqa, 13 July 1998; Khalil Haddadin, interview by author, Amman, 9 July 1998.

23. Reported in Hussein Abu Ruman, 86.

24. See Russell E. Lucas, "Do Elections Matter in Jordan?: The Regime, the Opposition, and the Election Law," a paper presented at the 32nd Annual Meeting of the Middle East Studies Association, Chicago, Illinois, December 3–6, 1998.

25. *Majlis al-Nuwab, Mulhaq, al-Jaridah al-Rasmiyyah, Muhdar al-Jalasah*, 26 January 1997, 19–21. Hereafter *Mulhaq*.

26. *Mulhaq*, 26 January 1997, 21.

27. *Mulhaq*, 26 January 1997, 22. Dissenters included Abd al-Karim al-Dugami, Ahmad al-Qadhah, Mahmoud al-Howimel, Hatim al-Ghazawi, and Hani al-Masalhah.

28. *Mulhaq*, 26 January 1997, 26–27.

29. *Mulhaq*, 26 January 1997, 30–31 (Ahmed al-Kasasbah), 33 (Abd al-Rahim al-Akor).

30. *Mulhaq*, 26 January 1997, 28 (Talal Obeidat), 43–44 (Bassam Haddadin).

31. *Mulhaq*, 26 January 1997, 41–43 (Bassam al-Amoush).

32. *Mulhaq*, 26 January 1997, 58–59.

33. *Jordan Times*, 9 July 1997.

34. *Jordan Times*, 12 July 1997.

35. Samih Mu'aitah, interview by author, Amman, 15 March 1998; Abdullah Hassanat, interview by author, Amman, 23 June 1998; other analysts pointed to a reduction in the IAF's sixteen seats as well.

36. See Glenn E. Robinson, "Can Islamists Be Democrats? The Case of Jordan," *Middle East Journal* 51, no. 3 (Summer 1997): 373–388; Glenn E. Robinson, "Defensive Democratization in Jordan," *International Journal of Middle East Studies* 30, no. 3 (August 1998): 387–410; Quintan Wiktorowicz, *The Management of Islamic Activism: Salafis, the Muslim Brotherhood, and State Power in Jordan* (Albany: State University of New York Press, 2000).

37. Ahmad Jamil Azem, "The Islamic Action Front Party," in Hani Hourani, ed., *Islamic Movements in Jordan* (Amman: UJRC, 1997), 113.

38. See lists compiled on UJRC's Internet site: http://www.ujrc-jordan.org/research/elections/.

39. Khalil Haddadin, interview.

40. *Middle East International*, 29 August 1997; *Jordan Times*, 20 September 1997.

41. *Middle East International*, 29 August 1997; *Jordan Times*, 22 September 1997.

42. *Jordan Times*, 20 September 1997.

43. *Jordan Times*, 30 September 1997; UJRC analysts later "outed" fifteen NCP stealth candidates, *Jordan Times*, 16 October 1997.

44. *Middle East International*, 17 November 1997.

45. Human Rights Watch; Article 19; Hani Hourani et al., *Press and Media Freedom in Jordan*.

46. *Jordan Times*, 5 October 1997; Toujan Faisal, interview by author, Amman, 22 June 1998. Faisal lost her seat in the 1997 elections.

47. *Jordan Times*, 5 November 1997.

48. The draft law was printed in *Al-Destour*, and *Al-Rai'* on 17 June 1998, the translated text appeared in *The Jordan Times* the same day.

49. Abdullah Hassanat, interview by author, Amman, 23 June 1998; a similar reaction was provided by Mahmoud al-Sharif, interview by author, Amman, 30 June 1998.

50. *Jordan Times*, 17 June 1998; Asma Khader, interview by author, Amman, 20 June 1998; Faisal, interview.

51. *Jordan Times*, 23 June 1998. Note that the draft was sent to the National Guidance Committee, a new committee for the Parliament, rather than the Law Committee.

52. *The Star*, 23 July 1998; *Jordan Times*, 23 July 1998. The six in favor were Raji Haddad, Abdullah Jazi, Mohammad Quz, Mohammad Rafaʿat, Nayef Moula, and Amjad Majali. The three dissenters were Mahmoud Kharabsheh, Bassam Haddadin, and Hamadah Faraʿneh.

53. *Jordan Times*, 26 July 1998; 29 July 1998; *The Star*, 30 July 1998.

54. *Jordan Times*, 3 August 1998; 6 August 1998.

55. *Jordan Times*, 6 August 1998.

56. *Jordan Times*, 6 August 1998.

57. *Jordan Times*, 3 August 1998.

58. *Jordan Times*, 3 August 1998.

59. *Jordan Times*, 10 August 1998. It is unclear why a second vote was taken.

60. *The Star*, 13 August 1998.

61. *The Star*, 20 August 1998. The senators opposed were Abd al-Karim al-Kabariti, Mudar Badran, Layla Sharaf, Dhouqan al-Hindawi, Taher Kanʿan, Rajaiʾ Muaʿsher, Adnan Abu Odeh, and Hamdi al-Tabbaʿ.

62. *Jordan Times*, 24 August 1998.

63. U.S. Congress, *Country Reports on Human Rights Practices for 1998* (Washington D.C.: U.S. Government Printing Office, 1998), 1725.

64. Human Rights Watch, 18.

65. Khader, interview.

66. Khalil Haddadin, interview; Bassam Haddadin, interview.

67. *The Star*, 10 September 1998.

68. al-Sharif, interview.

69. Both were also former Ministers of Information. Layla Sharaf, interview by author, Amman, 16 June 1998; Adnan Abu Odeh, interview by author, Amman, 14 June 1998.

CHAPTER EIGHT

1. Lamis Andoni, "King Abdallah: In His Father's Footsteps?" *Journal of Palestine Studies* 29, no. 3 (Spring 2000): 79.

2. Ibid., 79. The letter was reprinted in the *Jordan Times*, 26 January 1999.

3. *Newsweek*, 10 August 1998.

4. Andoni, 80.

5. Curtis R. Ryan, *Jordan in Transition: From Hussein to Abdullah* (Boulder: Lynne Rienner Publishers: 2002), 95–97.

6. *Washington Post*, 5 September 1999.

7. Ryan, 98–102.

8. *Jordan Times*, 7 September 1999.

9. *The Star*, 9 September 1999, *Jordan Times*, 7 September 1999.

10. *Middle East International*, 3 September 1999.
11. *Middle East International*, 15 October 1999.
12. *Jordan Times*, 31 August 1999. Jordan had retained a "Vatican" over Christian and Muslim holy places in Jerusalem under the 1994 Jordanian-Israeli peace treaty.
13. *The Star*, 12 October 2000.
14. *Jordan Times*, 20 May 2001.
15. Jillian Schwedler, "Occupied Maan: Jordan's Closed Military Zone," *Middle East Report Online*, 3 December 2002, http://www.merip.org/mero/mero120302.html; International Crisis Group, "Red Alert in Jordan: Recurrent Unrest in Maan," *Middle East Briefing*, 19 February 2003, http://www.crisisweb.org//library/documents/report_archive/A400897_19022003.pdf.
16. *The Star*, 11 February 2001; 25 February 2001.
17. *Jordan Times*, 11 October 2001.
18. *Middle East International*, 31 May 2002.
19. Russell E. Lucas, "Jordan: The Death of Normalization with Israel," *Middle East Journal* 58, no.1 (Winter 2004): 93–111.

CHAPTER NINE

1. Ellen M. Lust-Okar, "The Decline of Jordanian Political Parties: Myth or Reality?" *International Journal of Middle East Studies* 33, no. 4 (November 2001): 545–569.
2. Adam Przeworski, *Democracy and the Market: Political and Economic Reforms in Eastern Europe and Latin America* (New York: Cambridge University Press, 1991), 69.
3. Abdeslam M. Maghraoui, "Depoliticization in Morocco," *Journal of Democracy* 13, no. 4 (October 2002): 24–32.
4. Gregory White, "The Advent of Electoral Democracy in Morocco? The Referendum of 1996," *Middle East Journal* 51, no. 3 (Summer 1997); Guilain Denoeux and Abdelsam Maghraoui, "King Hassan's Strategy of Political Dualism," *Middle East Policy* 5, no. 4 (January 1998).
5. Henry Munson Jr., "The Elections of 1993 and Democratization in Morocco," in *In the Shadow of the Sultan: Culture, Power, and Politics in Morocco*, ed. Rahma Bourqia and Susan Gilson Miller (Cambridge: Harvard University Press, 1999), 259–281; Susan E. Waltz, "Interpreting Political Reform in Morocco," in Bourqia and Miller, 282–305.
6. Denoeux and Maghraoui, 113.
7. White, 400.
8. Michael Herb, *All in the Family: Absolutism, Revolution, and Democracy in the Middle Eastern Monarchies* (Albany: State University of New York Press, 1999), 8.
9. Jill Crystal, *Oil and Politics in the Gulf: Rulers and Merchants in Kuwait and Qatar* (New York: Cambridge University Press, 1990)
10. Mary Ann Tétreault, *Stories of Democracy: Politics and Society in Contemporary Kuwait* (New York: Columbia University Press, 2000).
11. Paul Aarts, "Limits of Political Tribalism: Post-War Kuwait and the Process of Democratization," *Civil Society* (December 1994): 21.

12. Tétreault, 164–172.
13. *The Economist*, 8 May 1999.
14. Mary Ann Tétreault, "A State of Two Minds: State Cultures, Women, and Politics in Kuwait," *International Journal of Middle East Studies* 33, no. 3 (August 2001): 213–216.
15. *The Economist*, 22 May 1999; *New York Times*, 4 July 1999; *The Economist*, 10 July 1999.
16. *The Economist*, 27 November 1999; *New York Times*, 20 December 1999.
17. Nikki R. Keddie, *Modern Iran: Roots and Results of Revolution* (New Haven: Yale University Press, 2003), 167.
18. Mohsen M. Milani, *The Making of Iran's Islamic Revolution: From Monarchy to Islamic Republic* (Boulder: Westview Press, 1988), 124.
19. Keddie, 214–239; Said Amir Arjomand, *The Turban for the Crown: The Islamic Revolution in Iran* (New York: Oxford University Press, 1988).
20. Robert Springborg, *Mubarak's Egypt: Fragmentation of the Political Order* (Boulder: Westview Press, 1989), 156.
21. Ninette S. Fahmy, *The Politics of Egypt: State-Society Relationship* (New York: RoutledgeCurzon, 2002), 64–65.
22. Daniel Brumberg, "Authoritarian Legacies and Reform Strategies in the Arab World," in *Political Liberalization and Democratization in the Arab World: Volume 1, Theoretical Perspectives*, ed. Rex Brynen, Bahgat Korany, and Paul Noble (Boulder: Lynne Rienner Publishers, 1995), 238.
23. Fahmy, 44–52.
24. Fahmy, 71.
25. Fahmy, 67.
26. May Kassem, *In the Guise of Democracy: Governance in Contemporary Egypt* (London: Ithaca Press, 1999), 92–101; Fahmy, 69–70, 87; Springborg, 189–191.
27. Kassem, 101–108; Fahmy, 73–74, 87.
28. See, for example, a series of articles in the *Middle East Journal*: Cassandra, "The Impending Crisis in Egypt," *Middle East Journal* 49, no. 1 (Winter 1995): 9–27; Eberhard Kienle, "More than a Response to Islamism: The Political Deliberalization of Egypt in the 1990s," *Middle East Journal* 52, no. 2 (Spring 1998): 219–235; Fawaz A. Gerges, "The End of the Islamist Insurgency in Egypt?: Costs and Prospects," *Middle East Journal* 54, no. 4 (Fall 2000): 592–612.
29. Kassem, 108–109; Fahmy, 87.
30. Jason Brownlee, "The Decline of Pluralism in Mubarak's Egypt," *Journal of Democracy* 13, no. 4 (October 2002): 9.
31. Kassem, 63.

BIBLIOGRAPHY

Aarts, Paul. "Limits of Political Tribalism: Post-War Kuwait and the Process of Democratization." *Civil Society* (December 1994): 17–22.

Abu Jaber, Kamel S. and Schirin H. Fathi. "The 1989 Jordanian Parliamentary Elections." *Orient* 31, no. 1 (1991): 67–86.

Abu Nowar, Maʿan. *The History of the Hashimite Kingdom of Jordan, Volume 1: The Creation and Development of Transjordan; 1920–1929*. London: Ithaca Press, 1989.

Abu Odeh, Adnan. *Jordanians, Palestinians and the Hashimite Kingdom in the Middle East Peace Process*. Washington D.C.: U.S. Institute of Peace, 1999.

Abu Rumman, Hussein. *Results of 1997 Elections: Facts and Figures*. Amman: Al-Urdun al-Jadid Research Center, 1998.

al-Akaylah, Abdullah. "Wujhat Nadhar Hizb Jabhat al-Amil al-Islami" [Theoretical Point of View of the Islamic Action Front Party]. In *Nedwat Tashryʿat al-Intkhab Hajar al-Asas fi al-Nidham al-Demoqrati* [Conference on Electoral Legislation, the Cornerstone of the Democratic Order], edited by Hussein Abu Rumman, 35–38. Amman: Al-Urdun Al-Jadid Research Center, 1995.

Amawi, Abla. "State and Class in Transjordan: A Study of State Autonomy." Ph.D. Dissertation, Georgetown University, 1992.

Amin, Samir. *The Arab Nation*. London: Zed Press, 1978.

Anderson, Lisa. "Political Pacts, Liberalism, and Democracy: The Tunisian National Pact of 1988." *Government and Opposition* 26, no. 2 (Spring 1991): 244–260.

———. "Democracy in the Arab World: A Critique of the Political Culture Approach." In *Political Liberalization and Democratization in the Arab World, Volume 1: Theoretical Perspectives*, edited by Rex Brynen et al., 77–92. Boulder: Lynne Rienner, 1995.

Andoni, Lamis. "King Abdallah: In His Father's Footsteps?" *Journal of Palestine Studies* 29, no. 3 (Spring 2000): 77–89.

Arjomand, Said Amir. *The Turban for the Crown: The Islamic Revolution in Iran*. New York: Oxford University Press, 1988.

Article 19. *Blaming the Press: Jordan's Democratization Process in Crisis*. London: Article 19, 1997.

Aruri, Naseer H. *Jordan A Study in Political Development (1921–1965)*. The Hague: Martinus Nijhoff, 1972.

Assaf, Nidham. Al-Intikhabat al-Niyabiah wa al-Mujtamaᶜ al-Madani: Arqam wa Dalalat Intikhabat 1993 [Parliamentary Elections and Civil Society: Figures and Indicators of the 1993 Election]. Amman: Al-Riada Center for Sciences and Studies, 1997.

al-Awdat, Hussein, ed. Al-Muwsuᶜah al-Sahfiyah al-Arabiyah: Buldan al-Mashraq al-Arabi [Encyclopedia of the Arab Press: Countries of the Arab East]. Tunis: Arab Organization for Education, Culture and Sciences, 1990.

Azem, Ahmad Jamil. "The Islamic Action Front Party." In *Islamic Movements in Jordan*, edited by Hani Hourani, 95–144. Amman: Al-Urdun al-Jadid Research Center, 1997.

Baaklini, Abdo, et al. *Legislative Politics in the Arab World: The Resurgence of Democratic Institutions*. Boulder: Lynne Rienner, 1999.

Bailey, Clinton. *Jordan's Palestinian Challenge, 1948–1983: A Political History*. Boulder: Westview Press, 1984.

Beblawi, Hazem. "The Rentier State in the Arab World." In *The Arab State*, edited by Giacomo Luciani, 85–98. Berkeley and Los Angeles: University of California Press, 1990.

Baram, Amatzia. "Baathi Iraq and Hashemite Jordan: From Hostility to Alignment." *Middle East Journal* 45, no. 1 (1991): 51–70.

Brand, Laurie. "Liberalization and Changing Political Coalitions: The Bases of Jordan's 1990–1991 Gulf Crisis Policy." *The Jerusalem Journal of International Relations* 13, no. 4 (December 1991): 1–46.

———. *Jordan's Inter-Arab Relations: The Political Economy of Alliance Making*. New York: Columbia University Press, 1994.

———. " 'In the Beginning was the State': The Quest for Civil Society in Jordan." In *Civil Society in the Middle East, Volume 1*, edited by Augustus Richard Norton, 148–185. New York: E. J. Brill, 1995.

Bratton, Michael and Nicholas van de Walle. *Democratic Experiments in Africa: Regime Transitions in Comparative Perspective*. New York: Cambridge University Press, 1997.

Brownlee, Jason. "The Decline of Pluralism in Mubarak's Egypt." *Journal of Democracy* 13, no. 4 (October 2002): 6–14.

Brumberg, Daniel. "Authoritarian Legacies and Reform Strategies in the Arab World." In *Political Liberalization and Democratization in the Arab World, Volume 1: Theoretical Perspectives*, edited by Rex Brynen et al., 229–260. Boulder: Lynne Rienner, 1995.

Brynen, Rex, et al. "Trends, Trajectories or Interesting Possibilities? Some conclusions on Arab Democratization and Its Study." In *Political Liberalization and Democratization in the Arab World, Volume 1: Theoretical Perspectives*, edited by Rex Brynen et al., 333–338. Boulder: Lynne Rienner, 1995.

———. "Conclusion: Liberalization, Democratization, and Arab Experiences." In *Political Liberalization and Democratization in the Arab World, Volume 2: Comparative Perspectives*, edited by Bahgat Korany et al., 267–278. Boulder: Lynne Rienner, 1998.

Brynen, Rex. "Economic Crisis and Post-Rentier Democratization in the Arab World: The Case of Jordan." *Canadian Journal of Political Science* 25, no. 1 (March 1992): 69–97.

Cassandra. "The Impending Crisis in Egypt." *Middle East Journal* 49, no. 1 (Winter 1995): 9–27.
Committee to Protect Journalists. *Attacks on the Press in 1994*. New York: Committee to Protect Journalists, 1995.
———. *Attacks on the Press in 1995*. New York: Committee to Protect Journalists, 1996.
Constitution of the Hashemite Kingdom of Jordan with All Amendments. Amman: Department of Press and Publications, n.d.
Crystal, Jill. *Oil and Politics in the Gulf: Rulers and Merchants in Kuwait and Qatar*. New York: Cambridge University Press, 1990.
———. "Authoritarianism and Its Adversaries in the Arab World," *World Politics* 46, no. 2 (January 1994): 262–289.
Dann, Uriel. *King Hussein and the Challenge of Arab Radicalism: Jordan, 1955–1967*. New York: Oxford University Press, 1989.
———. *King Hussein's Strategy of Survival*. Washington D.C.: Washington Institute for Near East Policy, 1992.
———. "A Democratization Scorecard: Political Parties in Jordan." *Jordan Issues and Perspectives* 15 (June/July 1993): 4.
Denoeux, Guilain and Abdelsam Maghraoui. "King Hassan's Strategy of Political Dualism." *Middle East Policy* 5, no. 4 (January 1998): 108–109.
Fahmy, Ninette S. *The Politics of Egypt: State-Society Relationship*. New York: RoutledgeCurzon, 2002.
Fischbach, Michael R. "British Land Policy in Transjordan." In *Village, Steppe and State: The Social Origins of Modern Jordan*, edited by Eugene L. Rogan and Tariq Tell, 80–107. New York: St. Martin's Press, 1994.
Fukuyama, Francis. *The End of History and the Last Man*. New York: Free Press, 1992.
Gause, F. Gregory. "Regional Influences on Experiments in Political Liberalization in the Arab World." In *Political Liberalization and Democratization in the Arab World, Volume 1: Theoretical Perspectives*, edited by Rex Brynen et al., 283–306. Boulder: Lynne Rienner, 1995.
Geddes, Barbara. "What Do We Know About Democratization After Twenty Years?" *Annual Reviews: Political Science* 2 (1999): 115–144.
Gerges, Fawaz A. "The End of the Islamist Insurgency in Egypt?: Costs and Prospects." *Middle East Journal* 54, no. 4 (Fall 2000): 592–612.
Glubb, John Bagot. *A Soldier with the Arabs*. London: Hodder and Stoughton, 1957.
Hagopian, Frances. "After Regime Change: Authoritarian Legacies, Political Representation, and the Democratic Future of South America." *World Politics* 45, no. 3 (April 1993): 464–500.
———. "Traditional Politics Against State Transformation in Brazil." In *State Power and Social Forces: Domination and Transformation in the Third World*, edited by Joel S. Migdal et al., 37–64. Cambridge: Cambridge University Press, 1994.
Halliday, Fred. "Monarchies in the Middle East: A Concluding Appraisal." In *Middle East Monarchies: The Challenge of Modernity*, edited by Joseph Kostiner, 289–304. Boulder: Lynne Rienner, 2000.
Hawatmeh, George, ed. *The Role of the Media in a Democracy—The Case of Jordan*. Amman: University of Jordan Center for Strategic Studies, 1995.
Herb, Michael. *All in the Family: Absolutism, Revolution, and Democracy in the Middle Eastern Monarchies*. Albany: State University of New York Press, 1999.

Heydemann, Stephen, ed. *War, Institutions, and Social Change in the Middle East.* Berkeley and Los Angeles: University of California Press, 2000.

Higley, John and Richard Gunther, eds. *Elites and Democratic Consolidation in Latin America and Southern Europe.* New York: Cambridge University Press, 1993.

Hourani, Hani. *Al-Ahzab al-Siyasiah al-Urdaniyah* [Jordanian Political Parties]. Amman: Al-Urdun Al-Jadid Research Center, 1997.

Hourani, Hani, et al. *Jordanian Political Parties.* Amman: Al-Urdun al-Jadid Research Center, 1993.

Hourani, Hani, et al. *Who's Who in the Jordanian Parliament 1993–1997.* Amman: Al-Urdun al-Jadid Research Center, 1995.

Hourani, Hani, et al. *Press and Media Freedom in Jordan.* Amman: Al-Urdun al-Jadid Research Center, 1998.

Human Rights Watch. "Jordan: Clamping Down on Critics: Human Rights Violations in Advance of the Parliamentary Elections." *Human Right Watch Report* 9, no. 12E (October 1997).

Hussein ibn Talal. *Selected Speeches by His Majesty King Hussein I: 1989–1994.* Amman: International Press Office, Royal Hashemite Court, 1994.

The Jordanian National Charter. Amman: n.p., 1990.

Kamrava, Mehran. "Frozen Political Liberalization in Jordan: The Consequences for Democracy." *Democratization* 5, no. 1 (Spring 1998): 138–157.

Karl, Terry. "Petroleum and Political Pacts: The Transition to Democracy in Venezuela." In *Transitions from Authoritarian Rule: Latin America,* edited by Guillermo O'Donnell, Philippe Schmitter, and Laurence Whitehead. Baltimore: Johns Hopkins University Press, 1986.

Kassem, May. *In the Guise of Democracy: Governance in Contemporary Egypt.* London: Ithaca Press, 1999.

Keddie, Nikki R. *Modern Iran: Roots and Results of Revolution.* New Haven: Yale University Press, 2003.

Kedourie, Elie. *Democracy and Arab Political Culture.* Washington D.C.: Washington Institute for Near East Policy, 1992.

Kienle, Eberhard. "More than a Response to Islamism: The Political Deliberalization of Egypt in the 1990s." *Middle East Journal* 52, no. 2 (Spring 1998): 219–235.

Korany, Bahgat. "Restricted Democratization from Above: Egypt." In *Political Liberalization and Democratization in the Arab World, Volume 2: Comparative Perspectives,* edited by Bahgat Korany et al., 39–70. Boulder: Lynne Rienner, 1998.

Kuwaraswamy, P. R. "Israel, Jordan and the Masha'al Affair," *Israel Affairs* 9, no. 3 (Spring 2003): 111–128.

Law of Election to the House of Deputies: Law Number 22 for the Year 1986, with All Amendments. Amman: Press and Publications Department, 1993.

Levine, Daniel. "Paradigm Lost: Dependency to Democracy." *World Politics* 40, no. 3 (April 1988): 377–394.

Lewis, Bernard. "What Went Wrong?" *The Atlantic Monthly,* January 2002, 43–45.

Lijphart, Arend. "Proportionality by Non-PR methods: Ethnic Representation in Belgium, Cyprus, Lebanon, New Zealand, West Germany and Zimbabwe." In *Electoral Laws and Their Political Consequences,* edited by Bernard Grofman and Arend Lijphart, 113–123. New York: Agathon Press, 1986.

———. *Electoral Systems and Party Systems: A Study of Twenty-seven Democracies, 1945–1990*. New York: Oxford University Press, 1994.

Lijphart, Arend, et al. "The Limited Vote and the Single Nontransferable Vote: Lessons from the Japanese and Spanish Examples." In *Electoral Laws and Their Political Consequences*, edited by Bernard Grofman and Arend Lijphart, 154–169. New York: Agathon Press, 1986.

Linz, Juan J. and Alfred Stepan. *Problems of Democratic Transition and Consolidation: Southern Europe, South America, and Post-Communist Europe*. Baltimore: Johns Hopkins University Press, 1996.

Lucas, Russell E. "Do Elections Matter in Jordan?: The Regime, the Opposition, and the Election Law." A paper presented at the 32nd Annual Meeting of the Middle East Studies Association, Chicago, Illinois, 3–6 December 1998.

———. "Monarchical Authoritarianism: Survival and Political Liberalization in a Middle Eastern Regime Type." *International Journal of Middle East Studies* 36, no.1 (February 2004): 103–119.

———. "Jordan: The Death of Normalization with Israel." *Middle East Journal* 58, no.1 (Winter 2004): 93–111.

Luciani, Giacomo. "Allocation vs. Production States: A Theoretical Framework." In *The Arab State*, edited by Giacomo Luciani, 65–84. Berkeley and Los Angeles: University of California Press, 1990.

Lukacs, Yehuda. *Israel, Jordan, and the Middle East Peace Process*. Syracuse: Syracuse University Press, 1997.

Lunt, James. *Glubb Pasha: A Biography*. London: Harvill Press, 1984.

Lust-Okar, Ellen. "Divided They Fall: The Management and Manipulation of Political Opposition." Ph.D. Dissertation, University of Michigan, 1997.

———. "The Decline of Jordanian Political Parties: Myth or Reality?" *International Journal of Middle East Studies* 33, no. 4 (November 2001): 545–569.

Lynch, Marc. *State Interests and Public Spheres: The International Politics of Jordan's Identity*. New York: Columbia University Press, 1999.

Maghraoui, Abdeslam M. "Depoliticization in Morocco." *Journal of Democracy* 13, no. 4 (October 2002): 24–32.

Majlis al-Nuwab, Mulhaq al-Jaridah al-Rasmiyyah, Muhdr al-Jalasah [Supplement to the Official Gazette, House of Deputies, Proceedings of the Session:]. Various dates.

Majlis al-Ummah, Mulhaq al-Jaridah al-Rasmiyyah, Muhdr al-Jalasah al-Awali (Mushtarakah) li-Majlisi al-Ayan wa-al-Nuwab [Supplement to the Official Gazette, National Assembly, Minutes of the first (joint) session of the Senate and House of Deputies]. 20 August 1992.

Massad, Joseph A. *Colonial Effects: The Making of National Identity in Jordan*. New York: Columbia University Press, 2001.

Mdanat, Issa. "Wujhat Nadhar Hizb al-Tiyyar al-Dimoqrati al-Mowahhad" [Theoretical Point of View of the Democratic Unity Movement Party]. In *Nedwat Tashry ʿat al-Intkhab Hajar al-Asas fi al-Nidham al-Demoqrati* [Conference on Electoral Legislation, the Cornerstone of the Democratic Order], edited by Hussein Abu Rumman, 42–45. Amman: Al-Urdun Al-Jadid Research Center, 1995.

Middle East Contemporary Survey, various years. Boulder: Westview Press, various years.

Milani, Mohsen M. *The Making of Iran's Islamic Revolution: From Monarchy to Islamic Republic.* Boulder: Westview Press, 1988.

Al-Mithaq al-Watani al-Urduni. Amman: Directorate of the Military Press, 1990

Mufti, Malik. "Elite Bargains and the Onset of Political Liberalization in Jordan." *Comparative Political Studies* 32, no. 1 (February 1999): 100–129.

Muhasanah, Mohammed. "Tatawwur al-Tashry ʿat al-Intkhabyah al-Urduniyah" [Development of Jordanian Electoral Legislation]. In *Nedwat Tashry ʿat al-Intkhab Hajar al-Asas fi al-Nidham al-Demoqrati* [Conference on Electoral Legislation, the Cornerstone of the Democratic Regime], edited by Hussein Abu Ruman. Amman: Al-Urdun Al-Jadid Research Center, 1995.

Munck, Gerardo L. "Democratic Transitions in Comparative Perspective." *Comparative Politics* 36, no. 3 (April 1994): 355–376.

Munson, Henry Jr. "The Elections of 1993 and Democratization in Morocco.," In *In the Shadow of the Sultan: Culture, Power, and Politics in Morocco*, edited by Rahma Bourqia and Susan Gilson Miller, 259–281. Cambridge: Harvard University Press, 1999.

Nevo, Joseph. *King Abdallah and Palestine.* New York: St. Martin's Press, 1996.

O'Donnell, Guillermo. "Tensions in the Bureaucratic-Authoritarian State and the Question of Democracy." In *The New Authoritarianism in Latin America*, edited by David Collier, 285–318. Princeton: Princeton University Press, 1979.

O'Donnell, Guillermo and Phillipe C. Schmitter. *Transitions from Authoritarian Rule: Tentative Conclusions about Uncertain Democracies.* Baltimore: Johns Hopkins University Press, 1986.

Offe, Claus. "Designing Institutions for East European Transitions." In *Strategic Choice and Path-Dependency in Post-Socialism: Institutional Dynamics in the Transformation Process*, edited by Jerzy Hausner et al., 47–83. Brookfield: Elgar, 1995.

The Political Parties Law: Law Number 32 for the Year 1992. Amman: Press and Publications Department, 1992.

The Press and Publications Law of 1993: Law Number 10 for the Year 1993, with All Amendments. Amman: Press and Publications Department, 1997.

"Proceedings of the Royal Committee for Drafting the National Charter." Unpublished Documents of the Royal Hashemite Court. [In Arabic] Various dates.

Przeworski, Adam. *Democracy and the Market: Political and Economic Reforms in Eastern Europe and Latin America.* New York: Cambridge University Press, 1991.

———. "The Games of Transitions." In *Issues in Democratic Consolidation: The New South American Democracies in Comparative Perspective*, edited by Scott Mainwaring et al., 105–152. Notre Dame: University of Notre Dame Press, 1992.

Remmer, Karen L. "New Theoretical Perspectives on Democratization." *Comparative Politics* 28, no. 1 (October 1995): 105–108.

Riedel, Tim. *Who's Who in Jordanian (sic) Parliament 1989–1993.* Amman: Friedrich Ebert Stitung, 1993.

Roberts, John. "Prospects for Democracy in Jordan." *Arab Studies Quarterly.* 13, no. 3/4 (Summer/Fall 1991): 119–138.

Robins, Philip J. "Politics and the 1986 Electoral Law in Jordan." In *Politics and the Economy in Jordan*, edited by Rodney Wilson, 184–207. New York: Routledge, 1991.

Robinson, Glenn E. "Can Islamists Be Democrats? The Case of Jordan." *Middle East Journal* 51, no. 3 (Summer 1997): 373–388.
Robinson, Glenn E. "Defensive Democratization in Jordan." *International Journal of Middle East Studies* 30, no. 3 (August 1998): 387–410.
Rogan, Eugene L. "Brining the State Back: The Limits of Ottoman Rule in Transjordan 1840–1910." In *Village, Steppe and State: The Social Origins of Modern Jordan*, edited by Eugene L. Rogan and Tariq Tell, 32–57. New York: St. Martin's Press, 1994.
Ryan, Curtis R. "Peace, Bread and Riots: Jordan and the International Monetary Fund." *Middle East Policy* 6, no. 2 (October 1998): 54–66.
———. *Jordan in Transition: From Hussein to Abdullah*. Boulder: Lynne Rienner, 2002.
Satloff, Robert. *Troubles on the East Bank: Challenges to the Domestic Stability of Jordan*. New York: Praeger Press, 1986.
———. *From Abdullah to Hussein: Jordan in Transition*. New York: Oxford University Press, 1994.
Scham Paul L. and Russell E. Lucas, " 'Normalization' and 'Anti-Normalization' in Jordan: The Public Debate." *Middle East Review of International Affairs* 5, no 3: 54–70.
al-Shalibi, Iyad, et al. *Intikhabat 1993 al-Urduaniah: Dirasah Tahliliah Raqamiah* [Jordan's 1993 Elections: An Analytical and Quantitative Study]. Amman: Al-Urdun Al-Jadid Research Center, 1995.
Shryock, Andrew. *Nationalism and the Genealogical Imagination: Oral History and Textual Authority in Tribal Jordan*. Berkeley and Los Angeles: University of California Press, 1997.
Snyder, Richard and James Mahoney. "The Missing Variable: Institutions and the Study of Regime Change." *Comparative Politics* 32, no. 1 (October 1999): 103–122.
Springborg, Robert. *Mubarak's Egypt: Fragmentation of the Political Order*. Boulder: Westview Press, 1989.
Susser, Asher. "The Jordanian-Israeli Peace Negotiations: The Geopolitical Rationale of a Bilateral Relationship." *The Leonard Davis Institute Occasional Papers* 73 (1999).
Tétreault, Mary Ann. *Stories of Democracy: Politics and Society in Contemporary Kuwait*. New York: Columbia University Press, 2000.
———. "A State of Two Minds: State Cultures, Women, and Politics in Kuwait." *International Journal of Middle East Studies* 33, no. 3 (August 2001): 213–216.
University of Jordan Center for Strategic Studies. *Istitlaʿa lil-Raiʾ howl al-Demoqratya fi al-Urdun: al-Nataʾij al-Awaliyah* [Survey on Democracy in Jordan 1997: Preliminary Results]. Amman: University of Jordan Center for Strategic Studies, various years.
———. *Istitlaʿa lil-Raiʾ howl al-Alaqat al-Urduniyah al-Israʾiliyah: al-Nataʾij al-Awaliyah* [Poll on Jordanian-Israeli Relations: Preliminary Results]. Amman: University of Jordan Center for Strategic Studies, 1997.
Al-Urdun Al-Jadid Research Center. *Intikhabat 1989: Haqaʾiq wa-Arqam* [Election 1989: Facts and Figures]. Amman: Al-Urdun Al-Jadid Research Center, 1993.
U.S. Congress. *Country Reports on Human Rights Practices for 1998*. Washington D.C.: U.S. Government Printing Office, 1998.

VanDenBerg, Jeffrey A. "Democratization and Foreign Policy in the Middle East: A Case Study of Jordan and Egypt." Ph.D. Dissertation, University of Cincinnati, 2000.

Waltz, Susan E. "Interpreting Political Reform in Morocco." In *In the Shadow of the Sultan: Culture, Power, and Politics in Morocco*, edited by Rahma Bourqia and Susan Gilson Miller, 282–305. Cambridge: Harvard University Press, 1999.

"Watha 'iq al-Intifadhah," [Documents of the (Jordanian) Intifada]. *Al-Urdun al-Jadid* [New Jordan Review] 14 (Summer 1989): 56–84.

White, Gregory. "The Advent of Electoral Democracy in Morocco? The Referendum of 1996." *Middle East Journal* 51, no. 3 (Summer 1997): 389–404.

Wiktorowicz, Quintan. *The Management of Islamic Activism: Salafis, the Muslim Brotherhood, and State Power in Jordan*. Albany: State University of New York Press, 2000.

Wilson, Mary C. *King Abdullah, Britain and the Making of Jordan*. New York: Cambridge University Press, 1987.

INDEX

Abbadi, Ahmed, 54
Abdullah II, King, 21, 125, 127–136, 143–144, 155
Abdullah, King (Amir), 14–16
Abu Marzuq, Musa, 131
Abu Nowar, Ali, 33
Abu Nuwar, Maʿan, 100
Abu Odeh, Adnan, 32, 123, 129
Abu Ragheb, Ali, 135, 139
Abu Zant, Abd al-Munʿam, 33, 132
additional member district, 107–108, 111
agency, 6, 8
Ahali, Al-, 66, 100
Ahd, al-, 92
Ajloun, 14
Akaylah, Abdullah al-, 83, 90, 107, 114, 120
Akor, Abd al-Rahim al-, 57, 75
Albright, Madeleine, 131
Andoni, Lamis, 128–129
Anis, Dhib, 132
Arab al-Youm, Al-, 103
Arab Legion, 15, 18
Arab nationalism, 9, 17–19, 38–39
Arab nationalists, 8, 19, 22, 30–32, 38–39, 45, 74–79, 82–83, 98, 107–109, 111, 113, 138, 141–142
Arabiyat, Abd al-Latif al-, 56–57, 74
Arafat, Yasser, 132–133

Arar, Suleiman, 112, 116, 124
authoritarianism, 2–4; 155–156
Azaidah, Mohammad, 120

Baʿath party, 18, 33
Baʿath Party, Arab Socialist, 58, 98, 113
Badran, Mudar, 45–46, 49, 78
Bani Issa, Abdullah, 67
Barak, Ehud, 133
Batikhi, General Samih, 129
Bedouins, 14–15, 18, 27–28
Bilad, Al-, 66, 105
Bin Shaker, Sharif Zeid, 27–28, 53, 69, 100–102, 121
Black September, 19
Brand, Laurie, 45
Bratton, Michael, 5
budget security, 5
bureaucratic authoritarian regime, 4, 7
Bush, George, 51

cabinet, 22–23, 69
Camp David Accords, 82
Carter, Jimmy, 150
censorship, 63–64, 103, 120, 130–131, 135
Center for Strategic Studies, University of Jordan, 82, 94–96
Chechens, 21, 27–30

Christians, 21, 27–30, 107, 113
Circassians, 21, 27–30, 113
civil society, 3, 8, 46–47
Clinton, Bill, 81, 128, 133, 135
Committee for Resting Submission and Normalization (CRSN), 90–93, 114
Communist party, 18, 32, 39, 58, 114
conservatives, 30–31, 67–70, 79, 101, 110
constitution, 17–18, 22–23, 40, 76, 105, 109–110, 123
Constitutional Bloc, 53
Constitutional Front Party, 112
constitutional rules, 2, 8, 22–23, 67–68, 121–125, 140–141, 143
contingent choice model of transitions, 3–4, 31, 142–143
coups, 18
courts, see judiciary

Daqamisah, Ahmed al-, 89
debt crisis, see economic crisis
debt relief, 93–94
deliberalization, 2, 134, 138
Democratic Unionist Party, 113
democratization, 3–5
Department of Press and Publications, 65–66
dependent economic development, 2–3
Destour, Al-, 61, 100, 103
disengagement from West Bank, 9, 25–26
divide and rule, 8–9
dynastic monarchy, 146–147

East Bankers, 20, 26–27, 128
Eastern Europe, 3
economic crisis, 2, 9–10, 23, 26–27, 155
economic growth, 94, 96–97
economic structural adjustment, 10, 23, 96–98, 129, 135, 143, 155
Egypt, 16, 18, 19, 55, 150–155
election boycott, 10, 58–60, 75, 78–79, 104–106, 111–114, 116, 122, 139–140
election law of 1928, 27
election law of 1947, 28
election law of 1986, 27
election law of 1986, 1989 amendments to, 27, 77
election law of 1986, 1993 amendments to, 10, 71–81, 83–85, 106–107, 109–111, 138, 143
election law of 2002, 134–135, 140
elections laws, 27–30, 73, 106–111, 139
elections of 1989, 10, 27–31, 47
elections of 1993, 58, 72, 79–81
elections of 1997, 58–60, 102, 111–116
elections of 1999 (local), 129–130
elections of 2003, 134–135
electoral system, 28–30, 48, 73–76
Emoush, Bassam, 90
executive branch, 22–23, 105

Faisal, Toujan, 92, 122
Fares, 105
Farhan, Ishaq, 36–38
fedayeen, 9, 19
fiscal crisis, see economic crisis
foreign aid, 15, 20, 93–94
foreign policy, 5, 26, 44–46, 87–90, 93–96, 128–129, 131–136, 143–144, 155

Geddes, Barbara, 7
Ghoshah, Ibrahim, 131–132
Glubb, John Bagot "Pasha," 15, 18
Gold, Dore, 88
Great Britain, 14–15, 18
Gulf War (1991), 10, 44–46, 51–52, 67, 147

Hadaf, Al-, 105
Hadath, Al-, 105
Hamas, 131–132, 138
Hamzah, Prince, 129
Haqiqa, Al-, 66
Haram al-Sharif, 88–89
hard-liners, 4, 35–36, 67, 102, 120
HASHD, 98, 100, 107–108, 112
Hassan II, King of Morocco, 145–146, 155
Hassan, Crown Prince, 120, 125, 127–128

INDEX

Hawadeth Al-Sa'a, 105
Hayat, Al-, 66
Herb, Michael, 146–147
Higher Media Council, 135
Hiwar, Al-, 67
House of Deputies, 7, 22, 27–28, 57–58, 61–64, 68–69, 74, 101, 105, 109–111, 118–121, 134, 139
Huda, Tawfiq Abd al-, 17
Hussein, King, 17–19, 21, 44–46, 68, 71–73, 75–78, 81, 84, 88–90, 98, 114, 124–125, 127–128, 141, 144
Hussein, Saddam, 45
Hussein, Sharif, 14

institutions, 1, 6–7
International Monetary Fund (IMF), 26, 96–98, 129
intifada (Palestinian), 10, 26, 133–135, 139, 143–144
Iran, 149–150, 155
Iraq, 45–46, 134, 139
Islamic Action Front, see Muslim Brotherhood
Islamic fundamentalism, 1
Islamists, 8, 22, 36–38, 82–83, 101, 111, 123–124, 138, 141–142
Israel, 10, 16, 19, 52–53, 71–72, 87–90, 133–134, 143
Israelis, public opinion of, 95–96
Istiqlal party (Morocco), 16, 145

Jammu, Shaykh Abd al-Baqi, 54
Jordan Times, 66, 103
Jordanian Arab National Democratic Alliance (JANDA), 52–53
Jordanian Arab Partisans Party, 112
Jordanian People's Democratic Party, 58
Jordanian People's Unity Party, 112
Jordanian Press Association (JPA), 62, 68, 100–101, 104, 117–118
journalists, 62, 69, 104, 118, 140
judiciary, 22, 66–67, 100, 105, 121–122

Kabariti, Abd al-Karim al-, 88, 97–98, 101–102, 111, 121, 129
Kamhawi, Labib, 38–40, 44

Karak, 14, 98
Kassem, May, 154
Keddie, Nikki R., 150
Khalifa, Abd al-Rahman, 52
Kharabsheh, Mahmoud, 119
Khleifat, Awad, 35–36, 48
Kilani, Ibrahim Zeid al-, 109
Kuwait, 146–149, 155

Latin America, 3, 4, 7, 8
Law Committee of House of Deputies, 54–57, 61–64, 67, 109–111
Lebanon, 88
leftists, 8, 22, 30–31, 32, 39, 52–53, 58, 74, 78–79, 82–83, 107–109, 111, 113, 138, 141–142
Legislative Assembly, 15
legislative branch, 22–23
liberalization, political, 2–5, 46–49, 67–70, 129–130, 137–138
liberals, regime, 35, 67, 69, 100, 123–125
Lijphart, Arend, 76
linchpin monarchy, 144, 147, 151
Linz, Juan, 6–7
Lust-Okar, Ellen, 138

Ma'an, 14, 26, 98
Madrid conference, 10, 52–53
Maghraoui, Abdeslam, 145
Mahoney, James, 6
Majali, Abd al-Hadi al-, 112
Majali, Abd al-Salam al-, 73–74, 76–77, 100, 102, 110, 112, 114, 117, 120, 124, 127
Majali, Hussein, 54–55
Majd, Al-, 66, 105
mandate of Transjordan, 14–15
martial law, 18, 52, 61
Mash'al, Khalid, 89, 131–132
Masri, Tahir al-, 49, 51–53, 60, 67, 69–70, 72, 81, 94, 112–113, 116, 123–124
Mdanat, Issa, 39, 56, 107
Middle East International, 93
Middle East peace process, 10, 51–53, 71–72, 131–133
military, 21, 103, 128

INDEX

Ministry of Information, 101
Ministry of Interior, 58
Mithaq, Al-, 105
Mohammed VI, King (of Morocco), 145–146
monarchical authoritarianism, 7, 9, 21, 2–37, 144, 146–147
Morocco, 16, 144–146, 155
Muʿasher, Marwan al-, 101
Mubarak, Hosni, 151–152
Mufti, Malik, 27
Musaqbal Party, 112
Muslim Brotherhood, 18, 22, 30–33, 36–38, 44–46, 51, 53, 58–60, 74–75, 78–79, 84, 90–93, 97, 107, 111–114, 124, 129–132, 138

Naʿmat, Salameh, 66
Nabulsi, Faris al-, 56
Nabulsi, Suleiman al-, 18
Najoum Al-Arabi, Al-, 105
Nasser, Gamal Abd al-, 17, 151–152, 154
National Action Party (Haqq), 112
National Charter, 10, 27, 31–46, 47, 52, 54, 61, 141, 143
National Constitutional Party (NCP), 60, 112, 115–116, 138
National Democratic Party (NDP) (Egypt), 151–153
national identity, 35–39, 44, 48
National Pact of 1928, 15, 16, 141
National Socialist Party, 18
Nazzal, Khalid, 131
Netanyahu, Binyamin, 88–89, 131
1948 war, 16–17
1967 war, 19–20, 21
Noor, Queen, 128
Nsour, Abdullah al-, 62

O'Donnell, Guillermo, 3
Obeidat, Ahmed, 39, 91, 93, 112, 123–124
oil, 20
opposition disunity, 2, 8, 48, 56, 67–69, 75, 84–85, 108, 110–111, 113–114, 116, 122–125, 141–142

Organic Law, of 1928, 15
Oslo Accords, 72, 81

pacts, 31
Pahlavi, Shah Mohammed Reza, 149, 154
Palestine Liberation Organization (PLO), 19, 26, 52, 72, 81
Palestine, 15–17
Palestinians, 16, 19–21, 25–27, 52–53, 81, 87–93, 116, 128, 132–134
path dependency, 9
peace treaty, Jordanian-Israeli, 10, 72, 81–83, 91, 93, 100, 106, 112, 143, 155
Penal Code, 58, 64, 67, 104, 135, 140
Peres, Shimon, 88
political parties law, 10, 54–60, 138, 142
political parties, 7, 18, 30–31, 42–44, 58, 76–77, 108, 112, 138–139
political pluralism, 35–39, 41–44
Popular Front for the Liberation of Palestine (PFLP), 19, 52
postpopulist republic, 151
prerequisites for democracy, 2–3
presidentialism, 151
press and publications law of 1993, 10, 23, 60–67, 100, 102, 142
press and publications law of 1993, 1997 amendments to, 10, 100–106, 111–112, 115, 121, 139–143
press and publications law of 1998, 10, 117–121, 123–124, 139, 142
press and publications law of 1998, 1999 amendments to, 10, 130–131, 139
press, 7, 23, 99, 139–140
prime minister, 22
private sector, 16, 20, 21
professional associations, 91–92, 133–134
proportional representation, 74, 107–108, 111
provisional laws, 23, 72, 75–77, 84, 102, 105–106, 109, 121, 134–135, 139
Przeworski, Adam, 3, 6

Qʿawar, Fakhri, 69
Qarash, Yʿaqoub, 68
Qattan, Iyad, 35, 44, 48

Rabadhi, Farah al-, 110
Rabat, Al-, 53

INDEX

Rabin, Yitzhak, 81, 88, 93
Rai', Al-, 61, 93, 103
Rania, Queen, 134
Rashid, Prince, 129
Rawabdah, Abd al-Raouf al-, 55, 62, 129–131, 139
refugees, 21
regime coalition unity, 2, 9, 48–49, 67–69, 85, 115, 122–125, 135–136, 142–144
regime coalition, 21–22
regime-led state building, 4, 9, 13–20, 47, 143, 156
rent, 16, 20
rentier state, 5, 20
Rifa'i, Zeid, 26–27
Rimawi, Fahd al-, 66
riots of August 1996, 97–98
riots, of April 1989, 23, 26–27
Ryan, Curtis, 129

Sa'id, Hammam, 75
Sabah, Amir Jabir Ahmad al-, 147–148
Sabah, Sheikh Ali Khalifa al-, 148
Sadat, Anwar, 151–152, 154
Salt, 14
Sawt Al-Mar'a, 105
Sayad, Al-, 105
Schmitter, Philippe, 3
security threats, 2
Senate, 22, 57–58, 63
Sharaf, Layla, 123
Sharif, Mahmoud al-, 101, 123
Sharif, Nabil al-, 100
Sharif, Seif al-, 104
Sharon, Ariel, 133
Shbeilat, Layth, 33, 68, 75, 90
Shreidah, Abd al-Majid al-, 55
Shyab, Hosni al-, 56, 69
single member district, 107–108, 109–111, 134–135
single non-transferable vote (SNTV), 76–77, 79–81, 106–109, 116, 138, 141
Snyder, Richard, 6
soft-liners, 4, 123
southern Europe, 3–4
Springborg, Robert, 151
Srour, Sa'ad Hayl al-, 101

Star, 100
state bureaucracy, 21
state formation, 14–16
stealth candidates, 115–116
Stepan, Alfred, 6–7
subsidies, 23, 26, 96–98
succession, 128–130
Sufiyan, Caliph Muawiyah ibn Abi, 1
survival strategies, 1–2, 6–8, 32, 47–48, 54, 61, 67–70, 83–85, 105–106, 137–144, 155
Susser, Asher, 94
Syria, 72, 87

tabloids, see weekly newspapers
Tafilah, 98
Talal, King, 16–17, 21
Tarawnah, Fayiz al-, 120, 127, 129, 139
Tareq Al-Mustaqbal, 105
Theneibat, Abd al-Majid, 131
trade fair boycott, 92–93
transitions, regime, 3–4, 6–7, 31
tribes, 21, 81, 114, 116

Ummah, Al-, 105
United States, 51, 53, 93–94, 96, 135–136
Urdun al-Jadid Research Center, al-, 108
Urdun, Al-, 105

van de Walle, Nicholas, 5
vote of confidence, 52–53
voter turnout 31, 79, 115–116

Wafd party (Egypt), 16
Washington Declaration, 81, 90, 93
Washington talks, 71–72
weekly newspapers, 65–67, 99, 100–101, 103–104, 119, 121, 140
West Bank, 16, 19, 25–26
Wilson, Mary, 15
World Trade Organization (WTO), 129

Yanis, Hisham, 92
Yassin, Sheikh Ahmed, 89
Yousufi, Abd al-Rahman, 146

Zarqa, 115
Zayn, Queen, 17
Zo'ubi, Fawwaz al-, 94